The
LONG ROAD
HOME

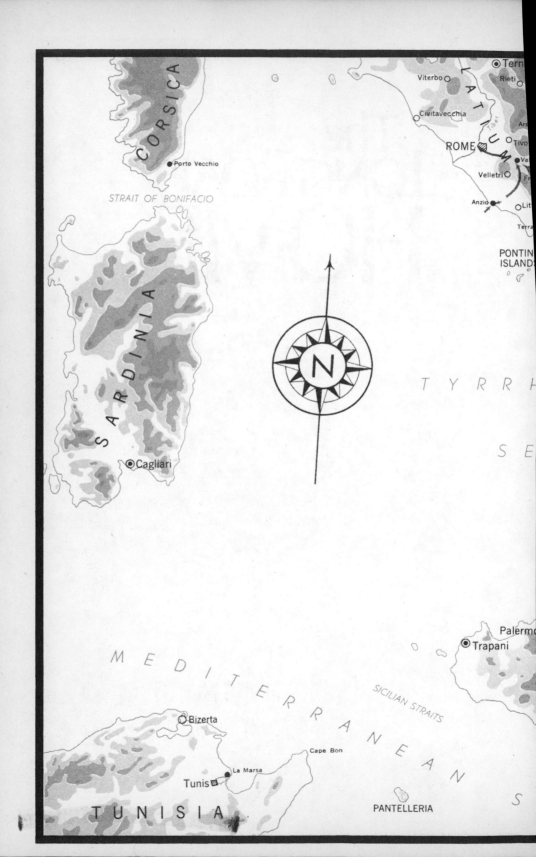

SOUTHERN ITALY
10 JULY 1943 — 9 JUNE 1944

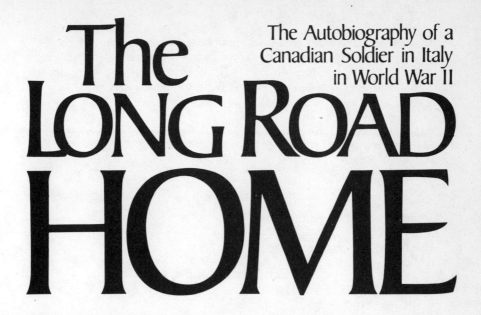

The LONG ROAD HOME

The Autobiography of a
Canadian Soldier in Italy
in World War II

Canadians in Battle Series

FRED CEDERBERG

Stoddart

First published in 1984 by
General Publishing Co. Limited
34 Lesmill Road
Toronto, Canada
M3B 2T6

Stoddart Publishing edition 1985

Third Printing September 1986

CANADIAN CATALOGUING IN PUBLICATION DATA
Cederberg, Fred
  The long road home

ISBN 0-7737-5050-9

1. Cederberg, Fred.   2. World War, 1939–1945 —
Personal narratives, Canadian.   3. World War,
1939–1945 — Campaigns — Italy.   I. Title.

D811.C43 1985   940.54'81'71   C85-099034-3

Line illustrations by Michael Glatt
Endmaps courtesy of National Defense Headquarters. The maps were drawn by Captain C.C.J. Bond and appeared in Lt.-Col. G.W.L. Nicholson's *The Canadians in Italy 1943-1945*.
Photographs courtesy of the author and Public Archives of Canada
Cover Illustration: Leoung O'Young

Printed and bound in Canada

*This book is dedicated to
every Canadian who marched
on the long road home.*

PROLOGUE

They told me, Heraclitus, they told me you were dead;
They brought me bitter news to hear and bitter tears to shed,
I wept, as I remembered, how often you and I
Had retired the sun with talking and sent him down the sky.

And now that thou art lying, my dear old Carian guest,
A handful of grey ashes, long long ago at rest,
Still are thy pleasant voices, the Nightingales, awake,
For Death, he taketh all away, but them he cannot take.

Callimachus of Athens

CHAPTER ONE

I saw the ranch wagon with its wooden side panels parked in front of our house as I came around the corner onto Maughan Crescent. A man in uniform was behind the wheel, one arm draped through the open window, his fingers drumming a tune on the door.

Uncle Gordon must be in the house, I thought happily, breaking into a long-legged trot.

I had four uncles, all MacNeils on my mother's side. But Uncle Gordon was the only one I really knew. Maybe that's why he was my favorite. A veteran of World War I (my father had been too old), he stood well over six feet, owned the biggest knuckled hands I'd ever seen and always brought me a present whenever he came by — a box of kilted, colorful, lead toy soldiers.

As I took the verandah steps two at a time, the door opened. I saw him standing in the doorway, his summer drill uniform almost white in the gloom of the hall. Behind him was my mother, Katherine Sarah, half his size.

"Almost missed you, young Fred," he greeted in his soft, east coast twang. "My Gawd, y're getting tall...'bout six and some?" He rapped me on a bony shoulder with his swagger stick. "How long's it been?"

"Four or five years," I said, grinning.

Mother laughed nervously. "Yes, he's tall, Gordon, but he's so thin, only about 155 pounds, although he eats like a truck driver."

Uncle Gordon looked me up and down. "He's gonna be barrel-chested and two axe handles across the shoulders...and scrawny legged, Kat, but he'll fill out. How old is he now?"

My chunky grey-haired father came out of the living room, his pale Scandinavian blue eyes unblinking, despite the flood of hard June sunlight. "He's eighteen, just turned," he said.

"Well," said Uncle Gordon, "no matter, he's big enough."

I continued to grin, oddly exhilarated without knowing why.

9

"Yes, he's big enough," repeated my uncle, looking first at my father then my mother. "I think he should go with me."

Now I understood why I felt the way I did.

My mother nodded. "I guess it would be better that way, Gordon. Yes, it would," she said softly.

Father rested his hands on his hips and stared out at the car. Mother turned her face away toward the darkened hall leading to the kitchen. "I'll get his things," she said. "You know, Gordon, he doesn't even shave."

My father turned and walked into the living room, taking my arm as he did. He jammed one hand into his trouser pocket, removed it and placed some rumpled bills in my palm, closing my fingers over them. "Here," he said gruffly, "it's all I have on me. Take them... because a man needs some money in his pockets. He can face whatever comes up much better with a few dollars."

"Pop..." was all I could mumble to the man I had known all my life, suspecting at times he was the reincarnation of a Prussian drill sergeant. He had relentlessly maintained a kind of impartial discipline in a small, rented family house (he'd been bankrupted in the Depression) populated by four sons, a daughter and a wife thirty-five years his junior.

He patted my shoulder, steering me back out onto the verandah. "I'll write your brother, Reg, and tell him you've joined," he said, gently. Reg was in the Victoria Rifles.

Twenty minutes later, without even time to say goodbye to my younger brothers or sister, I and my suitcase were stowed in the wagon and riding east on the Kingston Road, heading for the Connaught Ranges outside of Ottawa — and the Cape Breton Highlanders where Uncle Gordon was second-in-command.

It happened too fast for me. I had always known, I suppose, that I'd go into the armed forces sometime. But like a lot of teenagers — the age group I hung around with anyway — I had never finalized anything in my head. Sure, we knew there was a war on, but it only amounted to a blur of newsreels at the Friday night movies. And it certainly was never reported on the comic or sports pages of the Toronto dailies.

We were aware some of the older guys had disappeared from the neighborhood — Billy Rogers, Fred Bryan, George Campbell. At least we never saw them at Mass on Sundays. But then they had never played on the teams we did; they didn't skate at the Kew Beach open-air ice rinks. We only knew them because at church dances they actually danced. Despite Father McGrath's urgings we always lounged against the wall, lacking the nerve to approach the parish girls, girls we knew casually or eyed cautiously of a summer evening while they walked in pairs along the boardwalk, laughing, sometimes flirting with their eyes.

I was still in my Jeffrey's Drugs fastball sweater, dungarees and running shoes.

"You'll see your family in a few days," Uncle Gordon chuckled, reading my uneasy face. "The regiment will only be at Connaught for a short spell, then it's off to Camp Borden. And once you're signed in, you'll get a forty-eight-hour pass so you can take these clothes home."

I studied his angular face for a second, then stared out the window at the orchards flanking the roadway, at the radial trolley car swaying eastbound toward the Rouge River. It was packed with families and I could picture the kids shouting noisily at each other the way we did when we piled aboard for our year-end grade seven and eight picnics. And it made me remember Muriel Davidson, old Doc Davidson's pigtailed daughter, who had sculpted *I love you* with the toe of her sandal in the sandy soil by the river.

"We're motorized infantry — 'lorry borne' is the expression now — in the 11th Brigade of the 5th Canadian Armored Division," Uncle Gordon was saying. "Four rifle companies, headquarters, plus odds and sods. Remember that. It's all you need to know for now."

Sleep came unknowingly because I was abruptly aware the ranch wagon had come to a complete stop in an inky black world. And someone was jabbing me in the ribs with what felt like a teacher's pointer. "Up and at 'em, soldier," said my uncle, jovially, "we're here."

It was decided I would sleep off the rest of the night in the quarterstores marquee. "You'll be looked after and sworn in by 1000 hours," Uncle Gordon said. "That's ten o'clock in the morning. Take care of him Quarters — he's my nephew."

Quarters was Staff-Sergeant Cantwell whose face was dominated by a long, hooked nose. He smelled strongly of rum. "Will do, Major Gordie, will do," he replied amiably.

Bed was a groundsheet flung across stacks of packed duffle bags. "We're moving out shortly, son," he said, "and the men only take their packs with 'em on the troop train. Everything else has to be stowed, so I'm afraid this will have to do." He lit a Coleman lamp and it hissed bright light under the canvas roof.

Looking at me in my civvies, he said, "Yes, you're a MacNeil... long and blondish."

"I'm not a MacNeil."

"Then what are you?"

"A Cederberg, Fred Cederberg. Uncle Gordon is my mother's older brother."

"What the hell's a Cederberg?"

"Scandinavian. My father's a Swede."

"You born over there?"

"No, sir. Here."

"In Upper Canada?"

I knew from summers at my grandfather's Cape Breton farm that Upper Canada was Ontario. "No sir, Iona."

Quarters harrumphed. "Well, you're half MacNeil. And y're Major Gordie's nephew. That's better than nothing."

I took his words in stride. Hell, I'd been called a Squarehead, a Scandihoovian Beanpole and worse at home by buddies I referred to as Black Irish Micks, Limeys and dumb Scots. They were only words. Besides, I thought he was an officer and Uncle Gordon had stressed (somewhere along Highway 2) that you should never "sass the brass."

In the darkness, I couldn't even close my eyes. For a few minutes, I listened to the sounds in the night. I tried to picture myself in a uniform — in the army — but the fragments wouldn't jell. All the soldiers had faces like big Bern McAllister. Or Jimmy Chisholm. Or Jack Malloy. My boyhood friends. Besides, this wasn't the way it was supposed to happen... get drafted by your uncle even if he is your favorite. Where were the bands? The cheering girls throwing flowers and blowing kisses? The flags? I had to laugh inwardly when I thought of it — I didn't even have a girl. I didn't really know any, except for Gladys Smith. Some of us used to play cards on her verandah if it was raining and we couldn't play ball or football or lacrosse. Once, her mother had bent over my shoulder to help me play my cards (we were learning hearts). I had peered down the front of her dress and, fascinated, watched the free swing of her large breasts. A week later, on a Saturday night while Mr. and Mrs. Smith were at the movies, I sat in the dusk with Gladys.

"I saw you looking down my mother's dress," she announced airily.

I gulped, reddening.

"Are you going to deny it?"

I wanted to, but my mouth went dry.

My eyes must have bulged as she quickly unbuttoned her blouse and bared her very suddenly, very real chest. "Don't you think my breasts are prettier?" she grinned.

Their loveliness burned in my mind's eye and, muttering, "See you, Gladys," I fled, listening to her laughter as I crossed the Smiths' lawn and walked as quickly as I could down the street. Maybe, I thought, maybe I'll go and let Gladys see me in my uniform when I get home.

Regimental headquarters was a permanent wooden structure in the midst of a lake of Highlanders of all shapes and sizes.

"I'm Lieutenant Leif, the Intelligence Officer," he said after an orderly brought me to his desk. "So, you're Major MacNeil's nephew. OK, we'll fix you up in quick time. Let's start you off with Sergeant McIntyre."

Sergeant McIntyre was better known as Farting Joe. And I didn't need much time to find out why. While he checked if I could touch my toes, run on the spot for two minutes, looked down my throat and examined my teeth, he broke wind at least six times. "You'll do," he said, "you're warm. The MO will sign for you officially later."

I took my oath (without the King's Shilling) before Lieutenant Leif, confirming that I was in the Canadian Army, and assigned to the Intelligence section in headquarters. I drew messtins, a knife, fork, spoon and enamel mug and was told "Don't lose 'em, soldier, 'cause that's the last issue you'll get as long as this goddamn war lasts." Quarters said I'd draw my uniforms, webbing, packs, duffle bag, boots and weapon once the regiment arrived in Camp Borden. He pointed to a hut down the main camp road and said: "You'll sleep there."

I plunked my suitcase on a bunk, threw my pieces of army issue inside it and sat down on the cot.

"Hi, I'm Alex-Joe MacKinnon," said a Highlander as he came

through the door. He was solidly put together but soft muscled, brown faced, brown haired, brown eyed. "Y're Major Gordie's nephew."

"Does everybody know that?"

"Those that don't won't take long to find out. What's your name?"

"Fred Cederberg. You going to ask me where I was born? Everybody else does."

"Nope. I don't give a damn where you come from. But you gotta admit you can't hide very easy, looking like you do in that get-up." He laughed easily. "You gonna be an officer soon?"

"Why should I?"

"You're the 2/I-C's blood, that's why."

"Well, I'm not going to be an officer."

Alex-Joe's comments had touched a stubborn streak in me that my mother described as "combative." Then as I wandered through the lines of rifle company tents conscious of hundreds of pairs of curious, inquisitive eyes, I wondered if I shouldn't go home. Start over again. And while I knew I couldn't, the greasy stew served up at supper pushed me temporarily over the edge. Remembering how to use a public telephone without paying a nickel — and comforted by the forty-one dollars my father had given me — I called a cab and went to Ottawa where I checked into the Chateau. A snotty clerk made me pay in advance. He said I was lucky to get a room at all when I started to argue.

Surprisingly, I stared out my room window at the railway station and didn't even think of leaving. And I slept as I always had, dreamlessly. The next morning, buoyed up by a bath and bacon and eggs, I returned to Connaught Ranges. The guards at the gate, two soldiers flipping their long steel bayonets into a lone tree trunk, didn't even challenge me, just nodded in recognition. And when I walked into the headquarters hut, I discovered the army hadn't even missed me.

The night troop train to Camp Borden seemed to crawl, the ancient wooden coaches swaying rhythmically, steel wheels squeaking. We were seated, three to a rock-hard bench, facing another three men. Battle-dress blouses hung carefully from overhead racks, already jammed with large and small packs.

I grabbed a window seat. Next to me was Alex-Joe, like the rest of us wearing stark, heavy white braces over collarless, coarse khaki-colored shirts.

Alex-Joe thumbed his braces. "They bought 'em cheap from some fire department," he commented to no one in particular. "You don't smoke do you?" he asked.

I shook my head.

"Betcha he doesn't even drink, do ya?" The speaker had been christened Robert John O'Hanley, but nobody called him that but his family, the padre and paymaster. His nickname was Pithorse for the simple reason Mr. and Mrs. O'Hanley had spawned lots of kids, too many with a John in their names. Besides, his grandfather had handled pit ponies in the coal mines.

"Don't pay any attention to Pithorse," said Alex-Joe.

"Yeah, well, you look like you don't smoke. Or drink," said Pithorse. "Why do they always move us before payday, when we got no money for nothin'."

"Just so we'll all show up, I guess," said Alex-Joe, looking at Pithorse's buddy, sitting next to him. "You know, Cowshit?"

Cowshit MacKeegan had been born Alex-Joe. But the platoon already had an Alex-Joe, so he required a nickname. It hadn't been tough. Showing up as a recruit, he had lumbered into the platoon hut, over six feet of black-eyed hayshaker, with a mouth organ in one fist. He confessed he couldn't play a tune. "Y'see," he apologized, "I traded my fiddle for it. But I'll get the hang, don't worry."

"Where you from?" another hayshaker had asked.

"Coxheath."

"Yeah," said the hayshaker, "an' with the cowshit still stuck to your boots."

The name stuck, too.

The train shunted to a full stop. I peered out the window and made out the lights of a small nameless station. I got up and said, "I'll be right back," and worked my way between cars until I found it possible to climb down onto the platform. "What town's this?" I yelled at a shadowy man two cars down.

"What's the difference?"

I raced inside the small station and found an old man with a dark green eyeshade over his eyes. "You got any cigarettes for sale?"

"Nope."

I pulled a two-dollar bill out of my pocket.

"I got a couple you kin have," he said, opening the top drawer in his desk and handing me two large packs of Sweet Caps.

"You got change?" I asked.

"Nope. You keep 'em sonny. I ain't chargin' no soldier."

Passing around one deck, I leaned back. The ice had been broken, I sensed, as everyone lit up, exhaling clouds of smoke.

"Good boy," wheezed Cowshit when he choked on a puff. "We'll straighten with ya later. Okay?"

"You sure you aren't gonna be an officer?" whispered Alex-Joe.

"No way," I replied. And I meant it.

If the Connaught Ranges had been a lake of Highlanders, sandy Camp Borden was a sea of tam-o'-shanters, black berets, forage hats, glengarries, khaki berets, all caged in by military and regimental police and guard details who wouldn't let a dog on or off the base without a duly signed pass. There were regiments under canvas among stubby pines (like ours) and others billeted in wooden huts. And because there was very little wheeled or tracked equipment, tankers, artillerymen, infantry — everybody — route marched in endless columns or drilled on asphalt or gravel-covered makeshift squares.

And each evening, the defaulters — men and boys who fractured King's Rules and Regulations (Canada) — did pack drill, shouldering Enfield rifles that weighed about eleven pounds when they began at 1800 hours and almost 500 when the sergeant broke them off at 1900 to work in the cookhouses or pick up the inevitable litter between the lines of tents.

I settled into the Intelligence section Bell tent, stacked my battle dresses as prescribed, piled my packs, religiously cleaned my .303 and protected my hat badge from greedy scroungers who had given theirs to girls they believed they loved. Or could.

My five tentmates were older and married. And all they talked about was going into Barrie to get a piece of tail. When I ignorantly blurted, "You'd think you guys were single the way you spend all your evenings hunting for women!", I was told bluntly: "What the hell do you know? You're not even married, so you don't miss nothin'."

Blond corporal Johnny Kerr changed the subject. "How was your forty-eight-hour pass at home, kid?" he asked while I licked my verbal wounds, sitting cross-legged on the tent's wooden floor.

"Fine, I guess," I replied.

Kerr's face was burned a bright red. "Make you wonder why you joined up?"

"Nope." I lied a little because the two days had been streaked with mixed feelings — sudden waves of homesickness when my mother's eyes welled up with tears followed by inner quiet when I sensed my brothers and sister and father approved of my uniform.

My friends confused me. Big Itch McAllister and Butcher Brown just stared, half smiles on their faces. "You comfortable in that get-up?" asked Butcher. "You don't look it."

I went home, changed to my dungarees and sweat shirt. And it was like old times. We played pick-up ball all afternoon then went to the movies. Sunday evening, my father drove me to the bus station and I caught the last bus to Borden. Seated at the back while soldiers sang "Bless 'em All" up front, I suddenly realized why my being in uniform had unsettled the neighborhood gang: They had finally realized there was a war on.

Two weeks after the Highlanders' arrival at Borden, brawling erupted outside the wet canteens. By the third, there was a regimental riot between them and the 1st Hussars, a tank outfit. It took squads of MPs and my uncle, wading in with his big fists swinging at anything that moved in the swirling melee on Ralston Athletic Field, to break it up. I didn't get into it for the simple reason Alex-Joe grabbed me by the shoulders and yanked me back among the tents.

"That's for idiots, Fred, not for us," he snorted.

I half agreed with him then. After I saw the mess of split lips, broken noses, broken hands, the next morning, I knew for sure. "Somebody started slinging rocks," explained Cowshit, nursing his swollen cheek. "That's when it wasn't fun no more."

"You going into Barrie tonight?" asked Pithorse.

"Yep, soon's I get all cleaned up."

"What're you going to do?" I asked.

"A little whorin'."

I shut up. But after they had left, I crossed to the Knights of Columbus hut and went to the large *Webster's* dictionary chained to a pedestal. I looked up under the h's. Nothing. I might have had trouble with French, but I knew high school English, so I tried under the w's. There it was: whore, a woman who sold her body for favors or money. Christ, I thought, that's worse than a prostitute, a word I only vaguely understood.

Just before we received orders that the entire division was moving to Debert in Nova Scotia, preparatory to going overseas, my education was broadened. Screwball MacLean, one of my tentmates, climbed off his straw-filled palliasse and announced cheerfully, "I've got a drip," then amiably waddled his 200-pound bulk in the direction of Farting Joe MacIntyre's regimental aid post.

"What's a drip?" I had to ask Kerr.

"The clap."

"Oh."

Kerr split his ruddy face with a grin. "It's better than a chancre," he said.

"Oh," I repeated.

"Kid, I don't know where in hell you grew up, but I got the feeling you should still be playing with buckets of sand." He sighed. "The clap means gonorrhea and when you see a chancre on the end of your cock, you got syphilis...an' I wouldn't wish that on any man." He stared at me quizzically. "Hell, you don't even know what I'm talking about, do you! It's VD...venereal disease. You get it when you make it with a broad who's got it. A dirty broad."

I shivered despite the early July sunlight flooding through the open flap in the tent.

"Okay, kid, I don't mean to scare you, but it's a fact of life. They can cure the clap right quick with sulpha. But syphilis is tougher, like they lock you up in a box and drive y'r temperature up till they burn it out of y'r system. So, Screwball is lucky. Besides, he's had it before. To him, it's nothing more than a cold in his cock."

I paid a return trip to the dictionary in the KoC hut but it didn't tell me anything Kerr hadn't. And his details were more lurid.

In mid-September we moved out for Debert (although the shit-house rumors had begun in July with destinations as exotic as Texas and as far-fetched as Egypt because "someone in the know" had seen cases of British 8th Army shoulder patches or ten-gallon hats in the quarter stores). With endless clickety-clacks, the long strings of cars moved virtually unnoticed through eastern Ontario and Quebec, despite any number of stops to let fast freights through. But the first halt in New Brunswick, Campbellton, was different. It was late at night, but the town band (all old men) played ragged, enthusiastic marches, and "You Are My Sunshine" over and over again. And a steady parade of town girls marched back and forth along the platform, waving and calling to us, asking for names and addresses and pledging letters rarely written, or handing out sandwiches, soft drinks and candy. It made every man and boy feel good.

Debert was another Borden without the miles of sand and pines or the whores from Barrie. Nearby Truro had its own.

The 4th Division was already in the crowded camp, waiting to go overseas. "You guys?" they'd hoot, derisively, "y're gonna have to wait y'r turn. We were here first and we're the Fourth. Y're the Fifth. Know what we mean?"

But by early October, the Highlanders' colonel, Teddy Small, took a small advance party with him to the U.K., leaving Uncle Gordon I-C of the regiment. One evening, his batman showed up and, in front of a hut filled with Highlanders, said: "Major Gordie wants to see you, Private Cederberg." There were snickers as I left.

"You want a drink?" he asked. Before I could reply, he added, "It's time you had one," and passed me a half tumbler of whiskey. He chuckled when I made a face with my first sip. "Your mother would kill me if she knew I was teaching you to drink," he chuckled.

"Well, how do you like it, the regiment?"

"It's fine," I replied, fighting back the urge to throw up as the searing whiskey bounced around in my stomach.

"You've certainly gone out of your way to avoid me," he said. "I've seen you, but you apparently make it a point of not noticing me."

I shrugged. "After all, you're a major and I'm only a private. And I have to live with the men," I said slowly. "And Uncle Gordon, half of them already think I'm going to be an officer just because we're related."

"And what's wrong with that? Your grandfather gave me a leg up, his father gave him a leg up. The rest, you have to do yourself. Having said that, I also expect you to become an officer."

When I said nothing, he continued. "You remind me of my half brother, Albert, in A company. He'll never be anything more than he is, a corporal. Stubborn. Just because I'm a major. Goddamnit, Fred, don't you realize those men you worry about *expect* you to become an officer? And the reasons aren't important."

Silently, I vowed I wouldn't even take a promotion as long as my uncle remained with the regiment.

Albert introduced himself two nights later. And I knew why.

"Gordon said I should come 'round," he said, faintly shrugging his high shoulders. His big nose dominated a sharp face.

"You sure took your time," I countered, coldly, "you've known I was here, but I wasn't aware you were with A Company!"

This time, he did shrug and his almost homely face lit up with the most crooked, toothy grin I had ever seen. "You've got spunk, kid, you're gonna do. Let's go drink beer sometime and talk family."

"I don't drink."

"Gordon said you're learning."

"No thanks."

A week later, the regiment had its overseas medical. It began with the pipe band, some of them in their forties and fifties, trooping before a selection of doctors while Uncle Gordon stood by, an amused grin on his long face.

Piper MacMillan's old man, in his sixties, was first.

"You really want to go, old-timer?" asked the medic.

"Yes sir! My heart's set on it."

The doctor looked him over, standing in the raw, his skinny, veined legs planted on the chill floor. "Well," he said, "if that's what you want, you can go."

I was in line behind Regimental Police Corporal Joe Bonar, like everyone else, stripped. I was fascinated by the tufts of hair on his shoulders and the absence of hair on his head when he turned to me. "You got good eyes, eh?"

"I can read that chart from here, if that's what you mean."

"Good. Then you read 'em off and whisper 'em in my ear when my turn comes."

Joe passed with my eyes.

Another Joe, J.A. Gallant, broke up his doctor who had cupped one of his testicles in one hand and said, "Cough!"

Joe coughed.

The doc groped for the second testicle. "Where is it?" he finally asked.

Gallant played dumb while the lineup snickered by numbers. Every Highlander in headquarters knew J.A. Gallant had only one ball. "Where's what?" asked Joe.

"Your other testicle."

"My what?"

"Alright. Your other nut...ball?"

"Hell," Joe guffawed, "I only got one, yuh dumb bugger!"

Laughter exploded in the room. The medic reddened. "Next!" he said.

Bonar summed it up: "As long as you were warm an' didn't have VD you were healthy."

It took all day to load the S.S. *Orcades*, a peacetime Pacific & Orient liner, with its human cargo of Highlanders. By nightfall, in a chill rain, she rode at anchor in Bedford Basin. "So's nobody can change their mind and try to get off an' go home," said Alex-Joe to nobody in particular as we stood on deck and peered through the gloom at Halifax.

Albert was next to me. "That doesn't make sense," he said, "according to the paymaster, we got fourteen more bodies than we're supposed to."

"Where'd we get 'em?" asked Alex-Joe.

"I hear some of the guys on port guard duty just got into the lines and walked on."

"We gonna throw 'em overboard?"

"No. Pay says Major Gordie said to take 'em on strength so's they won't be listed as AWOL by the garrison command."

"Makes sense."

The November sun never shone during the eleven-day crossing. The skies glowered, raging with rain while the north Atlantic churned endlessly, but the 14,000-man convoy, escorted by U.S. Navy units (and the Americans weren't even in the damned war) steamed steadily eastward. We manned Bren machine guns, exercised in the windy rain, cursed the British food, and did boat drill endlessly. And we either carried or wore bulky life preservers every waking minute.

The *Orcades* docked at Liverpool and the Highlanders disembarked, loaded down like pack mules. Marching through the blitz-shattered streets to the trains was an experience. Buildings were half shattered, entire blocks had been levelled. But the people were friendly, yelling to us from their shops, windows and trams. Men, women and youngsters ran alongside, offering cigarettes, cakes and quickie cups of tea.

"We've come to turn on the lights!" yelled Cowshit.

"We 'eard your big brothers say that back in '39 — and they're still off!" a woman yelled back, cheerfully. "But glad to see you luv!"

The trains, we agreed, were a hell of an improvement over those we rode in Canada. "They got softer seats," said Farting Joe, feeling the coverings, "an' they don't jerk and squeal like ours." They raced through the night, neatly packed with three motorized infantry regiments, two armored brigades, artillerymen, medical corps, engineers, army service corps and assorted brigade and div formations, each for a specific camp in southern England. The locomotives hissed and hooted at the pale stars while we waited, collectively, for the Luftwaffe to send us to heaven or hell, according to our just desserts.

Nothing happened.

The Highlanders paraded into Aldershot, following in the footsteps of a thousand armies since Roman Legionnaires had built their first, antiseptically (for the times) clean bivouac twenty centuries earlier.

And the *London Evening News* headlined its November 26, 1941 tabloid edition: "Canadian Armored Division Lands" and the drop shrieked: "14,000 Fighting Fit Canucks and Equipment".

"We got any equipment? I didn't see any," said Alex-Joe.

"Outside of our rifles, I don't know," I said.

"You're supposed to know, aren't you in the Intelligence section?"

Alex-Joe knew I did nothing but study Morse code, route march, drill, learn map reading, route march some more and listen to the pipers play their chanters until everyone was driven from the hut.

"Okay," he said, "so I'm in the carrier platoon. We're supposed to have Bren carriers. Only we don't. I guess that answers my question."

"They must be saying that so the Germans will think we're loaded for bear," I said.

"If we don't believe it, why in hell should they?" Alex-Joe said, exasperatingly.

I tacitly agreed.

CHAPTER TWO

WE had landing leave, five days in early December. As the rest of the Highlanders left in pairs, I went solo to London's Waterloo Station and walked the rain-slick streets until I found the Strand Palace. On The Strand, of course. I also discovered how Brits gave directions: "Bear to the right, old chap, swing through the roundabout and it's on the left (or right) and you cawn't miss it."

It was bed and breakfast for seventeen shillings.

I was awed, wandering the crooked avenues of the historic city, taking in Westminster Abbey, the Tower, The Mall, Admiralty Arch, Trafalgar Square, St. Paul's, the Law Courts, the Tube with its color-coded arrows that directed everyone to Hammersmith, Leicester Square, Picadilly Circus, the Highgate. Every name rang a bell in my mind. Like Ludgate or Hampstead. I could almost see blank-eyed heads on pikes, ghosts patrolling stone walls, footpads prowling the blacked-out streets.

But it was the Londoners I fell in love with. I sensed they liked every one of us as we gaped at bomb-shattered buildings that left gaps in rows of stone-faced offices and shops. Queues were everywhere, but when a serviceman or woman went to a cinema or theater they moved straight to the head of the line and no Londoner ever complained, just motioned you up front, smiling.

Our first Christmas came and went swiftly. To a man, we were too homesick to enjoy it.

In February I turned down a promotion to corporal and a transfer to the carrier platoon. Captain Frizzell, better known as "Bootnose" for the obvious reason ("You could fill his nose with nickels and he'd be a millionaire," said Alex-Joe), pretended he was surprised. "You've earned it on your own," he said, "and I mean that."

I knew that. I'd mastered Morse, map reading and I could march farther than any man in my section and come back whistling.

I remember that day, specifically. Because later in the afternoon, quarterstores personnel came through the huts, collecting every man's second set of winter underwear — longjohns.

"Whatta ya want 'em for?" asked Bunny O'Connell, a pale-faced black-browed gnome who could recite most of what Robert Service had ever written and many poems he hadn't. "The generals up in London too cold?"

"Nobody tells us anything," the storesman said, "but I hear they're goin' to Russia."

"We on Hitler's side now?"

"Don't be so damn foolish. They're for the Russians."

"Jeez," wheezed Bunny, "I thought only the Germans were cold out there on the steppes." He fingered his spare longjohns, then tossed them across the room. "To think," he mused with his usual sly grin, "underwear is gonna decide the outcome of this friggin' war!"

Two weeks later, Uncle Gordon sent his batman after me again. "I'm going home and keep that to yourself," he said, pouring me a whiskey. "In fact, most of us old codgers are. So you won't have to turn down any more promotions."

Because it was only the second time I'd had a drink, I choked again, but partly because I realized I had hurt him at a vulnerable time.

"Going home?" I repeated.

"The colonel, myself, Major Joe MacLean (another relative), Angus MacDonald, Quarters, plus a few others who survived the old war. It's a young man's game and we aren't young enough."

"I'm sorry," I mumbled.

"You don't have to be sorry. It's the army, Fred. And while it sometimes can rile a man over the short haul, it knows what it's doing over the long run."

"Who'll take over?"

"Montrealers." He spat the word out, then paused, "But that's not why I wanted to see you. I hear from your mother now and then. And she doesn't know why you don't write more frequently. Is there a reason?"

"None. I just thought once every week or so was enough. I guess it isn't."

"No, it isn't. Fred, you remember what I'm going to tell you, and keep it under your glengarry. It's the folks back home — the mothers, fathers, wives, friends — who hurt most when there's a war. Soldiers only hurt when they're horny or broke or wounded. So, write. We don't have much equipment yet, but there's no damned shortage of paper or pens."

With the arrival of the Montrealers — Colonel J.B. Weir, 2/I-C Pete Sommerville, Regimental Sergeant Major Ralph Diplock and a covey of majors, captains and lieutenants — a wave of discipline engulfed the Highlanders. They took it for two weeks, then struck back, refusing to go on parade, shouting obscenities at the newcomers as they urged them to form up.

"You know what 'no' means?" a Highlander yelled from a window.

"I think I do," replied the new RSM.

"Then fuck off!"

The officers and men of the famed British 51st Highland Division across the roadway were literally horrified.

It took the appearance of Lieutenant-General E.W. Sansom, C.B., D.S.O., to settle the issue. He diplomatically suggested the Highlanders march to the parade square and have a talk with him. Defying a colonel was one thing, but telling a general to fuck off was another. The men formed ranks and, following their pipers, did just that.

Selecting the loudest striker, Jimmy Hec MacInnis, the stocky general turned complaints that the new officers were completely chicken shit (regs happy) around. He got Jimmy Hec to concede that regs, judiciously applied, were necessary if the Highlanders were to equal the glorious standards set by their forefathers in the old 85th Battalion at Vimy and half a dozen other battles. The snow job hit home. Then he gave everyone the rest of the day off.

I went out that afternoon with Albert and Alex-Joe, drank six pints of mild and bitters and threw up twice (once after punching out a Scottish corporal who had insisted we were a disgrace to British arms).

"He had it coming," said Alex-Joe, "because we aren't even British, we're Canadians."

The regiment settled down to an uneasy truce with its new command, bashing the Maida Barracks square, acquiring used Bren carriers, three and three-quarter ton trucks, servicing them until their motors hummed, route marched, practiced battle drill tactics and carried out regimental parades and guard duties with more and more precision. In between times, the ancient two-storey barrack-room floors were scrubbed and squeegeed clean. The men boiled and scrubbed their clothes or ironed shirts and battle dresses.

"There'd a-been no goddamned strike if those smart buggers hadn't tried to do too much too fast," allowed Alex-Joe. "Or if they hadn't tried to make us take down those friggin' daytime clothes-lines. When the hell did they think our shirts an' underwear would've dried? Not at night in this soggy land!"

Two weeks later, Captain Frizzell again offered me two stripes and a transfer to the carrier platoon in what was now support company. I accepted. And he intoned: "I expected you would. Major Gordie said to wait till he'd gone." I moved my kit that afternoon, after exchanging my .303 rifle for a Tommy gun, joining Pithorse, Cowshit, Alex-Joe and sixty others, including another transferee, Corporal Albert MacNeil. Later, I wondered if Uncle Gordon had arranged that, too. Or just maybe my mother had suggested it. She was a clannish woman and why not with her heritage.

Sergeant Coutt MacLean ruled the carrier platoon — officially designated as No. 4 — an integral part of a group which included pioneers, mortarmen, an antitank unit and signals.

Built like a grand piano, balding, and owning a high-pitched voice that always startled newcomers, Coutt could out-punch, out-arm wrestle, outlast and out-work any man half his age. Nearer forty than thirty and one of the few non-Catholics in the entire unit, he always took what he called "them black Protestant bastards" on church parade with one piper and one drummer while the rest of the Highlanders marched off behind the almost complete band.

He had two officers over him, Lieutenant Donald MacNaughton and Captain Tony Archibald — both had come with the new colonel. We rarely saw the latter, but MacNaughton was always on duty. He whined a lot. And his semi-British accent (known as la-de-dah by the men) irritated everyone. He made me think he must have grown up in Ottawa because my businessman father always referred to the natives of the capitol as "a bunch of damned half-English bureaucrats."

By mid-June, I could drink half a dozen beers and smoke without upchucking. I also met Joan Meeks at the local Royal Army Service Corps weekly dance.

She took my hand in hers, inspecting it. "Are you married?" she asked, her thin lips barely moving.

"No way."

"I know you're not wearing a ring, but a lot of Canadians take them off," she said.

Alex-Joe laughed. "Who the hell would marry a fuzzy-cheeked beanpole like him, lady!"

"I think he's cute," she sniffed at Alex-Joe. To me she said, "Let's dance, Freddie."

God, how I hated that name, I thought, as I took the plunge into the jumping, swaying couples.

Joan Meeks could dance, even jitterbug. And she patiently taught me how to control my steel-shod army boots so they wouldn't lacerate her shapely legs or ruin her hard-to-come-by pumps. Six Saturday nights later, I met her parents; he, a member of the local cricket club, she with the flower club. In minutes, they excused themselves, leaving us alone in the tiny living room where I learned (happily) that their daughter was a warm-hearted nineteen year old, but easily able to fend off my awkward attempts to carry everything I had learned (by doing a lot of listening in the barracks) to a successful conclusion. I was, I had to admit, hampered by the fact I didn't really know what it was all about in any formal sense.

In fact, I'd reached the conclusion my buddies (who told me she was ripe for the laying) were either boasting liars or completely out of touch with reality until a rainy night when the Meekses asked me to stay the night in the bungalow's spare room.

The slender Joan woke me from a fitful sleep, stretching out beside me in the delicious nude. She played with me for two hours while I strained and learned interesting techniques which fell short of the ultimate. "I shall wank you off, love," she whispered. And she did — into a handkerchief which appeared out of nowhere. I thought I was in love for a couple of weeks, but gradually came to realize it was the exercise that attracted me — and the large number of handkerchiefs she owned. Once, I tried to figure out whether she washed them out (and if she did, where) or simply bought new ones for use on picnics, in the living room or the cinema if we could get isolated backrow seats.

By July I wanted to break off with Joan but, because I'd never had a girl before, I didn't know how. The army solved my problem, moving the whole damn regiment to Crookham Crossroads. Training continued, interrupted by an outbreak of trench mouth that forced the medics to confine all of us — except the officers who could always swing a work order, a three-quarter ton truck or jeep to go with it, and a pass to their favorite hangouts.

Next came a bivouac in Sheffield Park outside of Hayward's Heath in corrugated metal huts, spending most evenings making toast over hot coals in the potbellied stoves which kept us from freezing at night. And the pay-night drunks fell into the slit trenches laboriously spaded out of small hillocks by our predecessors against German air attacks which never materialized.

The friction between the Montrealers and the Highlanders had simmered down to the point where anger had dwindled to displeasure aimed only at specific officers they wouldn't or couldn't accept. One way was to go to mess in long lines, precisely when a "target" officer was returning from his quarters. Every soldier would salute him, making him return each one separately until his arm was ready to fall off. Another was to steal his revolver and throw it into a nearby pond. It was kind of comical to see one of them, out on the pond late in the afternoon, dragging and probing for a service .38.

It was a 120-mile march to and from the Bisley firing ranges that ended the conflict. Colonel Weir and 2/I-C Major Sommerville walked with the men, striding out, singing along, tirelessly. In fact, Sommerville, whose battle-dress trousers were slightly too large for his ass, was tagged Pete the Tramp for the way he walked despite blisters.

But it was Majors Laird Nesbitt and Bill Ogilvy who extinguished the last embers of resentment. They provided barrels of good mild and bitters for the marching men at the end of the sixth day.

"Anybody who likes beer can't be all bad," said Alex-Joe, never for a minute realizing both much preferred whiskey or gin or champagne.

And the Highlanders as part of the 11th Brigade of the 5th Armored Division, played at war. Officially, Canadian Military Headquarters in London dubbed them schemes or exercises, like Tiger, Spartan, Harlequin. The first must have been a complete snafu because 4 platoon moved about the equivalent of four city blocks. It halted by the side of the road for forty-eight hours, until ordered to return to its lines.

Still, the army improved.

"Competition," snorted Pete the Tramp, one afternoon when he dropped around unannounced to inspect the platoon carriers, "that's what does it. But you have to instill it on a company versus company level here, regiment against regiment, then division against division. Why? Well, we're at war, even if we aren't fighting."

He grinned under his thick black moustache. "Looking back, I guess I tried too hard, too fast."

The platoon laughed, easily. He'd scored a point while conceding another.

"Major, when are we gonna fight?" asked Pithorse.

"Your guess is as good as mine. But the way I see it, we're not losing any more. The Russians are holding, the Yanks are doing likewise. And while the Brits aren't winning in the desert, they aren't losing; in fact, they're building up."

We were on a regimental exercise on the South Downs, driving our Bren carriers hell-bent up and over the rolling meadowlands, steel tracks slapping rhythmically against their iron skirts. The rifle companies practiced house-fighting in an abandoned village, and part of the Canadian Army overseas finally got into shelling and shooting action...at Dieppe.

It was August 19, 1942, when almost 5,000 infantrymen, tankers, sappers and a handful of Yanks and Brits went ashore in Fortress France.

We didn't know what was happening, sitting there in our light armored vehicles, counting parades of low-flying Spitfires and Hurricanes streaking through the high summer sky toward the English Channel and the French coast. Rumors flew alongside them.

"The second front has opened!" gasped Pithorse.

"Then that's why we're down here on the Downs, we're next," allowed Coutt.

Men clustered around the platoon carrier, tuning in the BBC. But except for flat-voiced announcers intoning that there was heavy air activity over the French channel coast, there was no news.

Lieutenant MacNaughton finally told us that the 2nd Canadian Division had "gone in," as he dramatically put it. It sounded like a phrase from a World War I movie I had seen sometime. It left every man alone with his thoughts.

Late in the day, the word was out. Green, untried elements of the 2nd Division had assaulted Pourville (west of Dieppe) and Puys. And under an Allied air umbrella, they had fought doggedly until enthusiasm had given way to reality and, finally, confusion. By 1358 hours the German batteries had fallen silent and there were 2,500 fewer Canadians in England.

In the gloom, I wrote a quickie, fold-up airmail letter home to my parents, describing the events from the hillside seats we had occupied, plus the fact I had become a section sergeant.

It wasn't my usual letter, a kind of I'm-fine, hope-you're-fine, your-loving-son effort. Dieppe had touched me for reasons I really couldn't explain even to myself. Perhaps, I was sensing that a reckoning was coming; perhaps I was trying to take stock of myself, wondering if I could cut it when the chips were on the table and the betting begun.

It also preserved my mother's sanity because apparently my promotion went through the day the casualty lists hit the desks in Ottawa. They must have all piled up in the same basket because Mr. and Mrs. A.H. Cederberg collected a we-regret-to-inform-you telegram, indicating I had been killed at Dieppe. But the day before, my airmail letter had been delivered by the postie, proving, said Alex-Joe, "Even the post office can move faster than this man's army."

Father, a stand-up sand-and-gravel engineer, quickly realized I couldn't have done both — written a letter from somewhere in England and died (in the service of his country, as the terse wire spelled out) on Dieppe's bloody beaches. But it took a telephone call to Ottawa where an information officer apologized for the mix-up before he could soothe my frantic mother's worst fears.

Two weeks later, my old principal at Riverdale Collegiate wrote solicitously that "We held a minute's silence for your beloved son, John Frederick, who was cut down in the flower of his life . . . a life so filled with promise."

Father had to make another call to Ottawa where another information officer regretted that they hadn't been able to correct the original goof before the casualty lists had been moved to the media from which Riverdale had learned of my untimely demise.

"I'm enclosing the letter from your high school," wrote my father, "because I have the distinct feeling that anyone who can read his own obituary is living under a charmed star, or, as your Catholic mother would say, a gifted guardian angel. I must tell you I find it rather humorous that Mr. Watson [my principal] would actually indicate you had promise."

"What's he mean by that promise stuff?" asked Cowshit after I gave him the letter to read.

I chuckled, feeling closer to my father than I ever had. "Cowshit," I said, "he spent several hours at that school, listening to old Watson tell him my marks weren't good enough, that I fooled around too much in class, and that unless I applied myself to my books the way I did in sports, I wouldn't amount to much."

"What'd your old man say to all that?"

"He'd repeat Watson's spiel."

"Nothin' more?"

"Nothing. Except he'd always make a point of saying that Watson did say I was polite and that I was never disrespectful...although I did hear him say to my mother once that some kids grow up a little slower than others, and that he hoped I was one of them."

Our second Christmas was without the successive waves of homesickness that had spoiled the first in those bleak Aldershot barracks — homesickness that had showed in our letters so much so it had alarmed the censors who in turn alarmed CMHQ which had informed regimental headquarters the "Highlanders have a serious morale problem."

"Christ," shrilled Coutt MacLean, "didn't they know half you kids were babies a long way from home?"

Joe Barter, a short-time apprentice fireman with the CNR, who had a mouth as wide as the Straits of Canso where he came from, protested, "I been all the way to Halifax before I joined!"

"How far's that? Eighty miles?"

"Far enough, Sarg, far enough. Just don't tell me I'm a baby."

Coutt glanced around the hut, staring in turn at the members of my section. "You, Cederberg, you shave yet?" he asked.

"Only when he's goin' out with some girl," snickered Cowshit.

Coutt growled. "Hell, look at you, a lance-sergeant and you've still got your issue of five Gillette blades. You thinking of getting married like a lot of other yahoos in this man's army?"

"No way."

"I am," said Albert. "And what's it to you?"

"You're almost twenty-eight, old enough to know better. But the rest of the ninnies in these here Highlanders — some eighty or ninety of 'em — they aren't. Hell, they don't know whether they're getting mothered or screwed. Can't tell the difference. Along comes a pretty little gal who won't put out and you're off to see the padre. Christ! You'd think we were gonna be here for the rest of our goddamned lives the way some of you're putting down roots." He shrugged, almost sadly, then smiled suddenly. "Mebbe that's it...a diet of steady tail is a cure for the homesick blues!"

Albert was married to Violet Wilson, the only and tiny daughter of an aging Scottish coal miner in Newtongrange. I was best man.

And later that night as the old men drank hoarded straight Scotch (while their wives sipped sherry) and sang mournful love songs, I came to the conclusion Coutt was right even if he didn't know it: The Canadians were putting down roots. The scene could have been switched to any small Canadian village or town and not a single guest would have known the difference.

In March of '43, the entire division was swept up into Exercise Spartan; an invading "German" army was pitted against two Canadian corps which included three British divisions.

The planners tried to make it as near to actual war conditions as possible through the use of umpires who rode the combat zones in jeeps, realistically writing off vehicles and men as out-of-action, destroyed, dead, wounded or prisoners. The umps — as they were called — tagged their victims under any one of such headings. If wounded, their wounds were described and they were shipped off to dressing stations, hospitals and POW camps, thus testing the support groups such as the medical corps.

Barter, upped to a corporal, and I were named umps and assigned a jeep and instructed to patrol the sector controlled by the Perth Regiment.

The roads were jammed with trucks, armored vehicles, scout cars, tanks, marching infantry while RAF and RCAF strafed or provided cover. In between all this, mobile artillery units careened down narrow, hedged lanes or across open fields.

I parked the jeep off the side of the road.

"You make any sense out of this?" asked Joe.

Looking at the map in my lap, I said, "Far as I can make out, we're on the left of the Limey Guards and the enemy is about three miles north and west."

Joe grunted. "I'm glad I didn't have to read maps when I was firing on the run to Halifax. Just followed the rails."

"Let's go and have a couple of beers."

"You know the rules, Fred," Joe said, "no beering, no nothing. We gotta stay out of pubs."

"Balls."

"What about that big Perth major with the little moustache? He's been watching us...taking this friggin' exercise seriously. He could report us and it'd cost us our hooks."

"Screw him."

"Yeah, well if that's your bent, here he comes, leading four truckloads of infantry."

The convoy halted, the major leaped out. "Hey, you, Sergeant! What the hell are you doing parked here? Don't you know the lead company is under fire and you're supposed to be umpiring?"

"No sir!" I shouted.

"Goddamn your lazy hide!" he screamed. "Get over here!"

Joe grunted. "Now we're in for it, buddy."

I swung my legs out of the jeep just as an "enemy" Hurricane roared above the roadway, its blank ammo machine guns spitting flame.

"We're under attack!" yelled the major, "take cover men!" He took a header into a ditch as the Hurry disappeared behind a low hill.

I removed a package of casualty tags from inside my battle dress and ran over to him. "Sorry, sir," I said, "you've been badly hit. And three of your trucks are burning."

He sat up. "Hit? Don't be so fucking ridiculous, soldier, I..." His eyes blazed. "You sonovabitch. Sergeant, you're doing this on purpose!"

I ignored him, scribbling "both legs broken, multiple shoulder wounds and heavy loss of blood" on the tag and fastened it to his battle-dress epaulet. Rapidly, I tagged the first, second and fourth trucks, then sixteen NCOs and men. "Corporal Barter, signal the medics that a company of the Perth Regiment has been badly strafed just outside of the village. Make it quick."

Joe did as he was told.

We had our two beers in the pub kitchen because the owner was aware he couldn't sell beverages to any soldiers while Spartan raged outside.

"You think he'll report us?" asked Joe.

"Nope."

"What about when he gets back to his regiment?"

"Joe, I gave him so many wounds the real friggin' war will be over before he rejoins the Perth. Drink your beer."

Corporal Joe Barter shook his head. "You're either smarter than I figured. Or lucky. 'Cause I don't think that's what you had in mind when you got outta the jeep."

Spartan ended in mid-March and the chief umpire ruled that, after a confused start, the defenders had thrown back the invaders. But the brass wasn't happy with the weather. It had been too warm, too sunny, and hadn't tested the participants. They didn't say anything about a Canadian sergeant and corporal who enjoyed the country-side and beer.

CHAPTER THREE

THE sign said: "Canadian spoken here: English understood". "It's gotta come down," snapped Coutt.

"How come?" asked Pithorse, the sleeves of his overalls twisted in a knot across his waist, under his bare, brown chest.

"Because the colonel says so. Some of the natives here in Hunstanton don't appreciate it. They called it 'outrageous.'"

"That's a big word; they know how to spell it?" asked Nine-Pence Holmes. "'Cause if they do, then that's another reason why Canadian and English is different."

"Take it down," said Coutt, gently.

Nine-Pence shuffled over to the entrance of the former Triton Hotel parking and carriage lot, reached up and pulled the offending cardboard sign off the brickwork. "There," he spat, "I hope they're happy."

The Bren carriers, tracked and lightly armored, squatted in the shade of the walls, like lazy water buffaloes trying to escape a hot sun.

"People can sure make a lot outta nothin'," soothed Pithorse as Nine-Pence returned to his carrier, climbed up on the spare battery box and shaded his eyes with his tam-o'-shanter.

None of the fifty-odd Highlanders was working very hard. They'd been off their last scheme with the Poles for two days. The real toil — track pins checked, split bogeys replaced, tracks tightened, Ford engines timed, greased and running easily — was finished until the next time it was required. In the warm sunlight, the Highlanders talked. Or smoked. Or dozed, carefully curled up and hidden, so the sudden appearance of Lieutenant MacNaughton wouldn't surprise them.

The occasional ping of a hammer against metal or the sputtering of the big wireless set in the lead carrier broke the silence.

"You get any more from the BBC on the invasion of Sicily?" yelled Pithorse.

39

Nine-Pence, sitting wide-legged on the carrier's engine frame, earphone bands circling the top of his crewcut, shook his head. "They tell us First Div's in action. They don't say another friggin' word."

"Ah, quit your beefing, Nine-Pence. They'll tell you when they're good and ready," I yelled, nudging Alex-Joe. "Has Nine-Pence got a brother in the Sicilian invasion?" I asked.

"How the hell would I know? I don't even know if Nine-Pence Holmes is his real name. Or if he's got any brothers." He looked up at Nine-Pence. "You got a brother in the First Div?"

"Nope, I'm just curious. Like a good hound."

Alex-Joe's eyes closed slowly, "There, Lance-Sergeant Cederberg, now you're as smart as I am. He doesn't have a brother in the First Div."

"You think we'll be next to go in?" I asked.

Alex-Joe's eyes opened. "There you go again, asking dumb questions. How would I know. Hell, I'm only a lance-sergeant, too. Remember?"

"Yeah, but I'm not getting any younger, waiting here in England ..."

"You're all of twenty, eh?"

"Now who's asking dumb questions? You know I'm the same age you are."

"Well, you sound like Angus the Goat MacKinnon. Like mebbe only fifteen."

I fished my cigarettes out of my thigh pocket, took two out and gave one to Alex-Joe. We lit up.

"Is The Goat only fifteen?" I asked. "He's big enough for more than that."

"He might be, but if you look at the hairs on his chin you'll figure out why he's called The Goat — and why he's not old enough to bother shaving."

"What the hell would make a fifteen year old want to join the army?"

"Why does anybody?"

"Because they want to, I guess."

"Well, I guess that was The Goat's reason," Alex-Joe drawled, languidly. "And it's as good as any I can think of. Me? I went because the regiment went. And because it had to..."

"The regiment didn't have to go anywhere," I said, softly.

Alex-Joe blinked. "Yes, it did...because we had to finish up where the other guys left off in 1918."

I thought about the afternoon I had come home to find Uncle Gordon on the verandah and how everything had happened so fast. It seemed like a long, long time ago.

Alex-Joe interrupted my mental game. "How's by that dark-haired little broad in the big house on the High Street?" he asked languidly. "You laying her?"

"No," I lied.

"Hah! You didn't take her away from Lieutenant MacNaughton and Captain Archibald just to hold hands, buddy," he snorted.

I had met Francine Powell-Jones when on rear-party duty while the Highlanders were training with the Guards Armored Division, chasing each other across Norfolk's desolate heath country.

With a dozen men, it was our duty to guard the rows of one-time gracious summer hotels fronting on The Wash, currently home for the regiment, reporting to Captain Frizzell.

I had casually watched her playing mixed doubles with an older woman and MacNaughton and Archibald on the farther of the two asphalt courts across the Esplanade from the Triton. The women were better than the officers who consistently hit lobs so high they often cleared the surrounding high wire fence.

One Saturday afternoon, I went to see Padre MacDonald, borrowed a tennis racquet, climbed into my exercise army-issue anti-passion khaki shorts and asked the older woman, politely, if I could join them. Her name was Mem Custance, a lively fifty year old, who enthusiastically said, "Yes, young man, do come in."

Five minutes of small talk later, I played singles with Francine, beating her twice. The first time, she insisted, was a fluke. But in the second set, my timing came back and I routed her. I walked off the courts with the distinct feeling she didn't like me at all.

Captain Archibald called me aside. "Sergeant," he said, evenly, "tennis is for officers only. OK?"

I turned to Mem. "Is that true?"

Mem brought her straw-colored brows together in her lined face. "Unless the Canadian Army has requisitioned *my* courts," she said too sweetly, "that's not the case at all. Has your army done that, Captain?"

Archibald allowed that it hadn't.

"Then the young man is my guest. He can play here any time there's a court free."

I was aware that Francine Powell-Jones was watching me curiously, beads of sweat running across a trace of freckles under her black-brown hair. "Thank you for the use of *your* courts, Mem. And thank you, Sergeant, for the two sets," she said.

We sat on the sandy beach under the sheer bluffs, her two-year-old son, James, endlessly filling and emptying a bucket with small stones and shells. I saw the puff of thin grey smoke billow skyward from the heavily mined fields between the Esplanade and the sea, before I heard the explosion.

"What was that?" Francine asked, startled.

"I don't know, but I'll have to find out...just in case the rear guard officer isn't at HQ."

The minefields had been sown during the 1940-41 invasion scare, clearly marked in half-a-dozen languages, surrounded by coiled high rolls of barbed wire. A local police officer (too old to even join the Home Guard) and Ronson were already there, staring at a multicolored beach ball, gently bouncing around inside the barbed wire.

"What happened?" I panted. "Somebody lose their ball? And it set off a mine?"

"Nope," said Ronson. "Look over to the right of the ball...that lump. Looks like a piece of a carcass."

It did look like a carcass, the legless one-armed torso of a bloodied human being.

"Anybody call Frizzell?"

"Not yet."

"I've sent for help," the old policeman said. "We'll have to get him out. He's a sailor, on leave. That's his wife over there, and their baby."

I decided to go into the minefield armed with a lifeguard's safety pole with a small curved hook on one end, and an extra large gunny sack under my arm.

"You're nuts," whispered Ronson, hoarsely.

"Who else is going to?" I asked, my mind already made up to follow the sailor's clearly imprinted footsteps until they ended, then try and hook what was left of one of His Royal Britannic Majesty's tars into the sack. Silently, I prayed he was no more than 170 pounds, my weight. "How many stone in 170 pounds?" I asked.

"What'd you say?"

"Nothing."

The footprints were safe. I stopped close enough to pull the remains into the gunny sack and cautiously retraced my steps.

Francine and her son were waiting when I sneaked through the same opening in the barbed wire the sailor had used when he tried to rescue his baby's beach ball.

"Come over and visit tonight, Fred, after supper," she said, "please." Her words were so soft I took them for a continuous hiss.

I lost my cherry that night — awkwardly — in a flurry of bare legs, arms and wet kisses.

"That was the bravest thing I've ever seen," she said later.

I stubbed out my cigarette. It wasn't, I said to myself, because I only followed the tar's footsteps.

"It's been an exciting day," she said, stroking my chest.

"Let's do it again, before I lose the hang of it," I said.

She giggled. "Yes, let's. But you must kiss my breasts first — you're in too much of a hurry."

Alex-Joe jolted me out of my reverie. "What's with Cowshit?" he prodded. "He looks like he has muckled onto the troubles of the entire world. Hey, Private MacKeegan, c'mere!"

Cowshit wiped his hands off with some rags and walked across the vehicle yard, grunted and squatted on his heels. "Yeah?"

"What's bothering you, soldier, you got problems? Like, are you sick?"

Cowshit sighed. "I'm getting married next week."

"For Chrissakes!" exploded Alex-Joe.

"To the little doll we met that night out at the Fox and Hounds?" I asked.

"Yeah. Clare Spooner."

"For Chrissakes!" repeated Alex-Joe.

"You aren't old enough to get hitched," said Nine-Pence.

"I'm almost twenty-two."

"That's not old enough."

"Hell," said Cowshit, spitting, "my old man was married at sixteen."

"For Chrissakes!" repeated Alex-Joe.

"Will ya cut that out!" snapped Cowshit.

"I can't see you all married up," said Alex-Joe. "That's what's throwing me."

"Yeah, I know," said Cowshit, sadly. "It throws me, too."

"You tell Pithorse?" I asked.

"Yeah. He's gonna be best man."

"Then what's your problem?"

"You sound like a man going to be shot, not married," said Alex-Joe.

"You got the army's okay? Or you going to do it civvy style?" I asked.

"I got the Old Man's okay. I asked for it two weeks after I met her. An' it's come through."

"Then what the hell are you sad for?"

"I ain't sad."

"You got a dose?" asked Alex-Joe, sarcastically.

Cowshit looked at him, half scowling, half smiling. "Naw. An' don't be funny."

"It's your family. They don't like the idea of your marrying a Limey. That's it."

The scowl disappeared. "Naw. I wrote the old lady an' the old man an' told 'em I was marryin' Clare whether they liked it or not. I ain't heard back. But that don't matter. I'm marryin' her anyway.

"But some guys think I'm marryin' her because I couldn't get it any other way," Cowshit went on.

Alex-Joe grunted.

"You guys think that?" asked Cowshit, his black eyes on Alex-Joe then me, his virility at stake.

I stared across the sand at Zwicker, in the back of the platoon jeep, his nose buried in a comic book as usual. Zwicker. Christ, I wondered, how many guys in this platoon don't seem to have first names? Like Zwicker. Just Zwicker. Nothing else. Pithorse. Or Cowshit. Or Shrumpski.

"You guys think that?" repeated Cowshit.

"No," I said.

"Me neither," said Alex-Joe.

"It's important to me," Cowshit said finally, "because it ain't true. I almost busted Shrumpski a shot between the horns when he said it last night. Everybody laughed. So, I couldn't do it. Did you know she was engaged to a Limey air force officer when she met me? An' she took his ring off and chose me."

"Smart doll," said Alex-Joe, humorously.

Cowshit blinked at Alex-Joe. "You think she chose me because she'll get a bigger allowance than she would from one of them skinny Limeys?" he asked.

"No, Cowshit. You're just a sweetie, a real live doll."

Cowshit's relieved smile was quick. Awkwardly, he shoved Alex-Joe violently and the stocky sergeant keeled over, then righted himself. "And y'r stronger, too. Every broad likes a strong man. You should know that, Cowshit."

Across the vehicle park, Coutt came out of the transport office. He spotted Zwicker and bawled, "Damn you and your little fat arse! You got to have that vehicle ready for 1730! Captain Archibald wants you an' four wheels at the officers' mess at 1745 sharp, an' you're sittin' in the back reading them damned fool books!"

Zwicker looked around, impassively. "I'm improving my mind, Sarg," he said, lazily.

Coutt exploded. "You ain't going to improve your lumpy Deutsch mind if you live to be a hundred and eighty."

Zwicker stretched.

"Now get movin'!" screamed Coutt. "You got to top up with gas an' you need a work order!"

Slowly, Zwicker climbed out of the jeep, mumbling aloud. Wide-legged, he plodded by Coutt, a bland expression on his face, the comic book stuffed in the hip pocket of his soiled denims. Coutt watched him, a half smile on his face, shading his eyes against the sun, until he disappeared inside the transport office door. Almost sorrowfully, he shook his head, and ambled across the park, between the brick pillars and out to the street. He turned right toward the company office.

Cowshit said, "I only asked for your opinions," he said, "because you guys know what's right. You got more schoolin' than most of us. You're no better. Just book smarter, like knowin' what's right and wrong socially." He looked at his feet. "I just ain't had that much schoolin' if you know what I mean."

I raked some sand with my fingers.

"All I know is I'm crazy about Clare," he added. "Christ, she's got more sense in her little finger than I got in my whole frame. And she's a right good girl."

Because he can't lay her, I thought.

"Funny thing," Cowshit said, "I get along great with her people.

Especially the old man. He's a little fellow, a retired army officer and a little deaf because he don't hear so well since the last war. Her old lady is okay now. At first, she was kinda stunned if you know what I mean. No, maybe a little queer an' old-fashioned. But I gave her the ol' rowdy-dow, the 'mother-I-love-you' bit and she came 'round, like the Grand Narrows ferry, slow but sure. Hell, you guys know somethin'? I don't even drink or swear when I'm around her. The old lady, I mean. But I drink a little with the old man."

I couldn't picture Cowshit as a mother's boy with the old lady, so I laughed. And in a swell of affection, I looped my left arm around his neck and dragged him to the ground.

"You crazy mixed-up bastards!" said Alex-Joe.

We wrestled like two dogs, rolling in the swirling sand and dust until exhausted, we lay flat on our broad backs, panting.

"You comin' to the weddin'?" gasped Cowshit.

"You asking us?" said Alex-Joe.

Cowshit rolled over until his head and shoulders were in the shade. He grinned, a streak of grey dirt on the side of his face. "Askin'? Hell, no! I'm tellin' you!"

"I'm going to borrow a kilt," said Alex-Joe.

I sat up, slapping the dust out of my coveralls. "Me, too. Where'll we get 'em?"

"I'll see Black Jack MacMillan in the pipe band. He'll line them up." Alex-Joe crossed his legs. "You're gettin hitched in the kilt, aren't you Cowshit?"

"Yep. I got Gunner Sutherland's."

"You going to wear underwear?"

"Christ, yes! It's my weddin'!"

"You got no sporting blood, Cowshit."

Cowshit grinned, like a poor man peering into a pot of gold. "The sport'll come, buddy, the sport'll come!"

The wedding was at 1400 hours in the Anglican church. The bride was pure and virginal in a white gown once worn on a similar occasion by her mother. It had been let out to the danger point to accommodate Clare's much more generous assets. She was given away by her father, Captain R.A. Spooner, M.C., retired, formerly of the King's Own Infantry. And because she was the daughter of a lowland Scottish mother, she stood on a gold sovereign (as her mother had) for good luck while the good and reverend R.P. Muchmore dutifully made them man and wife before the eyes of God and most of 4 platoon.

The Highlanders were a model of genteel decorum at the reception despite the fact Colonel Weir and Major Sommerville donated a single case of whiskey and gin.

"I really had my doubts," I explained in the half-light filling Francine's bedroom, "I was sure some of the boys would get likkered up and the inevitable fight would result."

Francine rolled over, exposing her shapely buttocks. "They do fight quite a bit, though...more than the English boys who were here before them."

"Who says so?"

"Everybody."

"Balls."

"That's a disgusting phrase, darling," she murmured, her face half buried in the thick pillow.

I ran my hands over Francine's bare, warm skin. "If they fight, it's because some of them have nothing else to do."

"English soldiers aren't always fighting."

"Francine, Canadians aren't English. And we're a long way from home," I said.

She lifted her head clear of the pillow and made a face. "Well, if they aren't English, what are they? They've got English — well, British — names, they speak English. And no matter, they should be better mannered."

"I won't get into that with you." I patted her bottom again. "And we make love differently."

She giggled. "How would you know?"

"Hearsay, ma'am, hearsay."

Francine Powell-Jones rolled over onto her back and opened her slim legs. "Well, if that's what you believe, now's the time to prove it."

Later, she asked, "Can you stay until morning?"

"No, sorry. I'm due back at 2359."

The warm, lazy night air in the elderly Triton Hotel was still and stifling, heightened by private Toasty MacDonnell's B.O.

"Even cigarette smoke and the smell of stale beer and whiskey can't kill it," muttered Shrumpski, lifting a half bottle of Scotch off the floor where it rested between myself and Pithorse. He took a mouthful. "Ach!" he whispered.

"He oughta get a regimental bath," Pithorse said.

"To hell with Toasty, tonight anyway," I said.

An insistent throbbing filled the night sky, drifting into each open-windowed room of the three-storied hotel.

"There they go again," Toasty said. "By day, it's the Yanks. By night, it's the RAF. There won't be anything left of the friggin' Squareheads by the time the army decides to move us onto the continent."

"Who says so?" asked Pithorse.

"Me. I think so."

"Mebbe you should do more washin' and less thinkin'."

Toasty sat up on his bunk. "I ain't so bad. After all, this ain't no palace."

"Yeah, an' you ain't no prince, either."

Toasty grinned lazily and stood up. "Pithorse, I got no grudge with you. An' seein' as we're pals, I'm heading for the cookhouse to see if I can rustle up some bread. An' hot tea." He stretched. "Ain't nothing I like more than hot, hot tea and lots of sugar an' some dry toast. You want some?"

"Why not?"

"Okay." He clumped out of the room. We listened to his footsteps die away on the narrow stairs.

"He's got to be the laziest, smelliest bastard in all the armies," said Pithorse, wrinkling his nose, disgustedly.

Shrumpski handed me the bottle. I drank and passed it to Pithorse. Pithorse studied the label. "That had to be a great weddin'," he said. "Ol' Cow all married up." He drank and returned the bottle to Shrumpski who leaned forward and gazed up into the night. "Don't hear those bomber fellas any more," he said.

Nobody spoke. We lit cigarettes.

Pithorse laughed. "With my luck, my bride will have the flag up an' I won't be makin' out on my wedding night!"

Shrumpski's wrinkled face twisted in a beatific grin. "That shouldn't stop you."

"Old man," Pithorse said, indignantly, "you friggin' Polacks might do it then, but not me. I got notions about things like that."

Shrumpski sighed. Only thirty-six, the years in the coal mines of first Silesia and then Cape Breton had taken a heavy toll, physically. He looked fifty. His round, Slavic face hid a mind that had long since stopped questioning the behavior of his fellow humans. He said: "What the hell does a twenty-one-year-old farmboy know about biology? Or behavior?"

"That had to be a great weddin'," repeated Pithorse.

"And that's the extent of it," said Shrumpski, "a great wedding between two kids who hardly knew each other but wanted to go to bed."

Pithorse ignored Shrumpski. "Like we promised Cow, there were no fights and no drunks. Not one," he said.

"Why didn't they just find a bed and climb in and screw?" Shrumpski asked no one in particular. "Then they could have had what they wanted without any commitment."

"You heard what happened last night in King's Lynn?" asked Pithorse, trying to change the subject.

"Then again," mused Shrumpski, and taking a long drink from the bottle, "maybe, just maybe, they would've still got married." He placed the bottle back on the floor.

"Yeah. Zwicker an' Ronson and Big Bonnicks beat up on some Limey redcaps," I said.

"One of 'em was an officer."

"Tough," someone said.

"Not tough," I said, "stupid. There'll probably be an identification parade tomorrow or the next day."

In the soft light, the high bones in Pithorse's smooth-skinned face left his eyes in dark shadows. And the bones seemed to shift as he said, "When you think we're going up against the Squareheads, Fred?"

The question caught me by surprise. So, I thought, that's why there's no post-wedding spree. The 1st Div's assault into Sicily has had a sobering effect. "I don't know," I said at last.

"We going down into them stinkin', waterlogged pits?" interrupted Shrumpski, drunkenly.

"What'd you say, old-timer?"

Shrumpski blinked. "Nothin'. Pithorse, have a drink. Nobody promised Cowshit we wouldn't get drunk in the Triton."

There was no ID parade the next day. Or the next. But Coutt fell in three men who marched Toasty to the company showers where he was rudely stripped, rudely scrubbed down with stiff brushes, and rudely guarded until all his clothes had been boiled, washed and dried. The next time he appeared in the vehicle park, he smelled no better than anyone else in 4 platoon.

Captain Frizzell, as usual, stared down at his large hands which half-covered his desk.

"Sergeant Cederberg," he said, "there's a divisional officer's training exam school coming up next week down in Eastbourne, and I think you should attend. I'll nominate you."

I shifted my weight from foot to foot. Hell, I thought, Uncle Gordon's doing what he thinks best again — all the way from Camp Aldershot in Nova Scotia. "Anyone else going, sir?" I asked, stalling.

"We're sending company Sergeant-Major Raff MacAuley and Sergeant Roy from the Pioneers. You'll make it three."

Remembering how I had pained my uncle the last time we had met, I heard myself say, "Yes sir, thank you."

The course was a snap. Middle-high-school math, English, history, geography, and how you handled your knife and fork in the school mess. I finished first, Sergeant Roy third and CSM MacAuley, who had studied hard, was up the track. With the week over, it was back to Hunstanton where the warm dry weather continued.

CHAPTER FOUR

I N August, the Highlanders moved. Headquarters, parts of support and the four rifle companies were loaded on troop-carrying vehicles and convoyed to the historic Salisbury Plains where they settled under canvas. Four platoon and the mortars went by flatcar, their armored vehicles chained to the wooden-floored rolling stock. A thousand kids, girls and aging parents saw us off.

"You remember the kind of welcome we got when we landed in Hunstanton?" asked Albert as he climbed up into his carrier.

"Yes, I remember," I replied. "There wasn't a soul on hand. Not even the kids looking for gum or chocolate."

"An' why would anybody have been there," said Coutt, "didn't some old minister advise the townspeople to stay away from us, that we were a bad bunch..."

I watched the Hunstanton belles hugging Highlanders, the little boys waving and crying out. Well, I thought, so much for old ministers.

Two days were needed before the regiment settled in — twenty-eight miles north and east of Christchurch. Routine training resumed.

And more than 900 men schemed incessantly to avoid route marches, cookhouse duties or regimental guard; or how to snaffle a pass into Christchurch where the newly arrived U.S. Army whites fought U.S. Army blacks over beer, whiskey and white women until frantic American authorities decreed Mondays, Wednesdays and Fridays as "Negro nights" and all others as "white nights."

Sundays were days of peace.

Outwardly, it was the same regiment which had disembarked at Liverpool in November of 1941. Internally, it had changed. Personnel had been shifted from one company to the other, older men returned to Canada or attached to nonactive depots. Younger men had begun shaving, others had become NCOs. Officers had been invalided out or promoted. They were orderly progressions despite the personalities involved. And if men were always shifting, coming and going, the order remained.

Boys and men who had come together, fresh from schools, farms, mines, their parents' homes, had replaced many of the originals who had gone active with the Highlanders in September, 1939. They had grown quickly, yet shucked family ties and freedoms slowly, submitting, without consciously realizing it, to army rules and regulations. In the beginning, most relationships had been on a personal basis, when companies, platoons, officers and NCOs had come out of individual towns, counties, valleys. But the shifting of personnel had begun a breakdown of the regionalities; training and time had ended them.

Order began with (as far as they knew) the Old Man in the Regimental Orderly Office. The rebels, the misfits, tested it. The smart ones watched and learned and survived. Joining the army, Alex-Joe had once allowed, was like breaking your leg and learning to live with it.

And no matter how much the ranks bitched, the regiment had become home. It offered refuge when they were broke, provided them with three squares a day (although this was a loose interpretation of what each man considered a square meal) and if a man got into trouble with the military police, a woman or civilian authorities, the regiment stood up for him. No one said this, it was merely accepted without the saying.

In early October, Albert and I headed for Scotland and his bride in Newtongrange on a nine-day leave just as the Highlanders were on the move again, this time to Eastbourne. The overnight train out of London's Euston Station was oversold (as usual) mostly to Canadians who had been marrying Scottish girls in such numbers that it had alarmed my mother. Her last letter had contained a Canadian Press clipping which claimed something like 35,000 to 40,000 Canadians had married in the U.K., the bulk of them to Caledonian lassies.

"Don't do it," she had warned. "There are plenty of nice girls back home. And you're a Canadian, don't you forget that."

Newtongrange was a drab little coal mining town housing pleasant people in row-on-row look-alike brick houses. And I came to the conclusion that Violet (Albert's bride) must have been the most popular girl in the entire shire because every time I turned around or went for a walk in the brisk autumn air I was introduced to another "girlfriend." All of them single. And there were pilgrimages to the Miner's Pub with Mr. Wilson where dozens of tough, dirty nailed, happy men (veterans of the mines and World War I) drank their Scotch in a gulp and sipped ale. Or played darts.

"Do you ever invite the women?" I asked Mr. Wilson.

"No, we don't," he said in his lowland burr. "And it's as well, for no lady would be seen in here. Or a pub, for that matter."

It made me wonder how the English and Scots could live literally cheek-by-jowl (in miles) and be so totally different. By the time we had ambled back to the Wilson home, I couldn't even remember where I was.

It was raining when we arrived back in Eastbourne, walking straight from the station to regimental headquarters where Coutt was duty sergeant.

"I got news for you, Cederberg," he greeted as he accepted our passes for the records.

"I've been made a general."

"You're going home..."

I gulped. "I've been accepted for officer's training?"

"...and we're going into action."

I sat down, abruptly, confused. "You got the details?" I asked as Albert edged across the room and stood beside me.

"Yep. You're to be struck off strength and shipped to the non-effective transfer depot in Cardiff to wait for shipping home."

"And the Highlanders?...No shit, Coutt?"

"Well," he looked at me curiously, as if he didn't know whether to feel sorry for me or offer his congratulations, "officially we're going to Ireland on a training exercise. But nobody believes that. We think we're going to the Mediterranean — Italy."

I winced, shaken by an almost uncontrollable sense of loss, of loneliness. I stood up. "Let's get out of here, Albert. Let's get out of here."

"Cederberg, you be here tomorrow at 1000 hours for your transportation order. Y'hear?" Coutt yelled as we left.

Albert opened a gill of Scotch his father-in-law had given him. "Here," he said, "you look like you need it."

I swallowed a mouthful and lit a cigarette.

"What're you going to do?" he asked.

"I've been thinking. I'm going to stay with the regiment...I can't leave now…not with all of you going to Italy…I can't." I leaked the phrases out slowly in fragments. "I just can't…any more than I could…ah, gentle Jesus…I just can't."

"If you're worrying about what the others would say, well I wouldn't," said Albert. "They'd understand, hell, they'd even be jealous."

I took a bigger mouthful of Scotch.

"Mebbe," said Albert, "Coutt's got it wrong. Mebbe we are just going to Ireland. The Italy bit is a rumor."

No, it's not, I thought. My instinct told me that. "Mebbe you're right," I said.

We finished the gill in silence.

"You made up your mind?" Albert said, finally.

"Yep. I'm going with the regiment. I'll tell the colonel I don't want the officer's bit."

"He'll tell you you're going, Fred. And that'll be it. You should know the army by now. They can make you do anything — except have a baby," Albert chuckled.

I had a bright, whiskey idea. "What time is it, buddy?"

"Just after six."

I got up. "How much money have you got?"

"About eleven shillings."

"I've got twelve, but together that's not enough."

"For what?"

"I'm going over the hill, AWOL to Scotland."

"On twenty-three shillings? You're nuts."

I grinned. "I'll use platform tickets and hide in the women's cans whenever the conductor goes through. Just for a few days. And when I get back, they'll cancel the NETD order. The army'd never send a guy home with a record." I mimicked the classic officer: "Just isn't done, y'know!"

"Shit…I'm going with you," said Albert, laughing. "Like the man says, let's move it!"

We did. And it worked. Four days later, Albert's wife gave us the money to return (and later paid British Railways, anonymously, for the two seats she insisted we had "stolen" on the ride to Scotland).

Coutt had covered for Albert, but apologized that he hadn't been able to do likewise for me. "You were supposed to be on transfer and I couldn't account for you for almost five goddamned days!" he said.

Colonel Weir reduced me to a corporal, then explained that because of my absence only Sergeant Roy would be going home. I felt he was laughing on the inside when he fined me five days' pay.

Four platoon's NCOs sat on lines of army-issue cots. Coutt stood with his back to the closed door.

"What I've got to say is not to leave this room, or I'd probably be shot at sunrise, if it ever stops raining." He licked his lips. "How I got the info doesn't matter, but you all know I was regimental orderly sergeant for the past couple of days. So listen and behave yourselves accordingly.

"It's named Operation Timberwolf, and we're going to Ireland on a training exercise."

Someone snickered.

Coutt looked around the room. "That's what it says. And all vehicles are to be delivered for dispersal to Southern Command.

"Think about that 'cause it means we're goin' to Ireland on a training exercise without any vehicles...unless, of course, we're gonna become cavalry division and ride those fine Irish horses.

"To get there, we go by train, at 2200 hours, on October twenty-sixth to Liverpool, if I remember correctly."

"That's twelve days off," said Alex-Joe.

"You thinkin' you might get leave? Or enjoy a Cederberg trip to Scotland on your own?" He paused. "Forget it. There'll be three-day passes for all ranks except those confined to barracks and servin' time in the cookhouse or digger...one-third to go at a time. And any man who doesn't return on time screws a man in the next batch because somebody won't go. First parties leave tomorrow at 1400. An' another thing, no heading for the nearest kiosk to phone a wife, broad, floozie or cousin. Got that?"

"When will the men know all this?" I asked.

"In about an hour. I'm telling you guys so's you'll be able to get to the kiosks before the lineups get so long a guy will need a one-day pass just to make a phone call." He laughed shrilly, enjoying his own joke. "Got it?"

The first batch of 300 Highlanders got off the train at Victoria Station and quickly disappeared in London's sodden, rain-drenched maze.

"There's a story my father used to tell me," Francine said, facing me across the small table in Bentley's Oyster Bar on Swallow Street, "that it's always raining on some part of London. It's just a small cloud, weeping for the Saxons who fell in 1066. Do you believe that?"

I sipped my whiskey. "No I don't. And besides, there's more than one cloud tonight, the sky's filled with them."

"You aren't very romantic tonight, my sweet." Francine wrinkled her fine nose and gently chewed a piece of Dover sole.

"I can be romantic. But not over a rain cloud. By the way, I'm glad as hell you came."

She paused, placing her slim fingers on the back of my hand. "My sweet, you knew I would come. And while you haven't told me, I know why you rang. You're going away."

I squirmed, uncomfortably.

"What's bothering you, my love? Are you afraid? No, that's not it." She smiled. "Ah, it's that I'm married, isn't it."

I lowered my head.

"Lover, I've sensed that from the beginning. Well, don't let it bother you. What a strange time for this to come up! I can assure you that Major Peter Powell-Jones, wherever he is, is enjoying some company, if there's any available."

Damnit, I thought, what a ridiculous conversation. "Let's talk about something else."

She shrugged, but her smile remained.

"You must come back after the war," she said, "then you'll dine at the real Bentley's. The beef is excellent, but the seafoods — lobster, clams, oysters — oh, Fred, in peacetime..."

Peacetime. What a strange word, I reflected. I wonder why I never think of it.

"...and with Picadilly Circus alight, it's so..."

I watched her face. Her teeth were small in her mouth. Her eyes were alive, her brows moving while she talked.

"The shops," she explained, "on Regent Street are simply divine ..."

I liked her more than I cared to admit, I thought, because I'd never met anyone like her. She wasn't like the girls I had known in high school. That was the difference. They had been girls. She's a woman. With a woman's ways.

Later, while Francine slept beside me, I tried to sketch Peter Powell-Jones and peacetime in my mind. But it was unconnected, like fragments of a restless dream. Reality, I concluded, was the woman beside me, her warm body, the slope of her hips, the texture

of her skin, the power of her. I recalled a question she had blurted
out one night in the beginning: "Am I your first?" And when I had
admitted she was, she seemed to catch fire in a frenzy of emotion.

We said goodbye at Victoria Station. She was gentle and too
talkative, I was uncomfortable, restless and edgy. I promised to write
and meet again. The train picked up speed quickly and hooted
forlornly at the grey skies as it moved between the rows of houses.

The troopship was the SS *Monterey*, tugging gently on her lines at
dock in the Mersey. The crew was American.

And because during their almost two years in the U.K. neither the
officers nor other ranks had noted the gradual darkening of British
bread, the bright whiteness of the U.S. issue at the first on-board
meal delighted them. They were like kids, turning the fresh slices
over in their hands, examining their whiteness, slathering them with
real butter and making sandwiches of real ham and cheese then
stuffing them inside their tunics.

"Take all ya want," the American dining-room orderlies yelled,
"an' help yourself to the apples an' oranges an' anything else 'cause
we only feed ya twice a day. But fill up!"

"I ain't seen bread like this since we were in Debert," insisted
Pithorse.

"Hell, you never had bread like that before you got in the army,"
said Alex-Joe. "All you ever got was halibut jaws and codfish balls."

"And balls to you," shouted Pithorse.

Quickly, the Highlanders bunked in, four sergeants to a cabin on
B deck, two officers to a cabin on A deck, and as many enlisted men
as could be squeezed in each lower deck cabin, the promenade deck
and dry swimming pool.

It was late afternoon. Gulls screamed and swooped over the
Mersey's black waters. The wreck of a destroyer poked its foremast
above the tidal flow while ships' cranes squealed while they stowed
supplies, equipment and gear.

We stood together on B deck aft. The American sailor had a
broken face that left him with a perpetual grimace. He leaned on the
rail, staring at the garbage and bluish oil slicks on the heaving water.

"Hey buddy," asked Pithorse. "Where are we goin'?"

The sailor turned toward us.

"Ireland, fathead," yelled Alex-Joe, munching a large apple.

"Yah!" said Pithorse. "Just because you birds got three hooks,
you figure you know it all!"

"You heard the colonel. He said Ireland. A training exercise."

Cowshit said, "Pithorse, you don't believe anything, do ya? Y'know, you're as mixed up as a neurotic whore."

"You don't even know what a neurotic whore is, do ya?" asked Zwicker.

"Sure. It's a broad with a five-pound ass who's peddlin' it for ten shillings," said Pithorse.

The sailor blinked.

"We going to Ireland?" repeated Pithorse.

"What thuh hell do you think we're runnin', anyway? The Hoboken Ferry?" fumed the sailor. He spat over the rail, watched it break up and disappear before it hit the water. "We're goin' a helluva lot farther than Ireland." Spitting again, he turned and walked away, swaggering a little, like he knew something he would never tell.

"Ah, the dummy," said Pithorse. "He don't know nothin'."

"Well," said Alex-Joe, "neither do you if you think we're going to Ireland."

We laughed nervously.

"Everybody's got to wear lifebelts all the time," said Alex-Joe. "And Pithorse, you haven't got yours on."

"Hell, Alex-Joe, we ain't even left port yet."

"I know. But with practice you'll get used to the idea. Get it on."

Glumly, Pithorse slipped his arms through the lifebelt straps. "There, ya happy now, Sergeant?"

"After you've tied it up."

"Ah, shit. Here, Cow, tie me up, will ya?"

CHAPTER FIVE

FOR eight days, the twenty-four-vessel convoy bucked the trackless Atlantic, flanked by American destroyers, cruisers and a single carrier. Then, on October 27th, we steamed in two lines through the Strait of Gibraltar as a near-tropical evening sun sank below the western skyline in a glowing red ball.

The merchantmen and liners carried 23,500 Canadians, including the 5th Armored Division, 1st Corps troops, reinforcements for the Palestinian Constabulary and ground-crew air personnel, who ate, roughhoused through boat drill, attended lectures, and studied pamphlets covering every subject from the perils of VD to basic Italian to how to count, using Allied script lira.

The next evening, as the first sitting straggled away from the stand-up serving counters, carrying their apples, oranges and sandwiches, a flight of German torpedo-carrying biplanes came low out of the dusk.

Escort warships opened fire, filling the skies with glowing tracers. At first, I thought it was a fireworks display. I watched and oohed like the other Highlanders. But the convoy scattered like cattle, shepherded by the quick-moving destroyers, their sirens wailing and hooting.

The noise was ear-shattering.

In the time it takes for a southern sun to disappear, it was over. A Dutch merchantman and U.S. destroyer had vanished in violent explosions, sending their crews and supplies to the bottom of the Mediterranean. Three swastika-banded planes had plummeted into the water, spewing smoke and orange flame. The troop-carrying liners steamed for the safety of nearby Allied ports, their nervous human cargoes hushed and subdued.

"If I'da known this boat ride was gonna get so serious," said Nine-Pence, "I'da paid more attention to that friggin' boat drill. Hell, I didn't know which end was up."

I nodded. When a Yank yelled "every man grab the nearest Bren and start firing" I knew it wasn't a fireworks show. And every time I emptied a mag into a Jerry plane, the vibration moved my helmet down over my eyes and I couldn't see a damned thing.

"An' when our three-incher went off, I thought we'd been hit. I was ready to abandon ship. Christ!" I said aloud.

"You should've been below decks," said Albert. "We didn't know what in hell was happening. You could hear explosions, planes, ack-ack. And smell panic — like something was going bad. For a minute, I thought there was going to be a wild scramble to get outside, but some guy hollered, 'Anybody want to buy a watch... cheap?' and everybody started to laugh. A little at first. Then belly laughs, and we felt better."

"Any troop ships get it?" asked Nine-Pence.

"Nope. I talked to Captain Archibald an' he said the div's still in one bunch," Coutt said, coming up on deck.

"What about the Squareheads? We get any?"

"Two. Three. That's the scuttlebutt."

"Where're we goin'?"

"Naples, they say. Tomorrow morning. First light."

"Jeez. It can't be too soon."

"Yeah?" asked Alex-Joe.

Suddenly, we were aware that the *Monterey* was stopped, riding the swells in the night.

"F'Chrissakes!" coughed Albert, "look at that!"

To our right, outlined against the faint horizon, was a liner, her stern deep in the water.

"Prepare to take survivors aboard!" the voice over the P.A. system intoned in a nasal Yankee twang.

Three destroyers, low in the inky night, circled slowly around us and the obviously stricken ship, like hounds trying to pick up a scent.

One by one the long scramble nets were flung over the side and we volunteered to go down their length to help Canadian nursing sisters aboard. It wasn't easy. The army had insisted we wear our woolen-issue gloves in any such exercise. But we had to get rid of them because they were too slippery. We couldn't hold onto the swaying ropes and carry a frightened nurse at the same time.

They were off the SS *Santa Elena*, they told us, which had been hit in the stern. But American officers had assured them the liner's bulkheads were holding.

Shortly after midnight there was a submarine alarm and the *Monterey*, with about 1,000 survivors aboard (the U.S. destroyers got the remaining 800) steamed for the safety of Philipville harbor in North Africa. We arose the following morning in time to see a deep-sea tug towing the *Santa Elena* into port. Suddenly the towing cable snapped with a sharp boom and she sank in two minutes, kicking up a tremendous rumble of foam, debris and froth.

Oddly, not a life had been lost in the rescue operation.

The *Monterey*, its bulk painted grey and flat blue, towered above Naples' bomb-blasted Royal Dock, disgorging lines of steel-helmeted Highlanders, carrying big and small packs, weapons and duffle bags.

I stood alongside Alex-Joe amid the shambles of the dock's paved surface.

"We all here?" he asked.

"Yeah. But where the hell are the trucks?" I jiggled my pack straps to make the weight of the pack more comfortable on my shoulders.

Pithorse, his back bent under the weight of his duffle bag and gear, said, "One of the crewmen tol' me Naples was just captured a few days ago."

A long boom swung out from the *Monterey* with a dozen packing boxes caught up in a huge landing net. Men were bawling orders, a steam engine panted.

"Where in hell are thuh trucks?" a Yank officer boomed. "If they don't come soon, we're gonna have more men than we can accommodate on this friggin' dock!"

Overhead, a pair of Allied fighter planes patrolled, lazily turning and circling in the grey skies. Across the bay, Vesuvius lifted its pointed crown upward toward the cloud, a thin wisp of smoke trailing from it.

White-helmeted American MPs were everywhere. A few drops of rain fell sending up tiny puffs of concrete dust.

"Four platoon..." bellowed Coutt. Whatever he said after that was lost. The trucks, a long line of them, crawled noisily onto the deck, MPs clearing a path for them through the mob of men.

Abruptly, everything began to work smoothly. As fast as the three-tonners pulled up, the men lurched aboard, thirty per vehicle, under the canvas-shrouded steel-tubed frameworks. No waiting was allowed. "You wanna be standin' around like a buncha dummies when the Krauts come in with bombers?" screamed an American MP top-sergeant. "Well, ya will, if ya don't get the lead outta y'r asses!"

Slowly, heavy duty motors roaring, the lead trucks negotiated Naples' narrow, rubble-littered streets. It was stop and go traffic. And we got our first view of a war-ravaged land, the filth, the frightened old people, the curious-eyed urchins who held their hands out and bawled, "*Chocolati?* Cigarettes for papa?"

Those jammed against the trucks' steel tailgates had the best view. The further toward the front, the less they saw. "Aw c'mon, Sarg," pleaded Cowshit, fighting to get a look and stay on his feet at the same time, "let's get 'em to take the canvas off, eh?"

"You nuts or something?" Coutt asked. "It's rainin'."

Pithorse, at the tailgate between Alex-Joe and I, stuck his hand out. "Hah, it ain't."

Coutt said: "The canvas stays."

Bumping and jolting, the convoy rumbled on, climbing higher and higher along a twisting, crater-pocked road. Neat, orderly olive groves lined the rolling slopes; fields opened on either side of them, studded here and there with scarred white-and-pink stone houses, their red-tiled roofs holed and splintered. No one spoke any more. Those who could see stared, wonderingly, at the scarred land, the tangled grapevines that clung like so many battered scarecrows to the wires strung from pole to pole.

Donkeys, scruffy and lean, plodded stoically along the verges, large wicker paniers strapped to their gaunt, ribbed sides. Behind them came their owners, barefooted in the chill, watery mud. They turned impassive, brown-skinned faces and black eyes on the moving trucks, insensible to the occasional hoots from the soldiers, or the gumbo muck splashed on their ragged pants and jackets by the big wheels.

"Lord Jesus!" wheezed Pithorse, one big hand clinging to the overhead steel frame to stay on his feet as the three-tonner literally bounced through potholes, "take a look at that!"

There was a mad scramble to the tailgate. At the same time, the truck hammered into a deeper than usual hole and the driver hit the brake pedal. Men were thrown against one another, falling over duffle bags, cursing and yelling. I managed to hang onto my corner by bracing my knees against the tailgate and clutching the framework at the same time. Looking out, all I could see was an Italian woman of gigantic proportions with a baby tucked under one arm. She was waddling downhill, against the flow of traffic. Then, suddenly and naturally, she halted, gathered up most of her billowing skirt in one hand, squatted and urinated. She turned to look at us, a placid smile on her broad face.

Howls of protest erupted from the ringside viewers.

"Hey, honey!" screamed Pithorse, "you can't do that in public!"

The woman's expression went blank. She shrugged her massive shoulders and looked away as a torrent splattered down between her dirty, bare feet. Finished, she straightened up and let her skirt fall. She patted the baby's head, hitched it into a more comfortable position on her fat hip and trudged down the road.

"Lord Almighty! Did you see that?" breathed Pithorse.

Alex-Joe's eyes were still bugged. "Well, when you got to go, you got to go," he croaked.

"Can you imagine doin' that at home?" asked Pithorse.

"It'd get ya thirty days, providin' the judge wasn't in bad humor," said Alex-Joe.

"Y'd get tarred an' feathered where I come from!" Zwicker piped.

"Didja see the sores on that ol' broad's legs?" asked Cowshit.

Talk died down, each of us struggling to keep from being bounced to death whenever the truck lurched.

From a particularly high turn, the Bay of Naples spread below us, like a peaceful green-grey mirror. We could see the high-decked *Monterey* still shedding its human cargo. They looked like long lines of worker ants as they moved from the ship's belly to the tiny trucks.

It began to rain again, quickly and in blinding sheets. And the sudden downpour drenched everyone near the tailgate before we could get the canvas flaps unstrapped and hooked together.

Alex-Joe was asleep, chin on chest, his flat steel hat tilted far back on his head. Each time the truck bounced, his head rolled from side to side.

Hours jolted by. I thought of Hunstanton and Francine. And, for the first time in almost two years, I felt absolutely alone.

"It's what I always pictured the moon would be," observed Albert. "I've never seen such destruction and poverty. See Naples and die! Hell, no wonder you died. The plague probably carried you off."

I could only nod in dejected agreement.

It was 2200 hours when the convoy halted in the late night. And it remained halted for several minutes, truck motors idling. Coutt unhooked the canvas flaps, bellowing, "Okay, men! Here's your new home away from home!" It was acres and acres of vineyards and olive trees. Once tiered like guardsmen on parade, they had been fought over by German and U.S. Fifth Army infantry. Now, in the rain and darkness, they were a maze of tangled wires, water-filled shell craters and mud.

Numbed from the jolting ride, we pitched small, two-man field tents. Inside, we laid our greatcoats and ponchos on the ground, then went prowling the strange landscape for the cooks who waited for us with steaming stew, hot coffee and thick slabs of bread.

It tastes, I thought, like Bentley's finest dish as I spooned the thick gravy and bread into my mouth, greedily.

Coutt called the platoon together by the light of a flaring gasoline fire. "Tomorrow," he shrilled, "you clean all personal weapons. And I mean clean 'em. Mister MacNaughton, himself, will be inspecting at 1000 hours."

In the shifting glow of the flames, he reminded me of a barbarian chief. The deep lines in his face stood out in black and his great, lumpy nose beneath his bushy brows could have belonged to a pitiless heathen.

"Then what?" asked Alex-Joe.

"We move off for the Adriatic side, across the country in the trucks."

The men of 4 platoon groaned.

"Well, the Infantry Div is over on the other side; it figures we'll join 'em."

A rolling, bumping series of explosions reverberated across the black skies. All eyes turned upward.

"What was that?" whispered Nine-Pence.

"Guns…?"

The gas fire, muck and gasoline worked together and ignited, flickered and hissed in the fine rain. For seconds, nothing happened, then a staggered series of jagged flashes lit the far horizon.

"Sure, it's guns!" croaked Pithorse under his breath.

The rumbling was farther away this time — several distinct, muffled explosions.

Coutt guffawed violently. "What a collection of soldiers you birds are!" he shouted, sarcastically. "That's nothin' but old-fashioned thunder!" He chuckled uncontrollably, slapping his thighs.

Foolish laughter filled the night. Embarrassed, one by one, two by two, we crawled on our hands and knees into our tents and slept. Some snored. I tossed restlessly.

For weeks, through November and well into December, the regiment, the division, played war games along the Adriatic. The weather worsened and tiny waterspouts danced across the grey, white-capped waters. And the generals and their staffs tried to fit an armored formation into a slugging, mountain-style war.

The incessant rains, torrential at times, turned tracked vehicle routes and the broken coastal highway into ribbons of mud. It forced engineers to lay steel matting over roadways to prevent men and vehicles from sinking out of sight. Soaked, we charged through swollen rivers, drilled in the use of rubber boats, until a bedraggled Pithorse muttered: "Those goddamned brassy tin gods of generals don't know anythin' else!"

We dug slit trenches. Big ones, little ones, perfect ones. All filled rapidly with the water that constantly dripped from the leaden heavens. And because we weren't allowed into the towns and cities, we lived off the land, liberating cows, chickens, anything to supplement the monotony of a diet consisting of bully beef, dehydrated potatoes, rice pudding and M and V. M and V was a can containing fragments of meat, globules of fat, a few peas, slivers of carrots and beans.

"If we ever get that s.o.b. Hitler," Zwicker cursed, "I'm gonna see to it that he's locked up in a room and force-fed nothing but M and V, dehydrated spuds and rice — everythin' cooked by our bastard cooks!"

Colonel Weir formally introduced us to Italy, Eyetieland, as he called it, two days after we had arrived in the Termoli area to begin prepping for the big day when we would "have a crack at Jerry."

He climbed up on the hood of his jeep and addressed us, legs apart, hands on hips, his tailor-made tunic and corduroy slacks as spotless as his batman could keep them. It was an afternoon when the skies only threatened rain.

Company commanders and junior officers surrounded the vehicle; we moved in, forming a large semicircle.

"Men!" he bellowed, "there are a few things I think you should get straight in your minds about this country, Eyetieland, facts that weren't in the *Introduction to Italy* booklet handed you while on board ship.

"The Eyeties are now officially considered our allies. That's the word. They've surrendered and they're on our side. Bully! Well, I'm telling you this: As far as I'm concerned, they're just defeated enemies and you can treat 'em as such!

"So help yourself to anything you want, providing it isn't nailed down or guarded. And if that's the case, I have an idea you'll know how to handle it. They're fair game, but don't get caught. Just think of what Eyetie soldiers would have done if they'd got loose in Canada. Remember Ethiopia and Mussolini and his strutting peacocks."

Cowshit whispered, "What happened in Ethiopia?"

"How the hell would I know?" answered Pithorse. "Shut up and let's listen to the Old Man."

"Don't worry about the local cops, the *carabinieri*. But if they do nab any one of you, I'll back *you!*" And he jabbed a pointed finger in the men's direction, dramatically. "And you know, I've got quite a bit of backing!"

A crackle of laughter began among the nearest men and spread through the ranks until, like a ripple on a quiet pond, it died away.

"That's a promise, men." Colonel Weir cleared his throat. "And something else. You're often going to see Eyetie men walking hand-in-hand. Like a couple of girls. Or lovers. Well, don't let it upset you. They aren't queers. It just happens to be an accepted custom, so don't go poking them in the nose.

"As for the whores in the streets, forget them. And any girl who can be had is a whore. Nice Eyetie girls don't screw. That's another custom you're going to have to get used to."

Another storm of laughter gushed from 900 throats. And two old women, damp firewood piled high on their heads, stopped on the road and stared curiously at us in battle dress and balmorals. The nearest stared back, grinning. The women resumed their shuffling march through the mud and water, chattering to themselves.

"There are, however, places where a man can get fixed up," the colonel went on, "legitimate places. And those of you who have disobeyed regs, know what I'm referring to — whorehouses, old-fashioned whorehouses. Which leads to why you've been kept out of the towns. There's a lot of old-fashioned VD around and the army is trying to make sure all of you don't get dosed.

"I know, some of you will. But don't say I didn't warn you."

Weir tilted his dress balmoral back on his head, switched his swagger stick from one hand to the other, and added, "I know you men better than you think I do. You'll get drunk and want to find some pussy. That's life. But for God's sake, and the sake of your wives and girlfriends, use the safes, the prophylactics, the Canadian taxpayers offer you free! They may not be as elegant as some of you are used to, but they're guaranteed *not* to break. And after that, if you can still walk, go straight to the nearest pro center and get a cock wash!"

The men stirred restlessly.

Suddenly, his face softened and he said, "Sometime around Christmas, or thereabouts, we get baptized. You and I. All of us." He looked around for RSM Diplock. "Sergeant-major," he began, then stopped and faced the troops again.

"We're going to be on the move, working hard for the next few weeks. If it gets you down — and it will — remember there is a purpose behind everything you're asked to do. It'll save lives in the long haul. Now, Sergeant-major, take over."

As Christmas neared, the Highlanders were billeted in a former Italian POW camp on the low hills overlooking Altamura. British soldiers and airmen and sailors had occupied it until Marshall Badoglio's surrender in September. It was windowless, chilly, but dry. The plumbing, if crude (concrete footsteps in front of holes over a trough full of running water), was indoors. Canvas was rigged over windowframes, candles lit and we settled in, happy after weeks of living in open fields around gasoline fires.

That afternoon, regimental orders, posted in each company office, announced: All ranks, except those on duty and regimental MPs, are free to leave camp between 1730 hours and 2300 each day until further notice.

Pithorse and Cowshit clomped into the platoon room, their boots muddied.

"Hey, Fred! They got a whorehouse in that crazy town!" Pithorse yelled.

"Can the big noise!" yelled Nine-Pence from a bunk.

"He means on the edge of town," Alex-Joe drawled, "where there's lots of riding."

"Yah. Listen to him! Once a cowboy, always a cowboy, eh, Alex-Joe?" said Pithorse, "and what in hell is a sergeant doin' in the men's room?"

"Pithorse, you know what the Old Man said about getting dosed.

You trying to catch all the VD in Italy all at once?" chided Alex-Joe.

"Aw come on, Sarg, there ain't no clap in this house. The army's runnin' it."

Alex-Joe's head appeared over the rim of the bunk mattress. "What'd you say, Pithorse?"

"As God's my judge, Alex-Joe, the Canadian Army's operatin' this cathouse. They got MPs outside an' issue pieces of ass inside. An' medics. Some of the guys from the tank outfits told me the joint's loaded with good-lookin' broads."

"That's what they say," I said.

"An' some of 'em are right young. Not ol' bags."

"I dunno. But it can't be big money. Not with the army in charge," said Pithorse, sitting down heavily on my bunk.

"Ah, shut up, everybody!" Nine-Pence yelled again.

"Yeah, this ain't no goddamned cathouse!" bellowed Cowshit.

Someone snickered. Pithorse lurched to his feet. "C'mon, Fred, we'll tell this bunch of preachers an' babies where all the fun is later. Like tomorrow."

Silence came with a rush after each man climbed noisily into his bunk to sleep with visions of bare breasts and buttocks.

The whorehouse, a two-story, whitewashed stone casa, was sited at the north end of the main road which ran in a straight line through Altamura. Four platoon arrived en masse, led by Pithorse, Angus the Goat and Nine-Pence. Only Cowshit and Coutt couldn't attend what was dubbed "cathouse parade." Cowshit said he couldn't take a chance, being married. Besides, he added, "Clare's expecting."

Coutt was on duty in the regimental orderly room, swearing profoundly.

For several minutes, we milled about aimlessly in the dark, beyond a small tent rigged over the entrance to the casa's main door. Two of the biggest MPs we'd ever seen were on duty, gazing indifferently at us.

"There's more of 'em, outside at the back," said Pithorse.

"What's the drill?" Alex-Joe asked one of the MPs.

The MP had two hooks on each sleeve of his tunic. He looked Alex-Joe over stonily. "Well, Sergeant," he said, "you pay your money, but you don't take any chances, providing you go through the tent." He nodded with his head toward the tent door. Alex-Joe could see a couple of hurricane lamps glowing inside. "And that's the only way in."

"What's the tariff?"

The MP's fleshy face twitched. "I don't know. I wouldn't be caught dead in there. Except if I have to go in and drag out a shit-disturber."

"Then we got to go through the tent first."

"Now you're getting the idea."

"What's in the tent?"

"Medics. They'll make sure you are clean and come out the same way."

"F'r Chrissakes!"

"You mean they're holdin' a short arm in there?" asked Shrumpski.

"That's about the size of it," the MP said.

"Well, I got nothin' to hide," Shrumpski announced, breaking away and going in.

Each of us produced his paybook, was registered, and the short arm followed. Alex-Joe snickered. "What's all the fuss about?" he asked the pear-shaped orderly checking him out.

"To make sure you simple bastards don't get dosed."

"You mean the broads ain't clean?"

"The MO thinks so. He checks 'em out every morning before they go to the can. But you guys, he doesn't. So, you got to be checked."

Pithorse belched. "Now, that's a job I'd like, checking out the broads!"

Shrumpski scowled, prodding Pithorse, to move along. "C'mon, ya stupid bastard! You wouldn't know how to check out a sick alley cat!"

I laughed nervously as we filed into the house.

The room was large, the walls covered with faded rose-colored paper. A cluster of naked bulbs hung from the ceiling by a rope of twisted black wires. The furniture consisted of benches against each wall. There was another door at the far end, revealing a staircase. But we didn't notice the decor, we focused on seven girls in very short singlets that came down to their hips. They sat together, their bare legs primly crossed, returning our stares, giggling and laughing.

"Lord Jesus!" breathed a pop-eyed Pithorse, "they're just kids!"

Shrumpski guffawed. "Ya, some of 'em can't be any older than you!"

I shivered, and I wasn't even cold.

A plump, laughing brunette came down the stairs, followed by a red-faced soldier in a Tank Corps black beret. His big boots crashed on the stone steps. "Hi men!" he greeted, trotting across the floor and through the doorway into the tent.

"Was she good?" yelled Zwicker.

"Find out for yourself, kid-oh!" he yelled.

The brunette smiled at Alex-Joe, flicked her singlet up, revealing a white, plump ass, then joined the other girls.

"I see the one I want," Shrumpski said under his breath. "The fat one."

"The one that just came down the stairs?" Alex-Joe asked.

"Naw." He pointed furtively at another black-haired girl with round breasts halfway out of the squared neckline trying to contain them. "That one."

Zwicker whispered. "How the hell do we start this?"

"Just help yourself," said Shrumpski. But he didn't move.

Pithorse licked his lips. "Can anyone get a drink in this dump?"

I said, "Nope. One of the MPs said no booze. That's another reason why they're around."

She came down the steps slowly with measured dignity, dressed from her high-buttoned shoes to her neck like a Victorian lady. She hesitated then came straight over to Pithorse and Alex-Joe. "You like my girls?" she asked in fractured English.

"Sure, ma'am, oh sure," said Pithorse, reddening slightly.

"Then you must introduce yourselves," she said. "The price is two hundred lira. Please pay the girls."

"How much is that in Canadian?" asked Angus the Goat under his breath.

"About two bucks," I whispered. I shifted from one foot to the other, feeling strange, as if I had stepped into an odd new world.

The woman gestured toward the giggling girls and spoke to them in Italian. They squealed and in a rush crossed the room, moving among us. A slim blonde grabbed my arm.

"You 'ave someone you weesh?" she asked. She had a pimple near one corner of her mouth. I looked down at her. She wasn't wearing a bra.

"Yes," I said, self-consciously, "but you'll do." I watched the plump brunette leading Alex-Joe up the stairs.

There weren't enough girls to accommodate everybody, immediately. Someone wailed, "Hey, what about me, baby?"

The babble of confused voices rose, boots scuffed the stone floor.

"Gentlemen!" the older woman's voice was thin, but piercing. "Be patient! Your turn will come, just sit down!"

I was halfway up the stairs, following the blonde when she reached back and took my hand, almost running down a long, narrow corridor illuminated by a single bulb at the far end. Girls leading soldiers disappeared through the rows of doors leading off both sides of the hall. Mine stopped suddenly and I almost knocked her down. She smiled without feeling, pushed me through a wooden doorway and slammed it shut.

The room was a cubicle, lit by a small lamp. There was a bed, a washstand with a basin half-full of water, and a chair. She pulled the singlet up over her head, turned and faced me, her hand extended. "You pay me?" she asked.

I dug two 100-lira script notes out of my trouser pocket and handed them to her. She quickly opened the single drawer in the washstand, dropped the money in, smiled again and threw herself on the bed, opening her legs as she lay back. "*Presto, amico!*"

I didn't know what she was saying, but I got the message.

It was all over inside a minute, a few expert caresses with her warm hands, a series of quick breaths in my ears and *finito!*

Downstairs, I met Alex-Joe while another shift disappeared in single file up the staircase.

Alex-Joe grinned stupidly. "I didn't even have time to get undressed," he said, slowly.

The room, its pinkish walls glowing, seemed warmer than it had been when we entered. I felt used. "Ah, hell," I murmured, dazedly, "let's go find something to drink!"

Angus the Goat staggered into the room. He looked like he had been caught playing with himself, a lascivious, wry expression on his face. "Boy," he said, softly, "wouldn't my mother blow her top if she knew I was staying out so late!"

The medical orderlies performed their pecker-check routinely and efficiently under the impassive eyes of two king-sized MPs. It was a warm-water-and-soap quick rinse followed by a syringe filled with purple fluid squeezed up the eye of every penis.

Angus the Goat smirked. "Christ, fella, that's more excitin' than when I was with the little whore!"

"Why can't we do this for ourselves?" asked an embarrassed Pithorse. "We ain't little kids y'know."

The medic didn't even look up. "Because you wouldn't do it right, that's why. It'd be like washing your hands, nothing more. An' we gotta get you guys home with clean cocks. You understand?"

Outside, the night air was chill and damp. We bunched together, waiting for the others. Already a fresh lineup was forming in front of the tent, heads with balmorals on them, berets and forage caps, shuffling, whispering crudely.

Nine-Pence and Albert came out, buttoning up their tunics. "We're the last," Albert said in the darkness.

"Now where?" someone asked.

"Let's go find some Eyetie screech!"

"You mean vino?"

"Yeah."

"Well, I can't drink that red stuff. It makes me sick."

"Okay, we'll find a joint where the goof's white," drawled Alex-Joe. "An' we stick together. The RSM told me that the Limeys who were here before us had some guys knifed."

"Who done that?" Nine-Pence asked.

"Fascist kids. There's quite a few in an' around the town," Alex-Joe said, "an' they like nothing better than to pigstick an Allied soldier, if they catch him alone."

We started down the road, sloshing through the mud and water like stray puppies turned loose outdoors for the first time.

I suddenly recalled my blonde piece. "What'd you think, Alex-Joe?" I asked.

"Once a philosopher, twice a pervert."

I looked at him. "You make that up?"

"No. Read it somewhere. But it makes sense. That kind of screwing will never replace loving."

Nine-Pence began to sing in a quavering tenor:

> *Frig 'em all! Frig 'em all!*
> *The long an' the short an' the tall!*
> *There'll be no more promotions,*
> *This side of the ocean!*
> *So, cheer up my lads, frig 'em all!*

And we all sang, booming our defiance at the black countryside, the war, the night and all the two-hundred-lira whores.

The *trattoria* was one block off the main street, half in and half out of the ground, with a flight of steps leading down to the door. Inside, it smelled of wine and sweat. Two large barrels were against the deep, end wall, battered tin pots sitting on the stone floor under the big taps. Low benches, like picnic tables, filled half the room. There was a high bar in one corner and, behind it, a fat, hairy-armed Italian, wearing a soiled white shirt and apron over black pants.

Alex-Joe, Shrumpski, Pithorse, Angus the Goat, Nine-Pence, Albert, Zwicker, myself and a Corporal Peters we didn't know too well from the Pioneers all sat around one table, drinking what the bartender called "cognac." We chased the shots with a dry, white wine.

The sweaty bartender poured another round of drinks. Pithorse grabbed his forearm. "Leave the bottle!" he said.

The man grinned, revealing a mouthful of bright teeth. "*Si, si!*" he said. He wiped his hands on his apron and said something in Italian.

"What's he want?" asked Zwicker.

"Probably money."

"Well, pay him."

Everybody tossed some crumpled notes on the table. The Italian picked several out of the scattered pile.

"Think he's gyppin' us?" I asked, looking up into the man's face.

"How the hell would I know?" asked Pithorse.

"Aw, crap. Leave him alone," drawled Alex-Joe.

The man said, "*Grazia, Grazia!*" and went back behind his bar.

I looked around the room. "All it needs is flies," I said, staring at the glistening, clammy, dirty whitewashed walls.

Everybody lit a cigarette except Angus the Goat. "My mother don't want me to smoke," he said. "Not till I'm sixteen."

"What'd you think of the whorehouse?" Pithorse asked.

Shrumpski rubbed his round, Slavic head. "I been in better," he said.

"Where?"

"Does it matter?"

"To hell with the whorehouse!" Nine-Pence said. "I had a better deal going when we were outside Hayward's Heath."

"Nobody wants to hear about your love life," Pithorse interjected.

Nine-Pence scowled.

"The Old Man says we're moving up into the lines right after Christmas," Zwicker said, puffing jerkily on his cigarette. "Or mebbe before."

"Yeah, he called it 'gettin baptized'!"

My wineglass was empty. "Hey!" I yelled at the bartender, waving the glass, "we need some more goof, pop!"

He hurried over, a liter bottle of vino in one hand. He set it on the table, smiled nervously and took another note.

Corporal Peters stood up, weaving slightly and said his first words of the night: "I gotta go," he said.

I refilled every glass.

"Wonder where it is?" Peters asked no one in particular.

"There's a door by the bar, probably outside there," said Zwicker.

Peters crossed the floor slowly, looked at the bartender who grinned back. "*Si, si!*" he gestured toward the door with his arms. Peters went out.

"Guess it'll be Ortona?" said Pithorse.

"What for?" I said.

"That's where the action is."

"There'd better be a river to cross," Angus the Goat said slowly, "because that's all we know. No river, no fight. We ain't fit for anything else."

Pithorse had started to laugh when we heard a strangled cry, then Peters reeled wildly into the bar. He started to topple forward but caught a table for support. Blood, red and rippling, was spilling down over his tunic and dripping onto the floor. The bartender, horror in his eyes, rushed from behind the end of the bar top, yelling hoarsely. He clutched Peters by the shoulders and staggered backward, his heavy features twisted and strained. "Holy Mother of God!" he shouted in broken English.

Snapping out of the shock which had robbed me of the ability to think, I wheezed: "Peters has been stabbed!"

The bartender wailed like a dying pig. Peters coughed, tried to say something. A fresh wave of bright blood gushed out of his throat. Slowly, like a deflated balloon, he began to fall over the table. The bartender stood watching him, helplessly. I caught him. And there was an odd smell that reminded me of a day, long ago, when I had seen a dog run over by a dump truck.

"Some wops! They must've done it!" yelled Pithorse. He broke for the door, followed by Zwicker and Shrumpski.

"Never mind them!" roared Alex-Joe, "we got to get him to the RAP! Quick!" He shouted at Nine-Pence. "Get outside and stop the first vehicle that comes down the road. You, too, Zwicker! Move!"

Pithorse had the bartender by the throat. "You bastard!" he snarled. "What happened? Who did it?"

The man made no attempt to defend himself. His face was puffed with fear, his eyes rolling. He moaned in Italian.

"Leave him alone, Pithorse," I said. "He didn't do it. That's for sure! C'mon, we got to get Peters out of here! Give us a hand!"

Gently, we carried the bleeding Peters out into the dark street. His eyes were closed, his face chalk white in the gloom, the blood seeping from his throat flecked with foam. His breath came in great gulps as if he were drowning.

Nine-Pence had flagged down a supply jeep. The driver, chattering inanely, helped us lay the rasping Peters across the back seat, his head in Angus the Goat's lap. Then he jumped in and with a clashing of gears, drove away, along the dark street, racing for the regimental aid post a mile up in the hills.

I shuddered and looked at my hands. They were sticky with Peters's blood. "Goddamn!" I breathed.

Pithorse was cursing and half crying. "You think he'll live?" he asked.

"If the medics get him in time," said Alex-Joe.

"God, was he ever gashed!" I said. "Right in the throat." I knelt on one knee and slid my hands into a puddle of water and frantically tried to clean them. Finally, I scraped some mud together and worked it into my palms, my fingers, then rinsed them, and dried them against the legs of my trousers.

"Let's go look for 'em!" snarled Zwicker, savagely.

"Who?"

"We got no weapons. An' they got knives," Shrumpski said.

"Who?"

Pithorse removed his web belt and wrapped it around his right fist, the dull brass buckles that held the ammo pouch straps on their shoulders, to the front. "I can handle any damned Fascist with this!"

"Yeah, but which one?"

"I wish I had at least my toad stabber," Shrumpski said, softly, referring to his army-issue knife.

"Any Fascists will do," hissed Pithorse.

We returned to the *trattoria*. But it was in darkness, the heavy door locked. Pithorse pounded on it, crashing his fists into it relentlessly. "I know you're in there, ya lousy Fascist!" he yelled, wildly. "Come out or I'll bust this goddamned door!" His words echoed down the dark street.

"Knock it off, Pithorse," I said, finally, "nobody's going to answer. You'll break your fists on that wood. It's too thick. And I don't think he had anythin' to do with it."

"I know," sobbed Pithorse, "but he could lead us to 'em."

We argued in the darkness for several minutes, rooting through the black alleys, pounding on doors, shouting and cursing. Not a window was opened. Not a door. It was as if we were in a damned, nether world where no one lived, no one breathed. Yet, in our frustration, we knew somewhere, behind a thick stone wall, at least one black-eyed, armed Italian youth was smirking and gleefully smiling. And the thought fueled our anger.

Finally, panting, we came together on the main street and without anyone saying it, began the long walk back to the regimental camp.

And while we moved silently up the winding road, through the slop and mud, our anger dissipated in the cold, raw air. And in its place, shock set in. Sober now, we thought only of Peters and the scarlet, running gash in his throat.

We had passed the regimental guards at the gate when someone said, "I'm going to see 3 platoon, the mortars, and we'll drop a few three-inchers on that friggin' town."

"That's the old play," croaked Zwicker, "teach 'em to mind their stinkin' manners!"

The mental vision of a cluster of high-explosive bombs raining down on Altamura, sleeping women and kids, jolted me. "Now, wait just a minute..." I began.

"Don't be chickenshit!" grated Pithorse.

"I'm not...and you know it," I replied.

"Just remember Peters. Mebbe he's dead. An' all he wanted to do was have a lousy pee!" Pithorse snarled.

"That's it, the mortars!" someone said excitedly.

I was horrified. "F'r Chrissakes! Mebbe Peters is not dead!" I shouted, looking at Alex-Joe. But Alex-Joe's face was bland. "You going to go for this?" I asked.

Alex-Joe shrugged. "I haven't said a word, buddy."

I stared at Pithorse, then Zwicker, then Nine-Pence and Shrumpski, searching for a shred of sanity. I was looking into cold, unresponsive eyes.

"It doesn't make sense to kill people —" I groped for the words "— like cats or dogs or crows!"

"They done it before. The RSM told us," said Albert thickly.

"But the women and kids in the houses didn't do it!" I said, heatedly, my hands suddenly damp and sweaty. "Not the ones the mortars will knock off!"

Albert asked, "You think of somethin' better?"

The wind blew across the hills and I shivered. "Wait'll I check and see if Peters is alive. How about that? You guys wait here and I'll find out and be right back. Okay?" I didn't look at them, now, but turned and raced along the roadway, splashing recklessly through water and mud.

I ran steadily until I met Angus the Goat. In the night, the lower part of his tunic glistened.

"Angus? How's Peters?" I panted.

"He's gonna live. At least the MO thinks so. The knife missed his juggler. But he's lost a lot of blood." He patted his wet tunic and lifted his hands, palms up. They were stained dark with blood. "Funny how it darkens after a while," he said almost wistfully. "When it was comin' out of Peters's throat it was bright red."

I shook him. "You sure he's going to live?" I demanded.

Angus the Goat's round face widened. "That's what the MO thinks."

"Good! Now come with me, Angus!"

"What for?"

"Never mind what for, we got to tell the others before they do something they'll be sorry for." We raced down the road. Only Alex-Joe and Albert were where I had left them, standing in the center of the ruts.

"Peters is going to be okay, guys!" I called. "Angus the Goat says the MO thinks he'll pull through." I looked around, quickly. "Where are the others?"

"Gone. Up on the hill."

"Where?"

Alex-Joe shrugged. "I've been thinking, Fred," he said. "It doesn't matter whether Peters lives or dies. They got to be taught a lesson."

I tried to interrupt. Angus the Goat glanced at me then Alex-Joe and Albert, unable to understand what we were talking about.

Alex-Joe held his hand up. "Wait, buddy. Sure some of 'em will be killed in town. But they're protecting those bastards who *tried* to kill Peters, who *did* kill some Limeys. It'll be a lesson to 'em."

"Christ! You're brave!" I hissed. "Not afraid to kill a few Eyetie civilians…"

"Aw, hell buddy, don't you think it's tough enough being in a war without having civilians knifing you in the throat?"

I sneered. "Maybe you'll be lucky and you won't kill any kids, eh? Just adults!"

"What's the matter with you fellas?" Angus the Goat bleated.

Alex-Joe half turned, as if to walk away. "Ask him," he said, nodding toward me, "he's making all the noise."

I started to say, "Some of the guys want to get the mortars to…" when there was a hoarse "Fire!" shouted in the night from a small hill dominating the camp, then a series of muffled cracks.

Angus the Goat swung 'round, sniffing excitedly.

Sickened, I realized the mortars had opened up. Crack! Crack! Crack! "My God, they're firing!" I cried hoarsely. Crack! Crack! Crack! The small cartridges in the bombs' tails exploded when they hammered against the steel firing pins, hurling the thin-shelled explosive charges back up the three-inch barrels. There was a succession of soft whispers as they sighed through the inky heavens.

Unable to breathe, I stared up into the dome of the night. I felt I could "see" the lethal bombs swinging on range, up, up, up, flattening out, then beginning their sharp descent.

Crumph! Crumph! Crumph! Flashes of lurid yellow light shot up in the darkness that shrouded Altamura. Again, and again. The light danced lividly then disappeared.

Someone screamed, "You don't quit until I holler 'Stop firing'!"

I shouldered by Albert and started up the road, but he grabbed me from behind. His strong arms pinned me as I struggled.

"You can't stop it!" Albert grated in my ear. "Nobody can stop it!"

With a violent twist, I broke free, but he punched me with tremendous force on the side of my head. All I could see was stars dancing before my eyes. I reeled backward, saw a second fist coming and ducked, then dropped into a crouch. My vision cleared. Albert was circling me. He jabbed, blinking.

Angus the Goat's face was frightened and white. A succession of explosions rippled down in the valley. People were shouting. The sharp "cracks" had ceased, but the mortars continued to crash into Altamura.

Panting, I lowered my fists because I suddenly realized Albert was staring down the roadway into the valley. Two fires had started, lean flames licking the night sky.

"What the hell's going on out there!" a voice boomed.

In the darkness, men scattered. The smell of cordite drifted down the road. Perspiration poured into my eyes. I trembled, my head ached, dully. The fires in the town were dying down as quickly as they had flared up. Only the echoes of the detonating mortars continued to rumble through the hills.

Someone pounded along the road, breathing heavily. It was Colonel Weir followed by Pete the Tramp. Both had their service revolvers in their fists.

"What's all the firing?" yelled Weir.

Major Sommerville bellowed: "Pithorse! MacNeil! Come here!"

Pithorse, grinning oddly, trotted toward them. Weir glared at him, then at me and Alex-Joe and Albert, ignoring Angus the Goat. "Will someone tell me what the hell's going on here, Sergeant?" he asked Alex-Joe.

"It all started with Peters. Corporal Peters, sir, was knifed in the throat," he said slowly.

The colonel looked questioningly at his 2/I-C.

"He's in the Pioneers, sir," Major Sommerville said.

"Well, sir," Pithorse said, "some Fascists down in the town knifed him..."

"Is he dead?"

"I dunno, sir, we shipped him to the RAP, fast as we could."

I said, "The MO thinks he'll live, sir."

"What the hell's that got to do with the mortars?" asked the colonel.

Still sickened, I couldn't speak.

Weir's eyes glittered in the gloom. "So," he said, softly, "they were squaring it, heh?"

Pithorse blurted, "Yes sir. Me an'..."

The colonel swung his revolver in a tight arc. "I don't want to know who was involved, Pithorse. In fact, I don't even want to know anyone was out. It could have been diehard Fascisti guerrillas, aiming at our camps, as far as I know. Now, all of you, get the hell out of here!"

Alex-Joe saluted.

Weir faced Pithorse. "You get your ass up to the mortar platoon area and tell your friends I want those barrels cleaned before daylight. You got that?" he barked.

Pithorse loped up the hill into the darkness.

"Okay, the rest of you, scram! Now!" said the colonel.

"Damned war!" I heard him snort, as he headed for his quarters. "How the hell did I ever get mixed up in it, wet-nursing a bunch of goddamned kids..."

We could hear a jeep, its motor racing, coming up the road.

"And now here comes the military cops. They always have to know what's happening! Over here!" The colonel cursed. Then I heard no more.

Every man in the hut was awake. "What happened?" someone yelled.

"Who was doing all the shooting?"

Tiredly, I slumped onto my bed.

"Is somebody going to tell us what..."

"The Lord said 'Let there be light!' and Shrumpski said 'Turn off that goddamned light' and there was no light," a voice said softly.

Albert undressed and climbed up into his bunk. I lay down. I couldn't sort fact from shame. Nothing made sense. I thought of Peters, perhaps fighting for his life. Then I heard again the mortars exploding in the town. I lit a cigarette, the match flaring briefly in the darkened room, and inhaled.

"You still sore, buddy?" It was Albert.

I puffed on the butt's stale smoke, letting it out slowly. "No, I guess not."

"I'm sorry I slugged you. But you couldn't have stopped anything. They'd gone too far. An' you'd have just made enemies. And nobody needs any more enemies than necessary."

"Good night, Albert."

"Good night."

I slept in my clothes, sliding into sleep's long tunnel of forgetfulness, confused and sorry. Sorry for Peters, sorry for the little people of Altamura who were, I finally conceded, stupid enough to believe they could live with a war without getting involved.

The squad of Italian *carabinieri* was obviously nervous, their tricornered cocked hats under their arms. They conferred with Colonel Weir, RSM Diplock and Captain Frizzell who were sympathetic, but cool. Later, they inspected the mortar platoon weapons, peered into their gleaming, shining barrels and went back to Altamura.

No member of the mortar platoon was interrogated. And Altamura was placed off limits to all personnel, except those on duty, hauling rations, mail and supplies.

The mortaring, the postal clerk told us, had been accurate. Thirty-four civilians, he insisted, had been killed, another two dozen injured. But a quartermaster, in town buying vino for the men's canteen, said only nine had died.

"In any case," he related, "the houses near the main drag are draped in black. An' there's been a lot of funerals. You know, a parade of priests and altar boys, women in black following big glass-sided hearses. A little gaudy, but impressive. Lots of guys carryin' tall candles and chanting in Eyetie, I guess."

Sad-eyed, Shrumpski shook his head. "Latin, you ignoramus," he said.

"Served them right. Now mebbe it'll be safe for a guy out doin' a little peein' or drinkin'," commented Zwicker, laconically.

Not a Highlander agreed. Or disagreed. They just stared into their souls.

The next day, Corporal Peters was moved to the Fifth Field Hospital where an army doctor stitched up the gash in his throat after removing the emergency trachiotomy tube that enabled him to breathe through the long night.

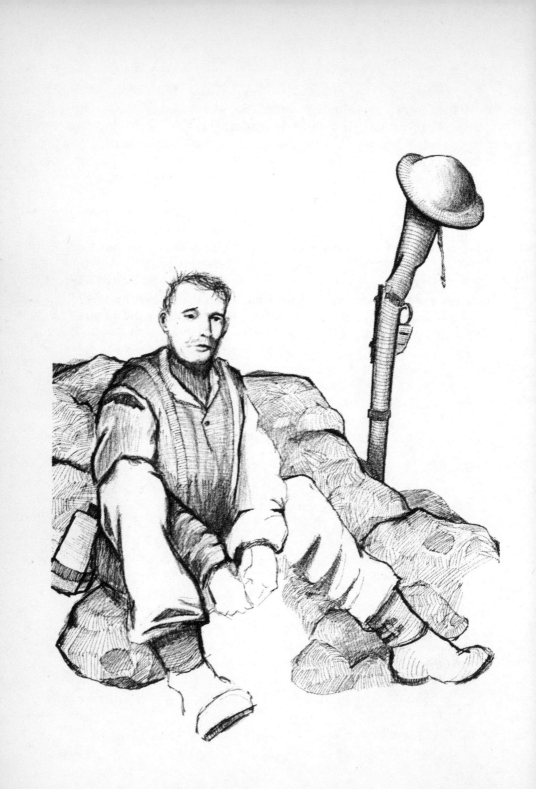

CHAPTER SIX

THE day after Christmas, 1943, at 0900 hours, the Highlanders, armored track vehicles leading, began the tortuous trek north along the devastated coastal road. We took over the line south of the Arielli River, held it for a few days, then were pulled back. At first light, January 17, 1944, in a misty rain and behind a thunderous barrage laid down by light and medium field artillery, together with the Perth regiment, we attacked the German positions on the high ground across the muddy, swirling river.

It was a fiasco. Men who had never been shot at before flopped face down for cover. The Irish, the battalion in a holding position in case of enemy counterattacks, accidentally shot up some bewildered, confused Highlanders, mistaking them for Jerries. All afternoon, unnerved and numbed, the remnants of the two assault companies clung to the soggy ground, pounded relentlessly by German mortars that churned the mud and water into great spouts. In the darkness, the living withdrew, shocked and tired.

Thirteen Highlanders died, thirty-three were wounded, and Toasty MacDonnell, long since transferred to a rifle company, was posted as missing.

In a field south of the Lanciano Road, leading inland to Orsogna, Colonel Weir laid it on the line: "It was a damned poor show!" he barked, clearly and coldly. "You've got much to learn and learn it you will. You snafued! Not once, but a dozen times. Like when many of you stopped to help the wounded. Nobody stops for the men who've been hit. Remember that! Men died who went to ground to aid a man already dying. No attack can succeed unless you keep moving!"

We stood, shocked by the death that had walked among us, impersonally claiming lives, flinching under the flow of biting, rasping words.

"And green men who go to ground will never get up ... it's tough enough for veterans!"

Faces still streaked with dirt were turned downward. Eyes levelled furtively on baggy trousers caked with mud. The stench of cordite and death was still with us.

"And — and this is worst of all, unforgivable! — some of you abandoned your weapons! Like scared goddamned rabbits, you bolted out of that valley! With your tails between your legs!"

Souls shrank under chill, grey skies and shame gnawed on the conscience of each of us who had, in his terror, raced up the hilly track, never pausing until reaching safety in the rear areas.

Weir, pale-faced and tired-eyed, spat.

"That's all. But I never expect to have to get up and say these words again." He turned to RSM Diplock. "Turn them over to their company commanders and get them to work on their weapons!"

As he strode down the muddy roadway avoiding the deeper holes, I heard him say to his 2/I-C: "What the hell did the army expect? Green boys going against crack paratroopers!"

Only my eyes, the bridge of my nose and upper cheeks showed through a knitted balaclava that swathed my head under a steel helmet. I stared over the shell-shredded sea of mud and wet snow. Whistling tunelessly, I stamped my cold, wet feet and swore, and watched my breath exploding into instant puffballs of steam in the freezing air, wondering if I would ever be warm again.

Nothing ever changed northeast of the village of Orsogna, deep in the province of Chieti.

The peaks of the Majellas, snow-streaked and jagged as if hacked out of ice and stone, ignored the puny men who struggled beneath their humped shoulders. The burned-out Sherman tank, thirty yards off from the northwest corner of our position, code-named Queen Ten, pointed its twisted 75-millimeter gun skyward. And the slit trenches guarding the defense perimeter were always half full of water — the damp snow that fell by night, and the cold rain by day.

It was stand-to when the two sections of 4 platoon ritually turned out thirty minutes before sunset and sunrise (what sun ever set or rose in the Godforsaken mountains?) through for another thirty minutes, guarding against attacks that never came.

I switched my Tommy gun from one shoulder to the other, reminding myself another dreary shift was almost over, that most of us would come down off the roofless second floor of the stone casa or climb out of soggy slit trenches, plod through the only intact room in the casa and take the ladder down the manway into the tunnelled dugout beneath the building — a dugout clawed out of the dirt by the New Zealanders who had originally wrested the salient from the enemy. There we could sleep between two-hours-on, two-hours-off turns on the roof or in the slits; or wait for the scrawny little Moroccans who brought the daily mule train up, carrying barely warm meals under cover of the abysmal darkness.

"They got a lot of guts," Albert said, "driving those bony mules along mountain paths that snake through minefields. I wouldn't want their jobs."

"Well, somebody's gotta do it," said Nine-Pence, "ya'd never get a truck or jeep up, not in this part of the world."

"How come it's named Queen Ten? Why not the Savoy Ten? That's even classier," said Pithorse.

"Because," said Lieutenant MacNaughton, "Queen stands for Q which is alphabetical code. And Ten merely differentiates between say, Nine, or Eleven, other fortified positions in our line."

Our line, I thought, is dozens and dozens of battered fieldstone casas, stretching to the Adriatic. And each is linked by fragile telephone lines laid by signallers who divided their time between laying the wire and repairing it.

"That right, Mr. MacNaughton?" asked Pithorse. Then he answered his own question. "It might be Queen Ten to us, but I'll bet it's only another goddamned little red pin on the maps back at headquarters an' mebbe a yellow one at brigade."

I thought about those pins as I stared into the misty evening at another shattered shell of a casa, housing Germans, and partially screened by a stand of leafless, stunted bushes.

"What color pin do you think that Jerry casa is on the Nazi maps?" I asked Albert.

Albert looked puzzled.

"Pithorse said that Queen Ten is just a yellow or red pin on the generals' maps. So what's the color of the pin for that casa on Hitler's maps?"

"Whoinhell cares!"

I looked again at the Jerry casa. In it lived the peeing Squarehead who had to be crazy. Every morning after first-light stand-to, he stood up in full view of us in Queen Ten, stripped to the waist, sponged himself wet, towelled himself dry, then peed at us.

The first morning Zwicker spotted the Jerry going through his act, he yelled to us down in the dugout. We rushed up, climbed to the upper storey's half walls and shattered windows and gawked, stupefied.

"Nobody," Pithorse said in awe, "should be goofy enough to try a trick like that!"

Strangely, not a man fired a shot at him.

Even when the raw winds whipped frozen rain across the stiff ground and forced the men to watch through hooded eyes, the German peed.

Someone had wanted to kill him the third time, but a rising protest forced him to slip the safety catch back on his rifle and forget about it. Even MacNaughton, whom the sections believed would shoot a sleeping bird, was against it.

"Aw hell," Shrumpski said, "he ain't hurtin' none."

We took a vote. There were only two dissenters, Pithorse and Zwicker. The rest voted with Shrumpski. "Okay," MacNaughton, ruled, "nobody shoots the nut." And so matters stood. Only the Squarehead had added to his act. After peeing, he thumbed his nose in our direction before disappearing behind a low wall of sandbags and railway ties.

A gust of surprised laughter followed him.

We looked forward to his antics, sometimes waiting a full hour after morning stand-down for the peeing to begin. Once, there had been a heavy ground fog and we couldn't see him. Pithorse and Nine-Pence had complained loudly, shaking their fists at the skies. "C'mon, God, lift that damned curtain, let the show begin!" Pithorse had shouted.

It began to rain, big drops that were half frozen. I shaded my eyes. Not a wisp of smoke from any casa, I noted, not a sign of life.

"Talking to yourself yet, buddy?"

I swung around and stared down the stairs at Alex-Joe. "Come on up," I said, "the view's fine. There's a nude broad getting a full tan in front of Jerry's positions. She's big, blond and busty."

Stepping carefully because the stairs were splintered and shape-less, he asked, "Is it beginning to get to you?"

"Hell, no, I can take it as long as those bastards can," I replied, jerking one shoulder in line with the Jerry casa.

The sleet was falling harder. We could see along the front about fifty yards in either direction. But only the one Jerry position was in view as well as Baker Company's extreme left flank strongpoint. The others were hidden in folds and sharp draws in the rugged ground.

"Where's MacNaughton?" I asked.

"The dear boy doesn't feel well," he said, mimicking the officer's affected vernacular. "It seems he has the trots."

I clucked. "He's got a lot of bullshit to get rid of."

"Don't be rough on him, buddy. He's not so bad."

"Just because he stepped on the S mine the other night?"

"Well, he had the guts to follow the drill, keep his foot on it after he heard the small explosion in the ground...even if it didn't explode."

"That's not guts, that's self-preservation. Take your foot off and make a run for it an' you'll get loaded with buckshot when it's blown hip-high out of the ground."

"Ah, he's tougher than I thought. He's also honest."

I frowned. "How's that?"

"Well, I got talking with him that night. Just after we had brewed up..."

There was a weird howl in the wind, as though someone was dying and fighting the inevitable end.

"He told me when his foot hit that prong and he heard the initial muffled explosion, he was scared shitless. He actually thought he'd had it. What hurt, he insisted, was all he could think of was what a silly bastard he had been all his life."

"You're kidding, of course."

Alex-Joe went on. "No, I'm not. And he wasn't. He said he couldn't think of one nice thing about himself...or anyone who'd miss him. Even his old man. It was a little odd. I felt like a Catholic priest sitting in a confessional, listening to a guy tell me what a shit he had been."

I pulled my greatcoat collar closer to my face. "Did you believe him?"

"He didn't have to tell me about it, did he?"

I could dimly hear Shrumpski and Zwicker halfway out of their waterlogged trenches, yelling across the mud to each other.

"No, I guess he didn't."

"Hell, I haven't heard him use that phony accent of his since...ah, Christ, since that night."

"Agreed. But he's still at least a partial shit."

I squinted at my watch in the dusk. "Fifteen minutes to go," I said, "then at 1800, Jerry shells for five minutes. Ever wonder why he's so punctual about a shoot?"

"Nope. And I don't give a crap. It's when he begins changing his timetable that I'm going to start worrying."

The sleet was pelting directly into our faces and we edged closer to the shattered wall for protection. There was a sudden flurry of sounds above the rush of wind and wet snow. Instantly we were alert.

I raced quickly to the full wall and peered through the lower half of a shattered window frame. At first I couldn't see anything but the driving sleet. Then, up out of a hollow, came a party of Italian civilians, all adults as far as I could make out, each waving a piece of white cloth attached to a stick. They were within fifteen yards of Queen Ten, working their way through the mud, the craters, slipping, falling, scrambling, crossing between the lines.

Albert whispered, "See anything?"

"Yep. Some Eyeties going through the lines. All adults."

Suddenly, they halted, waving their flags wildly over their capped heads, crying excitedly. They pointed at Queen Ten, then Queen Nine, shouting unintelligibly.

Nine-Pence and Angus the Goat waved back.

"Knock it off!" I yelled. They looked up, startled, and sank lower into their slit trenches.

"Aw, they're probably lost, tryin' to get their bearings, Fred," Albert said.

They milled about aimlessly in the muck, reminding me of frightened sheep. Then, as if they all thought of it at once, they plunged straight for the German lines across the uneven ground until the slanting sleet swallowed them up.

"Crazy, crazy, poor bewildered bastards!" Albert said, watching them disappear.

When darkness closed in, minutes later, the sections stood down and the sleet changed to snow. The night was long and bitterly cold. And those not on duty shivered even in the dugout, jamming their half frozen, wet feet in the knotted sleeves of their greatcoats, wrapping their single blankets shawl fashion around their shoulders and dozing, fitfully.

With every man doing two hours on duty, two off, those inside kept the pots of tea boiling hot. They also patrolled the roofless top floor and checked the men in the holes who sat on empty jerricans, watching the sides of the trenches, saturated by the snow and water, slide softly into the slop. Or they stared across the snow-covered land, until they imagined ghostly divisions of Panzers stealthily crossing the gap between them and the end of the world.

First light brought all the men standing-to, half of them in the sodden slit trenches. The snow had become rain that cascaded down on their steel-helmeted heads.

The first mortars crumphed in on target, tearing Johnny Gallant's left arm off at the shoulder before he could drop fully into his slit trench. Three hit the casa, sending shards of stone and shrapnel screaming through the air. I flung myself behind an open box of Bren gun magazines, trusting in God and instinct.

The harsh, grey skies seemed to be alive with hissing mortars. Between the sharp, ear-splitting explosions, Gallant yelled like a man who was both surprised and terrified.

I heard the cry: "Stretcher bearer!" before I pulled my head up from between my shoulder blades and peered over the wall.

Lieutenant MacNaughton, moving up the ladder from the tunnel out of the dugout when the first mortars hammered home, scurried into what was left of the living room. "Get your heads up when you can!" he screeched. "Look out for an infantry attack!"

Steel hats bobbed up, cautiously, then disappeared when another stonk crashed in. Gallant had stopped yelling. The air was filled with water, sleet, white-hot steel fragments and stone chips. A replacement, Ron Poulton, who had arrived the previous night with the mule train, leaped out of the hole he shared with Pithorse.

Pithorse lunged for him. The kid kicked free. "F'r Chrissakes!" Pithorse roared. He ducked as the next stonk came in.

"Stay put, you bloody fool!" bellowed MacNaughton.

The panic-stricken Poulton, head down, was going hard, scrambling, making for the rubble-littered ground entrance to Queen Ten. There was a livid flash at his heels and he seemed to come apart. His steel hat ricocheted off the casa's stone wall, landed in a puddle where the blast from another hit lifted it high in the air.

Someone swore.

I hugged the stone floor, thinking there must be some way to make myself smaller. The casa shook when another bomb crashed into the remains of the tiled roof. A stone chip struck my helmet, making my head ring. Sonofabitch! I said to myself, more to relieve the tension. Suddenly, I wasn't cold. I lifted my head, and all I could see was the dirty, grey stone wall.

Then, abruptly, it was quiet.

Cautiously, yet quickly, I climbed to my feet, crouched against the remains of the wall. "Alex-Joe?" I called.

"Down here, buddy."

I peered over the wall. Down in the muck, Alex-Joe was straightening up in his slit trench. Helmeted heads and shoulders appeared.

"If they're coming, they're coming now!" MacNaughton yelled. "Don't anybody relax!"

"Gallant's got it bad!" Pithorse cried. "For God's sake, where's the stretcher bearer?"

"Nobody moves, yet!" barked MacNaughton.

I ducked across to the other side of the floor. Layers of smoke and mist shrouded Queen Nine, like a shabby halo. "Queen Nine got it, too!"

"That you, Cederberg?"

"Yes, sir."

"How about Queen Eleven? Any smoke there?"

I peered into the misty rain. "Can't tell, sir."

It was still quiet. No men appeared in coal-scuttle helmets, stick grenades in their fists, carbines or machine pistols spitting fire.

"Corporal Cederberg!" It was MacNaughton again.

"Sir."

"I'm going into the dugout to check with Queen Nine or headquarters. You run it from up top. Okay?"

"Yes, sir."

Seconds stretched into minutes. Two dozen pairs of straining eyes searched the mist-shrouded ground for enemy. Nothing. The rain slackened. Zwicker's head appeared above the rim of Gallant's foxhole. "You can forget about that goddamned stretcher bearer!" he shouted savagely, "he's dead. Bled to death."

"You sure?" Albert called to him.

"He's got no shoulder and no breath. That's dead, ain't it?" he croaked.

"Okay, can it. You ain't helpin' matters by yellin'!" Alex-Joe said.

Zwicker glared, his face pale white, his eyes hard.

A Jerry machine gun burped. The men ducked. The bullets zipped off the burned-out Sherman.

MacNaughton's shout ended the stand-to. Alex-Joe crouched

over Gallant's slit trench and looked at him, lying on his side, armless at the shoulder, his face turned into the gooey, bloody slop.

"Come on, Zwicker," he said gently, "no medic could've saved him. He must've died right quick."

"Yeah, yeah, I know, Sarg. It just seems a little unfair."

Together they lifted the dead man out of the soggy hole and laid him next to the rear wall of Queen Ten while Angus the Goat watched in a fascinated, eerie silence. They had seen the dead carried out of the Arielli, but Johnny Gallant was the first man in 4 platoon to die. Poulton, oddly, they didn't count. He was a stranger. They hardly knew him. Besides, there wasn't enough of him left to suggest he had ever existed.

I stared at one of Poulton's footless boots. "Better find what you can, Pithorse, and bring it around for identification," I said slowly and went inside.

The muscles in the side of Lieutenant MacNaughton's face were taut as he spoke. "Headquarters thinks those Eyeties who crossed through the lines during stand-to yesterday evening tipped the Jerries off that we occupied the open ground every evening. Then," he said, "they figured the rest of it out — that we did it at first light, too."

I sat with my back to the earthen wall of the dugout, my greatcoat around my feet. "It cost us two men, sir," I said.

MacNaughton nodded. "And all because of some lousy civilians."

I lit a cigarette, carefully extinguishing the match because of the straw-covered dirt floor.

"Colonel Weir says in future, any Eyeties trying to cross to the enemy lines are to be stopped. If they don't halt, we're to shoot to kill."

"They lose any men in Queen Nine?"

"Headquarters didn't know for certain. Queen Eleven wasn't hit, but Nine, Baker Company, must've got it. Their line is out."

"Must've been cut by the stonk, sir."

"Probably. Captain Frizzell said he'd buzz back when he knew."

"Think I should take a contact patrol over and find out?" I asked.

"If we don't get any info in a couple of hours, okay. But I'd rather not risk it in daylight."

MacNaughton's dull eyes had big bags under them. He passed wind.

"Still got troubles, sir, eh?"

He grimaced. "Things have surely tightened up considerably since this morning, Cederberg," he said.

Angus the Goat and Zwicker were already dozing under their blankets and greatcoats. I inspected the cold, improvised fireplace, a blackened pit below a shaft that had been sunk through the stone floor and dirt under the original fireplace upstairs. I had an urge to light it, but I understood the rules: No fires by daylight, the smoke only invited a shelling or mortaring.

Outside behind Queen Ten, Johnny Gallant's bloodless body lay under a groundsheet, awaiting that night's mule train to take it out. And in a second groundsheet, lumped together like a tramp's belongings, was all that remained of reinforcement Ron Poulton, someone nobody had had the time to get to know.

MacNaughton held a scorched paybook in one hand and two dogtag discs. In the other was the shredded upper half of a second paybook. "Neither of them was married," he said.

Queen Ten's field telephone jangled, three long, one short. Mac-Naughton talked briefly. "Queen Nine was plastered. Four wounded, none killed," he reported.

I threw my butt into the blackened fireplace pit. "How long have we been here, Lieutenant?" I asked.

"Six days," he replied, "and twenty-six since we were chased out of the Arielli Valley."

The next morning, while a dank mist swirled across the broken ground, a Highlander in Queen Nine shot the peeing German full in the chest as a thin stream of Teutonic urine sprayed the earth. He went over backward and disappeared.

CHAPTER SEVEN

I answered the telephone simply because I was beside it when it rang. "Queen Ten," I said. "Corporal Cederberg."

It was RSM Diplock. "It's Sergeant Cederberg again," he said, "you can put three hooks back up. But that's not what I called about. Is the lieutenant there? Doc Boyden wants to talk to him about his problems."

Lieutenant MacNaughton's conversation with the MO was brief, ending up with "I'll do what you want, Doc, but the way I look at it, I can shit every half hour just as well up here as I can back at headquarters. OK, tonight. What's that? OK, I'll bring 'em."

He turned and faced Alex-Joe and I. "They want me back for treatment tonight, and both of you are coming along. There's something up. You'll come back the next with the rations. Corporal MacNeil will be in charge."

In the stinging sleet and lowering night, I blessed the Moroccans and cursed the mules as we plodded back to headquarters, scrambling to avoid the animals yet stick to the muddy trail that snaked across ridges and through upland mountain passes.

It was less than a mile as a crow would fly, but three by mule train to the collection of buildings housing the RAP, the wireless truck known as a gin palace (nobody in the ranks knew why, unless it was where the officers stashed their booze rations), the signallers, mortar platoon, Colonel Weir, his adjutant and RSM Diplock. And it took us three hours to cover the distance.

MacNaughton went straight to the RAP. "I'm sorry, boys, I guess I'm sicker than I thought, but I can barely stay on my feet. Go inside and report to the RSM." He closed his eyes and swayed slightly. "He'll give you the poop, if you'll excuse the shitty pun."

RSM Diplock, action or no action, was all business. "The colonel will do the talking," he said, "and you'll do the listening. And he'll supply the details. OK?" Then as if he had only become aware of our mud-covered uniforms and mud-streaked faces, he added, "You both look exhausted." He spread his hands.

"Well, Mr. Diplock," I replied, "it's not exactly Kew Beach in July."

He grinned. "Wherever that is. Anyway, it'll be a short and sweet briefing because the colonel's going to rear echelon in an hour, so Major Sommerville's replacing him for a week. You can get your sleep and rest during what's left of the night and tomorrow before you return to Queen Ten. Too bad about Gallant...he was a good soldier."

Weir came through a hallway door. "How's it going, men?" he asked, his voice thin in his grey face. "I've got a proposition for you — a competition, if you like."

The proposition was that we in Queen Ten try and cut out a German prisoner because brigade wanted to know specifically which enemy formation was facing us. "The details, I'll leave to you. And if you need support, let headquarters know — smoke, mortars, whatever."

The competition was that the men holding the other regimental strongpoints in the line had been offered the same deal.

"Whoever pulls it off first will get a Military Medal if he's one of the men, or a Military Cross if he should be an officer. And there'll be fifty bucks in lira and a week's pass to Campobasso or Naples," he said. "I don't need your answer now. You," he looked at both of us, "put it together. And there's no penalty for saying 'no thanks,'" he laughed wryly.

Doc Boyden lumbered into the room. "Well, my Colonel," he rumbled, "you're short another officer. Young MacNaughton's got dysentery so he'll have to go all the way out."

"And I suppose you're going to add jaundice to that," replied Weir.

"Ah, you know me better than that, I only give you the medical facts."

Doc Boyden, in his early forties, could tell a leadswinger from a sick man before the patient opened his mouth to say "ahhh." He faced us. "Good — whatever in hell it is — evening or morning, Cederberg and MacKinnon." He lit a cigarette, offering the pack around the room.

"How's your supply of whiskey, my Colonel?" he asked.

"Whiskey I have," Weir replied, crossing the room and extracting two bottles from a wooden box. "Here."

Doc stuffed them inside the pockets of his greatcoat.

"How's sick parade, Doc? The jaundice on the upgrade or are we levelling off?" asked Weir.

"About thirty cases a month — reported, that is. Some of 'em don't, you know, they prefer to sweat it out so they won't be shipped down the line, then wind up in another regiment.

"When that Eyetie sun comes out, they'll drop off — the numbers, I mean. And everybody will feel a helluva lot better, you'll see."

Alex-Joe and I slept until noon, then stripped to the waist, washed, shaved, scrounged messtins filled with powdered eggs and fatty canned bacon, washed down by mugs of coffee, then lit our first cigarcttes.

"Do we try it?" I asked.

"I've been thinking. We both can't go, not with the looie out. One of us'll have to stay in the casa, mebbe covering, using the field phone if we have to call for help."

"OK," I replied. "I know we're going to give it a hook, but who'll it be? If it's me, I want Zwicker."

"We'll toss."

"We haven't any coins."

"Then pick straws." Alex-Joe selected two from a nearby husk stack, cuddled them in his big hands. "Draw, the short one goes."

I selected. He was left with the short one. "It's me," he said, matter-of-factly, "an' I'll take Zwicker."

Partial sunlight danced on a thousand puddles and pools dotting no-man's land between Queen Ten and the German lines. But a swift wind would rush down from the Majellas, rippling the black waters and the dance would end only to start again. From the right, an enemy machine gun coughed, shrieking bullets. A slower Bren replied, hump-hump-humping regularly.

"Everybody out there's a little jumpy today," Albert said.

Earlier, before first light, Zwicker and Alex-Joe had ghosted out of Queen Ten, crawling and sliding through the muck until they had reached the mud track which ran behind the enemy gun pit. Then they had turned toward the German position to belly down in a maze of craters and ruts. Previous recce patrols had confirmed that the Jerries had a two-man post just where the track turned.

For two hours they had laid in the ditch, listening to the Germans change shifts and talk in low whispers. First light had given way to full daylight. Both sides stood-to, then down. But we, in Queen Ten, could see the tops of the Germans' helmets where they sat in their pit, straddling what had once been a dirt roadway.

The Highlanders lined the upper walls with automatic weapons. "After my grenade goes off," Alex-Joe had explained, "let go with everything you've got. Give us plenty. Queen Nine will supply enfilade fire. And keep it up till we get back."

We had worked the scheme out — a sneak approach, a quick thrust and fast getaway.

"Like cops and robbers," I had said.

Major Sommerville had given his approval.

Queen Ten's "garrison" was keyed up. Alex-Joe and I had done patrols, crept through two dangerous nights, urinating in little squirts to win release from the pain in our bladders. It would work. Our only worry was that someone else might beat us to the prize.

"This could be the damnedest scrap you ever saw," Pithorse hissed to Albert, "with real targets to shoot at."

"What do you mean?" asked Albert.

"If Zwicker an' Alex-Joe swing it, the Jerries might come out shootin'."

The grenade went off with a sharp crack. And as we watched, we jumped, caught by the suddenness of the explosion. Zwicker and Alex-Joe rose from the ditch like two grey spirits and dashed across the road, crouched over. A ball of bluish smoke erupted over what was the enemy gun pit. Zwicker leaped into it and, almost instantly, an inert body was shoved upward and onto the parapet.

Pithorse laughed nervously. "Everything's going like clockwork," he said, exultantly. "Christ! If this is war, it's a piece of cake!"

Zwicker was out of the pit and he and Alex-Joe yanked the fallen man to his feet. All three scuttled across the road and disappeared from our sight.

"Stay down!" bellowed Pithorse, "we'll get you outta there!"

But we couldn't. Every time each man inched a tentative head above the fold, long bursts of accurate fire forced them to duck quickly.

Every automatic weapon in both Queen Ten and Nine searched the Jerry positions for the machine gun pinning the patrol down. I put a call through to TAC, explaining the situation. Major Sommerville reacted quickly, ordering the three-inch mortars to lay smoke. They did. And, carefully, because the Germans were firing into the billowing clouds, Zwicker, Alex-Joe and their prisoner struck out on their bellies, crawling diagonally across the front until they escaped the cone of bullets. They covered the final yards on their feet at the double.

We shouted defiantly into the rolling, smoky sky as they scrambled into the casa, then emptied our Bren and Tommy gun mags in relief.

Albert stood up, stretched and swore softly. "They were lucky, the damned fools," he said.

"Naw," said Pithorse, "there was nothin' to it. Just a little crawlin' and creepin' and a big bang, they got themselves a Squareheaded prisoner worth a medal and a few bottles of real whiskey. An' in daylight, too!"

The prisoner's muddied face mirrored the shock of the violent action as he stood in the one-time living room, his dirty, trembling fingers clasped atop his head.

We eyed him curiously.

"He ain't no bigger than you are, Angus," Pithorse observed.

Angus the Goat shuffled over beside the prisoner, stood shoulder to shoulder with him, then moved away. "No, he ain't," he said, surprised.

Someone slid the bolt of his Tommy gun back and forth.

The German's green uniform was rumpled and stained with blood. But he didn't seem to be aware of it as he shifted woodenly from one foot to the other.

"He don't look so tough," said Pithorse.

"From what I've been told," said Angus the Goat, "I thought all Jerries were ten feet tall with jackboots clear up to their knees."

"I don't think he feels so good," said Pithorse.

I asked, "Where's Alex-Joe and Zwicker?"

"Down in the hole, telling the RSM how they did it," offered Albert. "Like heroes, gunning for medals, probably." He laughed.

"Yeah? Well, they didn't do so bad," allowed Pithorse.

Albert reached out and took the lapel of the prisoner's tunic in his fingers. He felt it, gingerly. "Real cloth."

"You expect he was wearin' steel plate?" asked Pithorse.

The bloodstains on the POW's uniform were darkening.

"They're supposed to be supermen, aren't they," Angus the Goat said.

"Mebbe they're savin' the supermen for the last," offered Cowshit. "They got to be. This guy's a shrimp."

"He's a rat," Zwicker said, emerging from the dugout.

Albert shoved a cigarette under the prisoner's nose. "Want one?" he asked.

The prisoner shrank backward until his shoulders were hard against the wall. His eyes exposed fear. He shook his head.

"Go on, take one," Albert said, gently, "it won't hurt you." He held it against the German's thin, bloodless lips. Again the POW shook his head, blinking.

Pithorse asked, "I wonder if these guys ever laugh?"

Pithorse grabbed the POW by the front of his tunic. "You ever laugh?"

The POW tried feebly to twist free while keeping his hands locked atop his head.

Pithorse shook him like a child. "Ya crummy bastard!"

I watched the German's head bob back and forth rapidly. "C'mon Pithorse, leave him alone, eh?"

Across the muck, a Red Cross flag fluttered in the wind above the German strongpoint. Cautiously, like students cutting classes, two men wearing Red Cross armbands and carrying a stretcher emerged from the casa. They hesitated momentarily then walked slowly down the roadway to the raided weapon pit. Roughly, they lifted a body out, stretching it on the ground. One man knelt over it, then straightening up, talked briefly to the other. Twice they looked at the man on the road. Finally, as if they had reached a decision, they rolled him on to the stretcher and carrying it between them walked back down the road, disappearing into the house.

The flag dropped out of sight. A machine gun, hidden by two soggy haystacks, coughed angrily.

Alex-Joe emerged from the manway grinning crookedly.

"Still got our guest, eh," he said.

"What's up? You guys gonna get the Victoria Cross to split between ya?" asked Pithorse.

"Don't be so foolish," Alex-Joe drawled, still grinning.

"Zwicker, you speak German?" I asked.

"A little."

Pithorse's eyes opened wide. "I never knew that."

"Ya never asked me. Besides, it's not a popular language in this man's army," he said. He faced Pithorse defiantly. "I'm Lunenburg

Deutsch, ain't I? What ya want me to speak, French?"

The prisoner shifted uncomfortably.

"His arms must be goin' numb," said Albert.

"Screw his arms," snapped Pithorse.

"Ask him what's his outfit, Zwicker," I said.

Zwicker spoke to the prisoner, haltingly, in German. The POW frowned. A blank expression came into his eyes. He shook his head. Zwicker thumbed the safety catch off his Tommy gun, yanked the bolt back and pointed the automatic weapon at the POW's belly. He spoke to him again, rapidly this time.

The prisoner's dark eyes seemed to expand into round, large Os. He licked his lips before several gutteral words escaped them.

Zwicker lowered the Tommy gun. "He says he's with the 334th Division an' his home's in Munich."

"Has he got a rank and number?" I asked.

Zwicker spoke softly this time and the POW answered quickly. "It's a boxcar number, Fred. His name's Corporal Gerhard Mueller."

Pithorse kicked some loose .303 casings across the rubble-littered floor.

"He says that all he's got to give us," Zwicker added.

I laughed. "The Old Man says he'll talk 'cause we aren't to let him pee until after interrogation gets through with him."

"That's not until tonight!" said Albert.

"That's right."

"Christ! A man can't go all day without peein', then walk a couple of miles through the mud. He'll piss his pants!"

"Right again, Albert. An' it'll be mighty uncomfortable, either way, dry an' holdin' it, or wet and stinkin'," Pithorse said.

I said, "Zwicker, tell him he can lower his arms."

Zwicker snapped out a short sentence.

The prisoner, warily eyeing us, lowered his arms, rubbing them roughly.

"You think they might attack to try an' get him back?" Nine-Pence asked.

"No," said Alex-Joe.

"Guess that means you wouldn't have gone out after me if I was cut out an' taken prisoner, heh."

"That's about the size of it."

"What a lousy way to run a friggin' war. Every man for himself," Pithorse complained.

The prisoner left that night with the mule train, Zwicker going along as his guard. Two hundred yards below Queen Ten, he made a break for freedom. But he ran blindly into a minefield laid six months earlier by methodical German engineers and tramped on an S mine. The exploding steel pellets shredded both his legs. He bled to death in the darkness while Zwicker emptied his Tommy gun in his direction and swore at the night.

And there was no medal — although Alex-Joe had decided that it would go to Zwicker because he led the charge into the gun pit — or fifty bucks in lira or passes to Campobasso or Naples. A corporal in A Company, a West Bay farmer, had earned them on the previous afternoon.

Standing silently that night in the chilled shadows, I listened as below me Nine-Pence relieved Shrumpski in the forward slit trench. A cold rain was falling.

"You're late, you lazy young bugger!" Shrumpski growled.

"I had to kiss my wife goodbye before I left the hole!"

"She still in your sack?"

"Sure. Where the hell you think she'd be at this time of the night? Out dancing? Why'd you ask?"

"I figure as how you're going to be out here, I'll take your place. Let her sleep with a real man," said Shrumpski.

There was a crackle of sarcastic laughter.

"Boy, when you're good enough to bed my woman, I'll pay you!"

"Okay, I'll remember that."

"You do that. Has the password changed?"

"Nope. 'Delhi' and 'Agra' are the good words."

"You mean if a guy don't answer 'Agra' I'm still supposed to shoot?"

"That's it. Last word I got was, there's a war on."

"Good night, old-timer," said Nine-Pence.

"Good night. See you in two hours. If you're still alive."

"Screw you."

"Keep your head up, the shelling's light."

"Yeah."

Albert shook me awake. "Up, buddy, up. We got something coming down."

I blinked in the half light of the burning wood in the fire pit.

"TAC buzzed. A big thirty-to-forty-man Jerry patrol, complete with a couple of dogs, has gone through Charlie Company's lines. They let 'em in, but TAC doesn't have any idea where they'll exit. So we gotta stand-to, just in case it's our front."

It was the Canadian way: Let an enemy fighting patrol in and hit them on the way out. None of us could understand why the Germans operated with so many men. We'd send four or five, maybe six.

Up on the top floor, we checked that all the Brens were loaded. My watch read 0450 and ticking.

The raw wind shushed through the leafless trees. A pale moon squinted occasionally from between silent, moving, low clouds. I shivered.

"I can hear 'em, I think!" hissed Alex-Joe. We squinted into the shifting gloom shrouding the humped, broken ground between Queen Ten and Nine. "Hear 'em?" he asked. We stared, eyes popping, gloved fingers opening and closing around the stocks of our weapons.

It was a soft, muted sound. And as it swelled, there was an almost rhythmical cadence to it. Then we saw them. I thought of a large, black caterpillar, flowing with a kind of undulating but deliberate surge.

"Christ!' squeaked Pithorse, "there must be a whole friggin' platoon!"

Silently, to a man, chilled fingers were eased out of woolen gloves and safety catches slipped off Tommy guns and Brens. Alex-Joe bent and selected two primed 36 hand grenades from their sturdy wood case.

"Nobody opens up till I say so," I whispered to Albert, "an' pass that on!"

Vaguely, I wondered what in hell I was doing in a Godforsaken Italian casa, responsible for the safety of two sections of 4 platoon and going into a firefight in the dead of night. Why me? I asked myself, why me? Who decided on that?

The Germans were halfway between Ten and Nine, closely bunched, their automatic Schmeissers at the alert, following their dogs, their eyes scanning the ground between the darkened casas.

"Okay, Alex-Joe, let 'er go!" I hissed. As the 36 left Alex-Joe's swinging hand, I bellowed: "Fire!"

The enemy patrol flinched when the first strings of .303s and .45s slammed into their ranks. Then the grenade exploded in a gash of bright flame. I aimed my Bren into the scrambling Jerries, watching the tracers thump home. A series of rippling flames flashed out of Queen Nine. Finally, sporadic bursts of bullets ricocheted off the stone face of Queen Ten as a desperate foe returned our fire. I was startled to realize that, in all the noise, I distinctly heard Zwicker and Nine-Pence loading and firing the two-inch mortar, cursing at each other.

A magnesium flare exploded dully, high in the sky, drifting with the wind beneath its tiny parachute, bathing the nightmare on the soggy land in pale purple-white. As it sputtered out, spewing smoke, the surviving German infantrymen were racing, doubled over, for their lines. The firing ceased. We had no casualties.

For three hours, we stood-to, listening to wounded Germans crying softly in the dark.

"We goin' to help 'em some?" Albert asked.

"No way. Not in the dark. We're taking no chances on losing anybody," I said.

Shrumpski groaned. "Mebbe we could throw 'em some shell dressings?"

"Never reach 'em."

Grey dawn revealed the remnants of the enemy fighting patrol. All were still. We counted seventeen. Two of them had almost made it to their lines.

A lone German seemed to grow right up out of the ground, waving a white flag. He hesitated, then walked slowly toward Queen Ten until he halted beyond our forward slit trenches.

"I am Lieutenant Ernst Broehm," he called up to us, "and I wish to speak to your officer under a flag of truce!"

"That's me," I responded.

"You are an officer?"

"No, but I'm in charge. What do you want?" I heard Pithorse gasp.

"I wish to arrange a short truce — some hour or so — to enable us to recover our dead and wounded."

I was conscious that the men of Queen Ten had their eyes on me. I shrugged. "Why not?" I replied. "Exactly how much time do you want?"

"One hour. Perhaps two." The white flag snapped as a strong gust of wind caught it.

"Make up your mind, Mister. One or two?"

"One should be enough."

"And none of your people will carry weapons or sidearms?"

"Absolutely not."

"Okay. You've got an hour."

"Thank you," he said, turning and loping quickly back to the German position. Two minutes later, a dozen Jerries, weaponless, carrying stretchers, dog-trotted across the ground.

I turned to Alex-Joe, "Better get down in the hole and ring TAC, if the line's still in. Ask for permission to grant a one-hour truce," I said quickly.

"But you already gave 'em the OK," said Alex-Joe.

"Yeah, but don't tell 'em that. Just ask for it. Right quick."

The Germans quickly checked out their fallen comrades, carrying out the wounded first.

Alex-Joe yelled up at me from the foot of the ladder. "You're lucky, Cederberg. The colonel says it's okay. And he's alerted artillery so there'll be no shelling."

The German officer neared us again. "I must ask a favor," he called. "We are short of stretchers. And morphine. Can you help?"

Hell, I thought, I've gone this far, why not? "Nine-Pence, go get a couple of stretchers and lug 'em outside will you? An' Angus, how're we for morphine?"

Angus the Goat nodded "yes" but said nothing.

"Give Nine-Pence what you can spare. Okay?"

In less than fifty minutes, the last of the German dead and wounded were gone. It was like it had never happened.

"An' there goes our goddamned stretchers," said Zwicker, "'cause you're never gonna hear from those bastards again."

Shortly before noon, Lieutenant Ernst Broehm reappeared with two soldiers carrying our stretchers and a cluster of morphine shots — all under his white flag.

"On behalf of my company, I thank you," he yelled, signalling his men to deposit the stretchers and morphine on the ground. "And to assist you to live with this cold, damp weather, I am including a bottle of good schnapps." He placed it beside the stretchers, straightened up, saluted and walked stolidly toward his own position.

"So, screw you, Zwicker," said Cowshit.

"When're we gonna drink that stuff?" asked Nine-Pence, handing me the bottle.

"It's probably poisoned," said Zwicker.

I pried the cork out with my issue knife and sniffed at it, then tenatively sipped. "Whoosh!" I wheezed, "that's strong enough to kill a horse!" I replaced the cork.

"You mean we ain't gonna get a slug?" asked Nine-Pence.

"Later, when it's too friggin' cold and the rum's run out — then you'll get some in your shift coffee."

The live-and-let-live stalemate on the Orsogna sector ended abruptly.

Nightly, three- and four-man patrols prowled the broken ground in front of and behind the Jerry lines, killing and being killed. In retaliation, the Germans pushed larger fighting groups through our lines, triggering vicious firefights.

Harassing mortar stonks demanded counterstonks. Counterstonks insisted on tank shoots. And the rotten weather returned, bringing hail, sleet and endless rain and an end to the false spring. The mechanical monsters, their crews protected by thick armor plate, shelled casas indiscriminately, driving the shivering infantrymen out into their slit trenches.

When brigade artillery was finally called on (like chips thrown in a poker pot as the bidding soared), it destroyed targets of maddened earth and stone, shattered water-filled tracks and blew apart burned-out tanks. The men cowered in tunnels or burrowed under tons of rubble.

Early in April, relief came. The Highlanders, together with the Irish and Perth regiments and their support troops, ignoring torrential rain, climbed into open trucks and carriers and moved westward to take up new positions in a 9,000-yard line five miles north and east of Cassino.

Meanwhile, the other formations in 1st Canadian Corps rolled westward, across traffic-choked roads that turned to dusty tunnels as the warm and sudden Italian spring sun dried out the land. Endless columns of soft-skinned vehicles, tanks, transport and troop-carrying trucks, their serial numbers, regimental and divisional emblems scraped off to mask the gigantic move from prying curious eyes, rumbled by night in endless columns. They clouded the horizon, streaking the roadside foliage with layers of dust, then spilled into the southwestern valleys where, in staggered ranks, they waited.

CHAPTER EIGHT

As usual, we stared upward at the Jerry positions. "That high ground you're looking at," I said to Cowshit, "is Castle Hill. And at the left end of the saddle, that's Monastery Hill."

"An' what's the big mountain?"

"Monte Cassino."

"How far's it off?"

"About seven to eight thousand yards, I guess," I replied, staring at the white walls of the partially destroyed monastery through the clear sunlit sky. "An' I'd guess it's about two thousand feet to the crown."

The skin at the corners of Cowshit's eyes crinkled as he squinted into the bright yellow-blue sky. "It's a god-awful piece of real estate," he said, slowly.

Alex-Joe spit against the wall of loose stones we had to use for our above-ground slit trench because the basaltic rock was impossible to dig into. "Who the hell would want to live here, let alone fight over it?" he asked.

I swept my eyes south and west, noting the shattered valley, the flattened farmhouses, the obliterated roads destroyed in two previous attempts to get by the Germans clinging to the ridges and mountains. "Somebody did, once," I said, "and they'll come back when it's all over and done with."

Cowshit took off his steel hat, smudges from the rubberized inner band staining his forehead. Then he pulled his rubber boots and socks off and examined his bare, sweaty feet. "Christ," he said, "when we were living in the mud an' rain at Orsogna, we only had issue leather boots that left our feet wet an' always cold. But now, now that we're in a rocky desert an' the friggin' sun's shining hot, the army supplied us with fuckin' wet-weather boots!"

The sun was a fiery ball, suspended from an invisible string in the sky.

113

I ran my tongue over my dry lips. "Yeah, I know how you feel," I said. "And the Jerries, up in the rocks, have 88s, Moaning Minnies and mortars...which they're more than willing to use."

"How come they're always up on the high ground and we're down below, getting shot at?" asked Alex-Joe, slyly.

"How the hell would I know? Maybe because they were here first."

We peered over the rim of the rocky wall at the blue-grey mountains which dominated the valley.

"You like your first tour of Eyetieland's little known and rustic beauty spots?" Alex-Joe asked Cowshit.

"Nah. Hell, I didn't even like it when I was in Orsogna. Then it was the lousy food an' the lousy weather. Up here, there's too much sun, too many Squareheads with big guns, and thuh food's still lousy." He laughed, "I guess I'm just the travellin' kind."

I stretched my legs to ease my cramped muscles, knocking a rock off the top of the low shelter. Picking it up, I slid it back into place. "I don't know which is worst, living behind rocks or in wet dugouts."

"Living behind rocks," replied Alex-Joe. "In a dugout, I never got the feeling my back was unprotected, naked as a baby's bum." He peered across the ground at the next pile of rocks and whistled, loudly.

Albert's close-cropped head appeared. "What's up?" he yelled.

"What's new with you?"

"Well, Lieutenant MacNaughton's back. And we're scratching more rocks together so we can build a wall right 'round us."

Albert shared what they called a "rock nest" with Angus the Goat and Zwicker.

A shell swished through the thin air and everyone ducked, instinctively. It exploded a hundred yards down the line.

I lifted my head and peered up at the saddle of rocky ground and beyond to the next peak. A tiny puff of smoke disappeared quickly. "Some stupid bastard is moving around and drawing fire," I said, quietly.

Cowshit, one cheek resting on his helmet, said, "Why don't the Jerries use ordinary little rifles?"

"They don't make enough noise, boy," Alex-Joe said. "In a war, you got to have guns that make lots of noise. Like in the movies."

A second shell whistled in, closer this time, wham! The echo bounced across the rugged ground until it struck the sheer face of the saddle and caromed into a jagged ravine and died.

I was annoyed. "Who the hell's moving around out there?" I asked, more to myself, rising up on one elbow and staring out at the stunted greening bushes, the twisted rocky landscape. There was no sign of life.

After a week, we had learned to exist below Monastery and Castle Hills and their formidable sister peaks. By daylight, we just sat, because the slightest sign of life drew pinpoint accurate fire from enemy guns sited above us.

By night, we gratefully ate lukewarm meals, backpacked into our positions by men who trudged along narrow trails even the mules couldn't handle. Or we patrolled or slept.

I moved my weight from one cheek to the other to relieve the numbness in my behind when the ring of steel-shod boots on rock and the blur of a battle dress jarred my personal alert system. I grabbed for the Bren.

"Don't hit the panic button, fellows, it's only me!" gasped Mac-Naughton, rolling into Alex-Joe and Cowshit, heavily.

"Lord whistling Jesus!" breathed Cowshit.

MacNaughton lay on the warm rock, gulping for breath. "Captain Frizzell was right," he wheezed, "the Germans don't like people running around up here!"

I grunted. "So, it was you they were potting at, eh?"

"The same." The lieutenant's shoulders gradually ceased heaving.

"Well, welcome back, sir," I said.

"Thanks, Sergeant. I'm glad to be here. Although I thought back there I might not make it. That second one was close. Too close. I almost started crapping again."

Cowshit laughed nervously.

"Something up, sir?" Alex-Joe asked, eyeing the officer carefully.

MacNaughton sat up, slapping the rock dust and dirt off his hands. He glanced over the rim of the rock wall. "Well, I don't know."

Cowshit frowned.

"A report came through to company from headquarters that a small group of Eyeties was trying to slip through the lines. I had just arrived from A echelon when I heard a runner was to go up to the forward platoon with orders to wave them back..."

"Why don't they try it by night?" I asked.

"Too many mines."

"And if they don't stop?"

"We shoot."

"Christ!" breathed Cowshit. "Can't somebody round 'em up before they get this far?"

"There are too many small draws and gullies. And the Eyeties know 'em all, meaning they can sneak through our lines. If we go out looking for them, we'd draw fire."

"Won't the Italians?"

MacNaughton shook his head. "The Germans will let 'em come through. Remember the night Gallant and the new kid were killed by a surprise stonk after we'd let that batch of civvies through? Well, we aren't going to let it happen again. Especially here, because our cover isn't as good as it was in Queen Ten."

We thought about it. Then MacNaughton said, "Who's out there on our left?"

I swung my head around and stared at a slight hummock, crowned by the inevitable rockpile. "Charley Company's right flank."

"Good."

Minutes passed. High above us a flight of what Alex-Joe insisted were Allied Mitchell bombers droned northward in a series of V formations.

"Much stuff behind us, sir?" I asked, thinking of the rumored offensive.

"It's a traffic jam already, Sergeant. And now I know why the artillery is called field guns — there are dozens of 'em in every field."

"I wonder when the balloon goes up?"

"Nobody tells a mere looie, Cederberg."

I smiled inwardly. MacNaughton wasn't the same officer who had given me the "officers only" routine in Hunstanton, I thought.

"I heard about the raid," MacNaughton said. "Tough luck with the prisoner."

Alex-Joe rubbed his hand against the two-day stubble on his face. "Tougher for the POW," he allowed. "If he'd been smart, he'd be in a camp somewhere in Canada or the States by now."

"Christ! I wish one of you guys would take me prisoner and ship me back. About as far as England would do," groaned Cowshit, shading his eyes.

I lifted one hand, held it motionless while looking toward Charlie

Company's rockpile two hundred yards away. Shimmering heat waves danced off the rocky ground, distorting my vision. I squinted. "I see 'em," I whispered, "I think."

It was a sea of bright yellow light and grey humped rock. But here and there a blob of green signalled that nature had defied the ravages of war, pushing life upward toward the sun.

"I see 'em!" breathed Cowshit.

Moving slowly in single file were several dark-coated figures. The leader waved a long stick with a slash of white cloth attached to it, holding it aloft. The cloth drooped in the calm air. A small dog ran ahead of them zigging and zagging, its nose to the ground, a curled-up tail high on its shaggy brown back.

Closer they came, walking through the stumps of oak and olive trees that had died in the winter's savage fighting, treading on the new shoots. Over the rise and then beyond was the Rapido River, a mere trickle compared to its early spring flood.

"How many do you think?" asked MacNaughton.

"Seven, I think. Mebbe eight. I can't be sure, sir."

"We gotta kill 'em?" asked Cowshit hoarsely.

We reached for our weapons, MacNaughton taking the extra Bren. Safety catches were slipped off. It was hot.

"No shooting, yet," he whispered. "I'm going to warn 'em." He straightened up on his knees as the range closed to fifty or sixty yards. There were eight of them, picking their way carefully up the trough, nearing the crest of a small spur. "Halt!" he bellowed, waving the light machine gun. "Go on back! *Presto! Presto, amicoes!*"

The Italians froze. Some pointed wildly at MacNaughton. Others shouted hysterically, their shrill voices carrying across the ground, the words telescoping into a jumble of frightened cries. The man with the improvised flag waved it toward the top of the ridge in the direction of the enemy lines.

"Go back!" MacNaughton boomed.

"Fire a shot over their heads, sir!" I urged. The hair on the back of my neck was tingling. "Give 'em a high burst!" I held my breath.

Five rounds erupted from the Bren's muzzle. The echoes filled the valley.

Eight swarthy faces stared at us in terror.

"Go back, *amicoes!*" Again MacNaughton motioned toward the rear with the Bren.

I looked up into the sky, wondering if some Jerry 88s or mortars weren't already on their way. I was sweating profusely.

Abruptly, the Eyeties broke for the top of the spur.

"We got to get 'em before they reach the top!" yelled Alex-Joe.

"Lord Jesus! I think one of 'em's a woman!" screamed Cowshit.

"Fire!" The word rushed out of the lieutenant's throat.

Calmly, deliberately, I squeezed the trigger. My Bren bucked. I swung the barrel in line with the man carrying the flag. Fired again. He fell forward, the flag-stick falling ahead of him.

Both Brens yammered thump! thump! thump! in short bursts of noise. Someone else was firing a Tommy gun. Alex-Joe, I thought.

"There *is* a woman out there!" Cowshit screamed.

My eyes shifted to my left. A woman was running up the slope, gathering a grey skirt in her hands as she did. Down she went, her hands flying outward, her skirt billowing up over her backside. She didn't move.

Another man was stumbling in circles, his face twisted, his mouth working. We couldn't hear him. The Bren coughed again and he was lifted sideways and flung through the air to crash against a rocky outcropping, as though some giant had hammered him with a pan shovel.

The firing ceased, the rolling echoes reverberating through the valley. MacNaughton remained up on his knees and I pulled him down, roughly. "For God's sake, get down!" I snapped. "Jerry's going to start throwing stuff. But soon. And you're going to need every bit of cover you can get!"

His eyes were slits. "Thanks," he panted.

We heard the shells at the last second before the world exploded, the crashing, flat eruption of sounds filling our ears. I was doubled over, mindlessly closing and opening my clammy hands.

Abruptly, it was all over. And the silence was almost as terrible as the noise.

"You okay over there?" we heard Albert shout.

MacNaughton raised his head, a silly grin on his face. "Are you grinning, too, Cederberg?" he asked.

"Not on the inside I'm not."

Cowshit rolled over. His chest was rising and falling. He stared, red-eyed at the sky, saying nothing.

"Alex-Joe?"

"Yep."

The smell of burnt smoke was strong. I peered into the trough, across the top rocks. Gossamer-light, grey-blue clouds drifted slowly toward Charlie Company's positions. "You know those things didn't hit any closer than thirty yards from here?" I said.

"That's close enough. I thought the goddamned things were going to land right in my pockets!" breathed Alex-Joe.

There was a piercing whistle.

"Everything's okay!" shouted Alex-Joe. "That goddamn Mac-Neil and his ear-splittin' whistle..."

"Anybody out there alive, Sarg?" It was Cowshit, his voice low.

I counted eight bodies, small and still, dotting the hard ground. "Don't think so."

Alex-Joe patted Cowshit's shoulder. "Cowshit," he said softly, "it couldn't be helped. There was no other choice. Not with the buildup behind us, or for the safety of the men, like you and me, holed up in these rockpiles."

"They were just going the wrong way," he said, his voice almost back to normal. "The stupid bastards, all they had to do was turn back."

I thumbed the empty mag out of the Bren, replaced it with a full one, and tucked the empty into my small pack. Flicking the safety catch to "off" I stacked it against the rock wall.

"We'll have to get a burial party out here tonight to pick up those dead civvies," I said. "A couple of days under this sun and they'll start to stink and it won't smell nice around here."

Alex-Joe's face glistened, beads of perspiration clung to his upper lip. His steel hat was on the back of his head, the shredded remnants of an issue camouflage netting hanging from it. "I'm hungry," he drawled, "an' my beef's all gone. Anybody got a little extra?"

"Take mine, Alex-Joe," Cowshit said. "I couldn't eat if I wanted to." The burly farm boy closed his eyes. "I don't think I like this war any more."

"Nobody likes it...it's just a temporary way of life," said Alex-Joe, busy turning the key to a can of Frey Bentos corned beef, probably packed originally for the Tommies, poilus and doughboys of World War I. "And all you got to do is remember that."

Two days later, a series of air bursts punctured the sky above our heads and showered us with leaflets, thousands of them, fluttering and gliding like the paper planes we used to make as school kids, only the wings appeared much larger. My curiosity got the better of my good sense and I crawled some fifteen yards across the rocks to recover one. We sat and chuckled over it the rest of the day. It was a good-quality drawing of a naked English woman sitting on the edge of a bed while a handsome — and obviously Canadian or American — soldier stood, buttoning up his shirt. The words, in excellent English, advised us: "Wake up Tommy! [slang for a Brit soldier]. While you're in Italy fighting for war criminals like Winston Churchill, those rollicking heroes from the west are sleeping with your women!" And they offered any Tommy who crossed the lines with a pamphlet safe conduct through the German lines and "the peace and quiet of a prisoner-of-war camp where you can rest until the Third Reich ultimately defeats its Communist and Imperialist enemies!"

"Hey," chortled Alex-Joe, "that can't be a Canadian, he's got a tie on!"

"Yep, it can," said Alex-Joe, "at home they wear ties now, just to match the Yanks."

"You've missed the point, fellows," MacNaughton said, "they think we're English, and if that's what they think, then their generals are all screwed up...don't know the Canadian Corps is even on the west side, facing their friggin' Hitler or Gustav Lines."

In the first week of May, the 11th Brigade of the 5th Canadian Armored Division was relieved by the South African Motor Brigade and went into reserve near Capua. And in a plot framed by the 8th Army brass, 1st Canadian Corps signallers assembled in and around Salerno, far to the south. There they sent out a steady stream of coded and clear fictitious signals, indicating that the 1st Div, supported by both 5th Div Armored Brigades, would hit the Germans with amphibious landings just north of Rome and well behind both enemy defensive lines.

Meanwhile, the 8th Army multiplied until more than 1,000 light, medium and heavy guns supported regiments of men and Sherman tanks covered by 4,000 aircraft, massed in the groves and valleys, tense and silent.

And I was sick. On my back, resting under a pup tent in my summer drill shorts (longs at night because of malaria-bearing mosquitoes) I felt tolerable. Twenty minutes after getting to my feet, I'd have to lie down. And I pissed pure yellow-orange whiskey-colored urine.

"You oughta go sick," Albert said.

"No way. Things are happening, and I've gotta stay. Besides, you go sick and next thing you know you're in another outfit. No thanks, old buddy."

For some reason I couldn't fathom, the sight of a messtin filled with army stew made me bilious, so Albert and Alex-Joe would scrounge chickens, cook them up, and feed me. It seemed to help.

At 2300 hours on May 11th, while nightingales sang in the olive and orange groves, the artillery boomed in tremendous concert. No one could sleep as the ground trembled while lightning from a thousand gun barrels shredded the calm night.

The generals, in their tents and villas and arks, believed it was a set-piece attack, a brilliant operation in which corps and divisions were governed by timetables which insisted on cohesion and clarity as regiments were fed into the maelstrom over the next ten days.

Instead, a thousand wild, breathless, brawling, cursing, tiny battles erupted, like spontaneous fires exploding in a rags factory. And as fast as one flickered out, another began while the wooden soldiers fought, lived or succumbed without ever realizing whether they had won or been overwhelmed.

The Highlanders stood-to and 4 platoon's dozen carriers laagered in a vineyard, hidden from the night in the tangled branches clinging to the wires supporting the vine's green tendrils and leaves. Above the Liri Valley, the May sky was dark blue, warm and punctured with stars. Silently, the drivers picked up gas from the petrol dump, hoisting the four-gallon tins on their shoulders. Then they tramped to their carriers, spilling the gurgling white, high-octane liquid into thirsty tanks.

Under a tarpaulin strung from the high side of a three-ton truck to slanting poles driven into the soft ground, the support company cooks worked, rationing bread, coffee, tea, bully beef, biscuits, sugar and powdered milk to platoon sergeants.

Breakfast came — hot mush, thick slices of bacon, bread and coffee — and still we waited. Coutt dished out the SRD (Service Rum, Demerera) as the overproof potion was tipped into each enamel mug then spilled into an empty stomach to ward off the chill and flu. It was strong and tasty, lacking the sweetish odor of the commercial drink, and a helluva lot better than mepacrine, the ersatz quinine tablets each man swallowed three times weekly to ward off malaria.

I asked Pithorse if Old Betsy II was shipshape.

Pithorse smiled sadly from atop the carrier's armor-plated side. "She ain't exactly like the Ol' Betsy we left in England, Sarg," he said, "but she'll go as far as the Squareheads will let us."

"You get all the extra rations packed away in the spare battery box?"

"Yep." Pithorse carefully fitted one of the engine panels into place, grunting.

"Room for the stone crock of rum?"

"Yep. Hey! You mean no shot before next breakfast?"

"That's what I mean. We'll hang on to it. Dish it up when the going gets rough."

"Christ! In all the army, I gotta get a smart-ass for a sergeant." He jumped down off the vehicle. "You hear about Cowshit?"

I worked my way to the back of the carrier. "No."

"He's a papa."

I lifted the lid of the battery box, bunched three large loaves of bread along one side and gently fitted the jug between them and the sugar, taking advantage of the padding they offered. "He tell you? Boy or girl?"

Pithorse wiped his hands with a blob of oily rags. He grinned, toothily. "A boy."

"Good."

I slammed the box lid shut, testing it to see if it would open when the vehicle leaped over the first hummock its steel tracks took in high flight. It wouldn't, I decided, and walked over to Albert's vehicle.

He was sitting, cross-legged before a flickering gas fire, writing on Legion paper. I sat down, lit a cigarette and listened to the scratch of his pen on paper. Finally, he said, "I don't think I have anything else to say." He bent over the pad, scrawled a few words and sighed. Capping the pen, he slipped it inside the pad. Tearing out the page, he folded it in the middle, then into three and fitted it into an already addressed envelope.

"You writing Violet?"

"Yep."

In the soft glow of night, vehicles and men were inky outlines that merged with the warm earth. Voices echoed and hissed through the sagging vines.

"Cowshit's a father," I said.

"I know."

Albert climbed to his feet. He lifted his small pack out of the armored carrier, unbuckling the top flap. Carefully, he slid the writing pad and letter inside the canvas pack, then buckled the flap, drawing the two straps tight.

"You going to mail the whole pack?" I asked.

"Nope."

"Then when are you going to post the letter?"

"When this show is over."

I took a long drag on my cigarette. "Christ! You're an optimist!"

Albert sat down, his face toward the firelight. He smiled a small sheepish smile. "I always do it this way, write a letter before we go into the lines. An' I hold it until I come out. Then I mail it."

I wanted to ask "What for?" but didn't. It was none of my business.

"Gimme a butt, buddy," Albert said.

I handed him one and stared into the night while he lit it. "Four platoon's been pretty lucky so far," he said, at last. "Only a couple. That's not bad." The shadows cast by the vines lengthened each time the fire flared.

"My old father used to say, a long warm summer is always followed by a cold, harsh winter," I said.

"What's that supposed to mean?"

"Nothing, then maybe something. Maybe the Fates have been giving us the big smiles because they're going to slip us the old fickle finger, but good," I said.

Albert's brown eyes were solemn. "Fred, my boy," he drawled, "you're a pessimist. You're supposed to count your winnings, not worry about your losses." He shuffled his outstretched feet, puffing lazily on his cigarette. "I have half a bottle of whiskey around here. You like a shot or two?"

"You mean we finish it off?"

"That's the general idea."

"Then what's holding you on the ground? Up off your ass and get it, Corporal. I think I'm thirsty."

"Yes, Sergeant."

We drank slowly and contentedly, wiping the brown glass neck of the bottle with our dirty hands before passing it back.

"I'm happy for Cowshit," Albert said.

"Because he's a papa?"

The rye burned our throats and warmed our bellies.

"Because he's happy."

"That's a crummy reason."

Albert soothed, "It might be, but I'm still happy for him."

"Even if you don't know why?" I belched.

"Even if I don't know why."

I thought about Albert's letter to his wife, tucked inside the small pack. And I hoped he would be around to mail it.

On May 24th, we jumped across the Melfa River and moved into our assembly area behind the convulsive, flaming front, but remained caught up in horrendous traffic for twenty-four hours while it began to rain. Traffic built up on the slick, track-churned routes as formations passed through each other, groaning and creaking in what seemed like all directions at once.

And the Germans, experienced in war, methodically shelled the assembly areas while they slowly retreated, initially caught with their critical reserves waiting for an assault landing that never came.

Forty-seven men were carted out by the dogged stretcher bearers. Four platoon had a dozen casualties, plus Zwicker. But he wasn't carried out. He filled the small shrapnel gash with powdered sulfa, bandaged it with his field dressing and stayed put in his slit trench, swearing indifferently.

The following day, the jams were dissolved and we plunged into the thousand battles, struggling mechanically until maddened by the noise, the death, the flies, the hot sun, the stench, we lashed out killing without conscience.

In the bitter struggle into the Liri Valley, the Germans abandoned Cassino to the Poles, as the 1st Canadian Division stormed into the Hitler Line after a series of frightful firefights, reaching Pontecorvo by May 24th. Switched to our left, we swung west of Highway 6 and doggedly struggled to our "Tom" objective when the Loyal Edmonton Regiment passed through us to take Frosinone on May 31st. When the fighting ended on June 4th — the day before Rome fell to the Yanks out of the Anzio bridgehead — 789 officers and men had died, 2,463 had been wounded and 116 taken prisoner.

Albert was one of the wounded, collecting an inch-long chunk of shrapnel deep in his side that sent him to hospital, grimacing in pain.

And I was on a hospital train, half in a daze, destined for the Fifth General. By the last week in May, I had still felt like a dog, but had added a temperature that rose and fell like a yo-yo. Sitting by a sunken road with Cowshit, guarding a half-dozen prisoners, I watched Farting Joe's red-cross-marked jeep heading toward us through glazed eyes. He drove alongside and braked.

"You look like death warmed over," he suggested.

I nodded. That's all I could do.

"Get in," he said, and without a word I climbed into the back, leaving the surprised Cowshit.

I vaguely remembered Doc Boyden's greeting in the chaos that was the RAP. "Cederberg…and I'll bet you've got the jaundice!" he snapped, peering into my eyes. "Yes, sir." He jammed a thermometer in my mouth after touching my forehead with his hand. "And malaria as well. Christ! How long've you been like this?"

Two minutes later I was lying on a stretcher. I closed my eyes and opened them on the hospital train. I closed them again. Next time they opened, I realized I was in bed, under canvas, listening to soft, girlish voices I hadn't heard in years. They belonged to Canadian nurses. I laid on my belly for over an hour, listening, savoring the soft sounds, homesick as I had never been before — even that night when the *Orcades* had swung-to in Bedford basin when, if there hadn't been so many other Highlanders aboard, I could have cried.

A soft hand touched my shoulder. I rolled over and looked up into the scrubbed face of the most beautiful girl I had ever seen. She wore thick gold-rimmed glasses, her hair was a mousy blond and she had tiny spaces between her front teeth. "I'm Sister Connie," she said, gently, "how are you today? You've been a very sick young man."

Our ward was filled with jaundice cases, dysentery cases and hopeless cases — soldiers who hadn't gone crazy, just run out of desire. "Battle fatigue," the medics termed it.

Next to me was a greying, lean sergeant. "Name's Roy," he said, "Princess Pats. Who're you with?"

"The Highlanders."

"Cape Breton? Forty-eighth? Seaforth?"

"Cape Breton."

He sighed. "I met a Highlander once. Months ago. When we were holding on at the Arielli. It's the goddamnedest story you ever heard. Want to hear it?"

I had the feeling I was going to anyway. I nodded.

"It was about the twentieth of January — maybe the twenty-fifth — just a few days after you guys got the crap kicked out of you in the Arielli. Remember?" he began.

How could I forget? I thought. "The First Div's never going to let up on that, is it?" I said aloud.

He grinned. "You brought it on yourself, telling us as you moved up how you were going to go all the way to Pescara — right through 'em."

I took my eyes off a fly crawling across my blankets and stared at the canvas roof of the marquee.

"Anyway, we were sitting on our side of the river, patrolling, bringing back the Brens and rifles you'd left behind. Doing what came natural since we'd landed 'way back in July in Sicily.

"About the twentieth or twenty-first, like I said, somebody in a forward slit trench reported he'd seen a faint flash of light down in the valley. On the Jerry side of that lousy river," he went on.

"But nobody else saw anything. How could you? What with the friggin' off and on again rain, that Adriatic mist that seemed to come in off the water and hug the mud. Next day, there was another short spell of pale sunlight and I'll be damned if a couple more guys don't swear they saw a light. It'd go on, then off. No, it wasn't a light, more like a signal.

"At first, we figured those goddamn Jerry paratroopers were trying to sucker one of our patrols. You know, ambush 'em all dead should they take a notion to check it out. So, me an' the looie decide we don't need that. And we sat tight."

I was listening now, ignoring that fly.

"Well, I'll be damned if we don't see it again the next afternoon, and I mean *we* 'cause I'd moved up to the forward position, just in case. Wanted to see for myself, y'know," he continued.

"That evening, I talked it over again with the looie. He was a good boy, a bit young and he'd seen too much. It made him a bit leery, if you get me. Finally, he said we could risk four men, under Corporal Savard, a cagey cuss with a big French-Canadian nose that could smell a trap before it was even set.

"They started out before 2300, so's they'd get across the river ford just about the time the paras would be changing shifts an' they wouldn't be too watchful, if you know what I mean..."

There he goes with that "if you know what I mean" business, implying that the Highlanders didn't. "Yeah," I said, "I know what you mean."

"Good. Anyway, they got back into our lines about three hours later, carrying a half-alive one-footed soldier, one of your Highlanders..."

My eyes snapped wide open, I struggled to a sitting position and the fly zoomed off my covers, straight up onto the ceiling. "What was his name?" I croaked.

"Ah...that I don't recall. Anyway, he had one foot blown clean off an' he'd been there for most of a week with it stuck in the mud. Y'know, he'd used his rifle sling for a tourniquet, so the stump was kinda healthy. He'd eaten cold bully beef and hard chocolate and drunk muddy water all the time. An' at night, he told us, he could hear the fuckin' Jerries movin' around and talkin' and he never once thought of calling to them and surrendering. Imagine the guts that took, lying there in the muck, cold as a whore's heart, tightening that tourniquet, then easin' it off, just like he'd been taught. You know how he had signalled?"

I felt woozy, but my mind was clear. "A piece of mirror he'd been carrying for when he had to shave?"

"Nope. Not at all. He'd polished — well partly polished — the bottom of that friggin' empty bully beef tin against his battle dress! Christ, can you imagine that!" he said.

"Did he die after you brought him in?"

The sergeant shook his head, almost sadly. "Nope, again. But he'd lost his mind. The poor, poor bastard...all he kept asking for, as we strapped him into a stretcher on the Red Cross jeep, was black tea with lots of sugar and a stack of dry toast..."

"Toasty MacDonnell!" I blurted, "Toasty." For some reason I felt like bawling, but I didn't. "He wasn't crazy, that was his favorite snack — sugared black tea and dry toast."

I laid back on my pillows. So, I thought, all the Highlanders didn't leave the Arielli the night of January 17th. Toasty needed another four or five days.

"In your platoon?" I heard the sergeant ask.

I shook my head. "No," I said, "but he was a friend."

It took me three weeks to convince the doctors that I had recovered and a record-breaking five days — so the other inmates told me — to clear the convalescent camp. I was trucked to the reinforcement depot at Avellino where I met Albert, still grinning crookedly but without any pain.

"They took me to a field operating room, in one of those big squared-off trucks," he explained, fingering the souvenir fragment of shrapnel the surgeon had given him. "Boy, was it noisy in there.

All you could hear was the plinking and plunking of pieces of German shells landing in the metal pans as the docs dug 'em outta the casualties. Hell, it was like an assembly line, moving guys through like so many goddamn Fords where the frame goes in one end and comes out the other all welded together and in one piece," he said.

"By the way, who mailed my letter to Violet? She got it, y'know."

"I dunno. One of the boys, Alex-Joe probably. It'd go out with the requisitions for ammo and food," I said.

"Thanks."

OUT OF BOUNDS

Chapter Nine

ALBERT and I sat under the awning in front of the San Marco sidewalk cafe, sprawled in wire-backed chairs, smoking. Two glasses half-filled with *vino bianco* were between us on the table.

Albert wiped the perspiration from his forehead and pushed his glengarry back on his head. "We're in a backwash war, now, buddy," he said, slowly.

"You mean since the second front opened?"

"That's about it."

"You mean we'll rate the comic pages from now on, eh?" In the heat, I really didn't give a damn, but wondered absently if the censors had insisted on no German accents in the "Katzenjammer Kids" strip.

A sloe-eyed Italian girl passed, her girdle-free hips struggling inside her thin skirt, her large breasts swinging free inside her blouse. The action made me forget the sores on her legs.

"You can't bed 'em, but they're allowed to suggest it would be a hell of an idea," Albert said. "There ought to be a friggin' law."

A mob of USAAF non-coms surged slowly into the bar-*ristorante*, talking and laughing.

Army trucks, Canadian three-tonners, American eight-wheelers and bareheaded jeeps snorted slowly in either direction, their speed governed by the plodding donkeys hauling high, two-wheeled carts piled with oranges, peppers, firewood, clothing, furniture, kids. Army drivers honked horns at the soldiers and civilians alike, one American Negro screaming in frustration at three slow-moving soldiers in shorts.

"Screw off, yuh bastid!" one yelled back, giving the Negro the two-fingered salute. He returned it.

A box-shaped ambulance, its large red cross standing out against a white background centered on its khaki body, followed the

131

Negro's truck, the driver with a soggy cigarette dangling from his lips.

And over everything, the yellow sun burned, boiling the concrete, the stone, the black glass windows, the vehicles, the donkey carts, the humanity, the whitewashed buildings, the windless air, the damp stench in the narrow, shadowy side streets.

The early summer sun shone over the old man with the concertina, standing in the gutter of Benevento's main street that led down toward the Emperor Trajan's sandbagged arch. His face resembled a crumbling copy of an Old Masters' portrait, brown-black and wrinkled. The breathless heat didn't seem to bother him. His skinny fingers worked nimbly, squeezing out "Lilli Marlene." Soldiers in bleached summer drill sometimes slowed to listen, their faces indifferent. Others bent slightly and dropped crumpled script notes into his upturned black hat. And he would smile, exposing two rows of jagged, stained teeth.

The sidewalks were solid with shuffling columns of people, spilling over onto the cobblestoned roadway, soldiers and airmen, fresh skinned, suntanned, sunburned, pale faced, erect, in their USAAF greenish-brown or 8th Army bush shirts, slacks or shorts, puttees, glengarries, black tams, berets and forage caps. Among them were Italian men looking like so many replicas of Hollywood's version of the James Brothers, slouched, caped, riding or walking donkeys, their dark-eyed, dark-skinned faces under high-crowned black hats.

I forgot about the "Katzenjammer Kids" and watched the girl until she was lost in the crowd.

Albert roused himself to an upright position and stared at his bare knees, bare from the hem of his shorts to a point where his puttees spiralled out of his army boots. "They look okay in front, but in back they're burned to a crisp," he said, sleepily.

It was our first pass since we had met at the depot in Avellino. Along with a hundred other non-coms and men we had been trucked to Benevento to enjoy a day free from saluting, drilling or working on excuses to avoid both. Others had gone to Salerno. Naples was out of bounds because of VD. We had elected for Benevento because it was closest, shortening the tiresome, jolting ride in the back of the three-tonners.

Dirty-faced kids darted barefooted among the sidewalk crowds.

"I need something stronger than this," Albert said, squinting into the bottom of his empty glass.

"You know what Farting Joe said about Benevento gin," I said.

"I know. But maybe they have some brandy."

"Wartime brandy with a prewar smell? It's made in the same bathtub, ol' buddy."

Albert grunted, signalling for the waiter. "You're beginning to sound like you should've been a padre."

A woman, her shoulders swathed in grey-brown shawl, her face fractured by wrinkles, walked doggedly by the table. A tall, round demijohn rested on a roll of cloth atop her head. Our waiter brought fresh glasses of vino, removed the empties and I paid him.

We sat and watched the shuffling crowds moving sluggishly in the muggy air. A curly haired boy, his shirt unbuttoned to the belt holding up his shorts, stopped in front of us. His black eyed face was grimy. He smiled. "Hey boy," he said to Albert in rapid, broken English, "you want-a jiggy-jig my sister?" He extended the thumb and forefinger of one dirty hand. About a half inch separated them. "She got small puss, Joe. Like this."

"How much VD's your little sister got, sonny?" asked Albert.

The boy frowned. He shook his head. "Only three hundred lira, Joe," he said.

I shooed him away. *"Via! Via!"*

He made a face, stuck his tongue out and bolted, hissing, among the sidewalk crowd. As the milling servicemen parted in his headlong dash, Pithorse, Cowshit, Zwicker and Alex-Joe appeared.

"F'Chrissakes! It's Cederberg and MacNeil!" Pithorse squealed. "What're you guys doin' here? On y'r way back? Like soon? Or tomorrow?"

I shook my head. "How in hell would we know? You know God and the army move in mysterious ways. We're both at the holding unit. Remember Captain A.O. Gunn? Well, he's I-C and running the show — he'll tell us when."

"Elephant Shit Gunn! I'll be damned. When he left suddenly back in the wintertime, I thought they'd be shippin' him home," said Alex-Joe. "How is he? In fact, howinhell are you characters?"

"I'm A-one, fit for duty, all sewn up. Cederberg's also fit for duty ...no more doggin' it with jaundice or malaria. Captain Gunn?" Albert laughed. "Still describing the war as real big stuff, like elephant shit."

"What about the rest of the platoon?" I asked.

"We're resting, kind of tidying up, near the Dragone-Alvignano area."

"I mean, did we lose any more guys after I left?"

"You knew Louis Hiley got it. And big MacDonald," replied Alex-Joe. "Couple of others, too. I forget their names…" He turned away, staring out into the street.

I coughed. "Who's he?" I asked, changing the subject and pointing at a U.S. Air Force sergeant standing next to Pithorse.

"His name's Vitunski," Cowshit said. They pulled chairs away from nearby tables and sat down.

The Yank said, "Hi, fellas." He was chubby.

Pithorse's tunic was open halfway to his web belt, the necks of two bottles protruding from it. He reached in, removed them and plunked both on the table. "Genuine Eyetie cognac. An' they cost one army boot," he said.

"One?" Albert asked.

"Yah," said Cowshit. "We got four for a pair an' we drank two of 'em already."

Everybody laughed.

"Hey! They haven't gone blind!" said Albert.

"Who says we ain't?" asked Zwicker.

I jerked my head toward Albert: "Fartin' Joe says this guck here in Benevento will blind a man."

"Yah!" exclaimed Cowshit, lifting one bottle to his mouth and trying to drink with the cork still in it.

"Cow," Pithorse cried, "You got no manners!"

Cowshit grinned. "Aw, c'mon Pithorse, a guy can make a mistake." He yanked the cork out and drank.

They all drank.

Vitunski smacked his chubby lips. "I hear you guys get real whiskey."

"Just the three-hookers an' officers," said Pithorse without rancor.

"Nobody gets booze in our army. It ain't considered good for us by our mothers."

"Your mothers? F'r Chrissakes!"

"Ain't you heard of our mothers? They're patriotic. They cry when we go away an' they cry if we get killed. But in between times, they don't want us to get likkered up. You ever hear of such damn foolishness?"

"Don't knock the mamas, Vitunski," Pithorse said.

The Yank looked at Pithorse carefully. He shifted in his chair. He wasn't sure how to take him. "Your last name's O'Donnell, ain't it?"

"Yah."

"That explains it. Irishmen are always respectful of their mamas."

"Yah. But my mama never said not to drink."

"What did your mama say, Pithorse?" I asked.

"Nothin'. So, I took to the drink."

Pithorse lifted the full bottle high, removed the cork. "Then I propose a toast to all the Irish mamas!" he said and took a long swallow. Both bottles passed from man to man.

"An' what about the American mamas?" asked Vitunski.

The bottles were passed around again.

"And here's to the Canadian mamas!" said Alex-Joe.

They drank again, leaving the bottles half empty.

Zwicker jammed a thick hand between their faces. "An' what's wrong with German mamas?"

"Nothin's wrong with any mamas," said Cowshit.

"Then here's to the German mamas!" mumbled Zwicker. He drank so long, Pithorse pulled the bottle from his hand and some of the cognac spilled over his chin and bush shirt. He yelped.

"Where are you guys from in Canada?" Vitunski asked, producing a pack of Camels and handing them around.

"East coast," drawled Alex-Joe.

We lit up, two to a match.

"I'm from Ohio," Vitunski said, exhaling a thin stream of smoke from his round nostrils.

A convoy of 8th Army trucks clattered through the street, gears clashing, steel tailgates banging against steel bodies. Across the road, at the curb, was a two-wheeled cart loaded with tangerines and nuts, an underfed donkey standing patiently in the traces. Beside him stood a stubby man, lighting a cigarette, his hands cupped around the flaring match.

"Vitunski's with the Yankee air force," Pithorse said.

"Bombers?" someone asked.

"No siree. I'm with the transport group, pushin' Libs between here an' England," said Vitunski.

"But he done his tour. Been over an' back twenty-four times, right buddy?"

"I saw a guy crash. Once. Near Pontecorvo. Bango! He piled her right in," Albert said. "No way I'd be a flyboy. Too fuckin' dangerous."

"One of ours?" I asked.

"Limey. Two engines. He'd been bombing ahead of us an' on the way back he started smoking...falling back. All at once he nosed over and started straight down. All guns firing. He tried to pull out, and might of made it except he ran out of air and the whole friggin' plane disappeared in a big, big ball of fire. Christ! Nope. No place for me…" Albert's words trailed off.

"Yeah? An' I think any bird in the infantry's got to be a little nuts," slurred Vitunski.

"What's the difference, whether ya die in a big bang or crawlin' aroun' in a hole in the ground?" asked Zwicker.

"There's no difference," replied Vitunski, amiably, "it's just a matter of preference."

"Shit! said Pithorse, "I'm glad to know we get a preference."

Alex-Joe giggled.

"What's the matter?" asked Cowshit. "Ya drink go down the wrong way?" He stared at Alex-Joe who was half-choking.

"No, I was just picturing Pithorse selecting his personal method of how to die."

"An' how would you like to go?"

Alex-Joe stopped laughing. "Like anybody else, you stunned bastard, screaming and moaning if you get the chance!"

The rosy, semi-purplish, pleasurable hue of late afternoon showered the street, shading the casas, hushing the sounds of day. The old vendor was sitting on the curb now, his head resting against the end of his cart, his hat brim over his eyes.

"We're out of cognac," said Pithorse, shaking the two empty bottles. "Now whatta we do?"

Two *carabinieri* walked slowly by and stopped at the far end of the block, one cleaning his nails.

"We drink vino," said Alex-Joe.

"Not me," said Cowshit peering at his watch, "it's almost seven an' there's a leave truck back to the regiment in eight minutes if I can make it…because, I think, I'm loaded."

Pithorse tried to talk him out of it, but no dice. Cowshit departed, Vitunski with him, both staggering slightly.

"When's the last truck?" Pithorse asked, blinking like a drunken owl.

"Twenty-ought hundred."

"Thas eight, ain't it?" asked Zwicker.

"Chris'! Y'r smart, Zwicker."

Zwicker laughed. "I'd like to get laid."

"See what I mean Alex-Joe," Pithorse said, "he *is* smart. Thas a hell of an idea."

"Well, you've come to the right country," I said, "half of it's screwin' and the other half's sellin' it."

We located a brothel less than one hundred yards from the ruins of a Roman theater. And while the ghosts of long ago classic Thespians recited their lines in Latin and Greek, we copulated. Zwicker, Pithorse and Alex-Joe made the last truck to Dragone, but Albert and I missed ours to Avellino. So we drank some more. And we found another brothel where the girls were younger and more aggressive even if the exercise was mindless.

"You know something, young Fred," Albert said as we wobbled up a dark street, "I'm hungry — let's eat."

It took half an hour to find a house where the mama reluctantly cooked up eggs and chips. When she overcharged us, Albert liberated an ornate clock that sat on a cabinet in the living room. It ticked steadily inside his bush shirt as we walked out of the city. And it chimed each half hour and hour while we hitched a ride almost to Avellino with a Free French truck driver, then plodded the rest of the way to the holding unit camp.

As we neared the guards in front of the one-time Italian cavalry barracks, Albert flung the clock into a roadside ditch where it bounced off a rock and settled face down in the dirt. The glass shattered, it stopped ticking.

The orderly said, "Captain Gunn wants to see you right quick, Sarg."

The whimsical captain, long-bodied and short-legged, was pale-faced despite the Italian summer sun. I saluted.

"Sit down, Cederberg, smoke if you got 'em," he said. I lit up. "Any news on Major MacNeil? I haven't heard a word since he was appointed camp commandant at Aldershot in good old Nova Scotia. He's well?"

"Yes sir."

"What about young Gordie, his son the captain. Last I heard, he was still with the West Novies."

"Haven't heard a word. Nothing. In fact, Captain, I haven't seen him since we landed in Italy."

He tilted his chair back. "Well, I suppose you're raring to get back to the Highlanders, right?"

I nodded.

"Unfortunately, I've got some bad news for you — not from home or the West Novies. It's army elephant shit, because it seems the Canadian Corps needs more infantry and less armor in this kind of slugging up-over-the-mountain-and-across-the-river war. So, in their wisdom, the generals are putting together another brigade of footsloggers. It will, I'm told, consist of the motorized Westminsters, an armored car regiment — the Princess Louise Dragoon Guards — plus the light anti-aircraft regiment, all of 'em to be the 12th Brigade in the 5th Armored."

"What's the bad news about that?" I queried, uncertainly.

He spread his hands. "You're going to have to join the ack-ack unit."

I groaned.

"I have no choice, my boy, none at all. My orders — along with every other holding unit CO — is to ship up one battle-experienced sergeant and one corporal at a minimum. And you're the only three-striper I've got on strength."

"These ack-ack, weren't they ever in action?"

Captain Gunn grinned. "I suppose in their terms you could say they were. But not really, because the Germans simply don't have aircraft in this theater. In fact, I've heard the only kite they ever knocked down was one of ours. So, in our terms, they've seen little action, and none as infantry."

"Sir, who's the corporal?"

"Let me see, there's..."

I interrupted. "Captain Gunn, seeing as I have to go, could Corporal Albert MacNeil accompany me?"

"MacNeil...Albert...isn't he old Major Gordie's half brother? Is he here?"

"Yes sir. Got hit in the Liri, but he's recovered and here."

"So be it." I got up. We shook hands. "Good luck, young fellow," he said. "Oh, by the way, you'll both be ticketed to the carrier platoon in the new outfit."

Later that evening, I shrugged off my disappointment and Albert and I consoled ourselves over a bottle of Seagram's VO as we sat on the grass outside the barracks while a fistfight raged inside between green reinforcements from Nova Scotia and Quebec.

"They'll learn that brawling is for kids," muttered Albert, "they'll learn."

CHAPTER TEN

THE 30 cwt rumbled to a stop and Albert and I climbed out to be greeted by a florid-faced sergeant. "I'm Scotty Morrison," he said in a loud, happy voice. "Welcome to the outfit without a name."

Our kit landed on the dusty roadway as the driver flung packs and duffle bags over the tailgate. "Here," he said, sweating profusely in the searing summer sun and extending our Tommy guns, "are your weapons."

"Sergeant Cederberg and Corporal MacNeil," I said, "reporting for whatever comes up, Sergeant Morrison."

"Call me Scotty, that's enough," he said cheerfully.

I judged him to be about forty.

"According to headquarters, we're supposed to get ten officers and 156 men. You're among the first. After you're signed in or checked off, whichever, I'll take you to your lines. Any idea what platoon you're booked for?"

"Carriers."

Scotty beamed. "Great! That's my platoon." He examined our shoulder flashes. "Highlanders, heh? That's a good outfit. Welcome again. Like I said, we got no name, so we're kinda screwed up. But it'll all fall into place. An' tonight we're throwing a bash in the sergeants' mess, Cederberg. Heh? What's y'r first name?"

"Fred. He's Albert."

"Okay, Fred, tonight you'll meet the rest of the gang in that big marquee down the track. It'll be a kinda welcome bash where we can all get conked."

"Conked?" Albert asked.

"Yeah, you know, start out on issue whiskey and gin and when it's gone, top up with Eyetie conk." He laughed, showing two rows of neat, white teeth.

Five minutes later, names entered on the 1st Canadian Light Anti-Aircraft Regiment ("That's why we call it the 'no-name battal-

141

ion,'" chortled Scotty), we were heading down a path leading to a shallow, wide gully cluttered with Canadian Army-issue pup tents, sited among half-flattened vines.

"I'm looking for Sergeant Eddie Kerr," I told a fuzzy cheeked soldier, squatting in front of a pile of web gear.

He straightened up, pointing at a youngish man, sitting, his elbows pivoting on his knees as he worked with a knife on a piece of wood. As I walked over, he looked up, squinted in the sunlight and brushed a handful of blond hair out of his eyes.

"I'm Fred," I said, extending my hand, "and this is Albert, Corporal Albert MacNeil." He took our hands firmly after switching the toad stabber to his left.

"An' I'm the Eddie Kerr you're looking for," he drawled. "I know, you're the new lance-sergeant and Scotty sent you. Both from the Highlanders. Well, glad to meet you. Tell me, how'd you wind up with us? Luck of the draw?" He smiled ruefully.

"Caught us in the holding unit, coming back from hospital. I'd been sick. Nothing glorious. Albert picked up some shrapnel in the Liri."

Kerr stood up, dusted off his denims. "I got some rye. Let's have a drink."

While we drank, he talked about the 1st Canadian Light AA Regiment.

South of Piedemonti D'Alife, while the July sun boiled the rolling landscape, the officers and men of the then Royal Canadian Artillery unit had fought flies and boredom or competed with 2nd Light AA gunners to find out which troop could handle their Bofors guns the quickest. Or swam in the nearby almost dried-up river. At night there were movies.

Training in the muggy air had been perfunctory, consisting primarily of vehicle and weapon maintenance and traffic control exercises. And there had been a steady parade of officers attending conferences with the AA C.O. Lieutenant-Colonel J.P. Thorpe. In turn, this had produced rumors that by July 11th firmed up around a single point: The regiment was to be converted to infantry.

On the 13th those rumors had details.

The Canadian Corps in Italy needed more footsloggers; the Germans had almost no air strength in the Italian theater of Ops, so with the demand for infantry up as a result of the opening of the second front, it was obvious to even the soldiers in the digger that the unit was destined to reform as PBIs — poor bloody infantry.

Eddie Kerr laughed in a low voice. "You know what they had to do? They completed a survey to determine which men were suited for infantry, and which weren't. Those that weren't were called 'surplus,' whatever in hell that meant. Now, we're part of the 12th Canadian Light Brigade." He kicked at a hillock of dirt. "We turned in our guns a couple of weeks back. It was kinda sad," he said.

On July 18th, Brigadier D.C. Spry had addressed all ranks.

"He didn't fool around with fancy words when he spoke to us," commented Kerr, smacking his lips. "He noted — get that word — he noted that a lot of artillerymen might not be too happy at the idea of being infantrymen. Just the same, the regiment was now a walking unit and we might as well make the best of it."

I caught a lazy fly with a quick swoop of my cupped right hand, squeezed it, then watched it fly away when I unclenched my fingers. "Lucky bugger," I said.

"What'd they do with the men they rated unsuitable?" asked Albert.

"Shipped 'em back to the arty reinforcement depot."

"Wonder if we could get rated 'unsuitable,' Fred?" Albert asked, grinning.

Eddie Kerr chuckled suddenly, catching us by surprise. "You guys unsuitable? No way. You're supposed to know what it's all about!"

"That's why we'd like to be rated 'unsuitable,'" I said.

"What is it all about?" he asked.

I looked at Albert. He lowered his head, scooped up a handful of dirt and flung it in the humid air. "Mostly an awful lot of fuckin' noise. You get used to it."

The mess party that night ended up in a no-holds-barred fistfight between a stocky newcomer from the Royal Hamilton Light Infantry who had won a DCM on Dieppe's beaches, Sergeant Tommy Graham, and RSM Stinson, a bull of a man out of the original ack-ack unit.

It really began after the first round of drinks, despite polite, formal — even friendly — introductions when an invisible, frigid wall rose between the newcomers and the remaining original battery sergeants. A complete stranger could have told them apart, even if they hadn't drifted slowly into two distinct groups. The former line regiment infantry three-hookers were neatly but almost casually turned out, boots polished, wearing their former unit patches. But those from the ack-ack batteries looked like British guardsmen. You could cut butter with the creases in their summer drill trousers. Their shoulder lanyards and hooks had been white-ohed, each tiny herringbone stripe done individually.

One infantry recruit sergeant snickered: "I wonder if these cannon soldiers polish the insteps of their boots?"

"Why not?" cracked Graham, loudly, "they never had anything else to do. Look at 'em, hell they ain't never even been shot at an' they stand around lookin' down their friggin' noses at us, like we were some kind of low life form."

"Forget them, Tommy," I chided. "They'll get over it when they find out what the infantry's war's all about."

But Graham had a pugnacious bent. And Stinson represented the artillery. One cutting remark led to another. Just as one drink led to another.

"You guys will forget all that chickenshit stuff," snarled Graham, casually flicking a finger across an ex-artillery three-hooker's stripes, glistening with their finely outlined white-oh.

"Graham," said Stinson, "it's too bad you infantry people never learned to dress like proper soldiers. When I look at you, I sometimes think..."

He never finished the sentence. Graham hit him flush in the mouth with a short, powerful righthand blow, driving the RSM into three of his friends. Good Scotch went flying, glasses clattered and shattered off the duckboard floor. Stinson, fighting for his balance, lunged at his attacker, but it was all over quickly, with the panting Graham astride the bleeding RSM.

The sergeants, stunned by the suddenness of an RSM on the broad of his back with a three-hooker on his chest, recovered their sense of discipline, forgot their infantry-artillery differences and broke it up.

The next day, the new C.O., Lieutenant-Colonel W.A. Dick, gave us a brief lecture, diplomatically suggesting we remember "You're all Canadians, you're all on the same side, and you all know what you have to do — help win a war we didn't start." He also told us one suggested name for the new regiment was the Second Battalion 48th Highlanders of Canada which didn't go over that well.

"We may be a bastard unit, but I don't like the idea being called a 'second' battalion," said Scotty, scowling.

The hot, sunny weather continued right through into August while infantry drafts poured in from corps holding units, swelling the rifle and support companies up to strength.

Private Fred Cederberg presents arms to no one in particular, showing off his new-found ''skill'' in Camp Borden, Ont., a few weeks after enlisting in the Cape Breton Highlanders.

Sergeant Eddie Kerr (left) parades down a western Canadian main street prior to going overseas with the Canadian artillery in mid-1943. That's Ed Johnson with him.

Tommy Burns (top left), Alex-Joe MacKeegan (center), Red Roper (right) and Cederberg (seated) ham it up in front of the grand entrance to a posh country home that served as 4 platoon's home away from home in Hadlow, in the south of England, during the early part of '43.

CT 43355

5

62

April of '43 and England. Cape Breton Highlander sergeant, Louis Hiley (left), is in the Bren carrier's driver's seat while Fred Cederberg stands in the commander's spot and Tommy Summerall drapes himself over the armor plate.

The Highlanders' 4 platoon, somewhere in England during the spring of '43. That's the writer "dead" center.

The Highlanders disembark from the SS *Monterey* at Naples, Italy, October 1943.
(Photo by Frank Royal, Public Archives of Canada, PA 114562)

Corporal Fred Cederberg (right) poses with his Bren carrier driver, Scottie, prior to going into action for the first time in Italy. Coveralls and braces were ''in'' during training exercises in the early Italian winter slop of mud and wet snow.

The Highlanders at "Snow Haven" rest camp at Fornelli, May '44.
(*Photo by Strathy E.E. Smith, Public Archives of Canada, PA 135902*)

Moving supplies westward to the front from the junction of the Liri and Gari
Rivers, May '44. The vehicles are those of the 8th Army and 1st Canadian
Corps troops.

A Highlander, eyes averted, passes by a dead German soldier at the Liri Valley, May '44.
(*Photo by Strathy E.E. Smith, Public Archives of Canada, PA 135904*)

This German antitank gun was positioned in the Hitler Line and knocked out in the assault on May 23, 1944.

Canadian transport moves through Pontecorvo on May 24, 1944, the day after the town's capture.

The Lanark & Renfrew Scottish pose for this one with six-pounder antitank guns.
(*Public Archives of Canada, PA 135903*)

A Sherman tank of the Lord Strathcona's Horse crosses the Uso River at San Vito on September 26, 1944.

A view of the infamous Lamone River, December 1944.
(*Photograph by G.W.L. Nicholson*)

Corporal Albert MacNeil (left) and Sergeant Fred Cederberg in a stilted pose, taken by an unknown Italian photographer while the Lanark & Renfrew Scottish were out on rest early in 1945.

Infantry training began in earnest after the unit moved to Caiazzo: bayonet drill, demonstrations highlighting the functions of our own and enemy minefields, crude bazooka and rifle ranges were built, all ranks were trained on the rifle, Bren, Tommy gun, two-inch mortar and grenades.

"I think we gotta get some other points across, Eddie," I said one evening. "Every man's going to need a slit trench and, while it sounds simple, it isn't. Like, sometimes…hell, too often…there isn't enough time to dig a regulation hole. You should know how to convert a tank rut into a slit in twenty seconds. Or know that a lousy little fold in the ground can save your ass when the 88s or mortars come whistling in."

"What about ditches?" he asked.

"Sometimes. But I don't like 'em. They're too friggin' wide open at both ends. Like if a mortar slams into one, the shrapnel will slice the shit out of you. And there's always the chance some Jerries have them covered with machine guns."

"You speak to Scotty about this?"

"Yeah. And he says to do what we have to do."

For the next few days, with Scotty watching curiously, Albert and I hammered home our points. "One more thing," Albert said, "most of you guys think your weapon is your key to survival. Well, it isn't. And don't laugh when I tell it's your friggin' shovel. Don't go anywhere without it." He grinned crookedly when the seated men laughed. "Hell," he held it up, "it can be a weapon, if that's all you got."

"What about when you're bayonet fightin'?" a round-faced kid named Robbie Crawford asked in a high-pitched voice. "Whatta you do then? Just stick an' jab like the pamphlet says?"

I pointed to a sallow-skinned one-time Loyal Edmonton private whose thin lips barely masked a perpetual small grin. "You tell 'em about bayonet fighting, Alex, you came in with the Eddies 'way back in Sicily in July of '43."

Alex Greenwood, a thirty-one-year-old general store owner, father of three and graduate of the University of Alberta, laughed lazily.

"I never saw a bayonet fight. And I never took part in one. I've walked a long way. I've been shot at with a variety of deadly weapons. And I was wounded in the Hitler Line. But I don't know anything about bayonet fighting."

Al Hall, a skinny, swarthy, sharp-talking son of a Tabor, Alberta,

Mormon cattle farmer, punched his muscular, light-haired younger brother. "I told you that last night," he crackled, "and you wouldn't believe me."

"Whoa, fellows, whoa. You might have to…somewhere… sometime. But like Greenwood, I never got into one," I said.

"Well," Alex went on, "let me say it another way: If I was that close to a Jerry, where we could use bayonets, one of us would have already surrendered!"

The platoon broke up, howling with laughter.

"What do we do when we meet up with a German tank? Like a Tiger?" asked Corporal Howie MacLeod.

"If you got time," said Albert, "get your ass out of the area. Right quick."

"And if I have a PIAT — a bazooka?" persisted MacLeod.

That's the trouble when you've been trained by pamphlets, I thought. They outline perfect cases and happy-ever-after results. "It depends on your choices," I replied aloud. "If it lumbers by you, like only twenty or twenty-five yards away, and your PIAT is loaded, and there are no German infantry with it, take a shot. Go for the shoulder. Or better still, get it in the rear end after it's gone by. Then, get your ass out of the area like Corporal MacNeil said."

"I met a British tank corps gunner once," said Norm Hall. "He'd been at Alamein, clear across to Tunisia, an' he said war was a big bollix when the fighting began. What the hell did that mean?"

Greenwood turned and looked up at the ham-handed Albertan. "While I don't have a specific translation in mind," he drawled, "I believe he meant it was a lot of confusion mixed with noise and motion — all stirred into one giant bollix."

Chuckles and snorts rippled through the ranks.

"Jeez, I wish I was educated, like old Alex," trilled Moose McAdam, a half-breed out of The Pas whose tremendous chest perched precariously on a small behind and two thin legs, "then I coulda said that."

That night, while mosquitoes swarmed around our netted heads, we showed 4 platoon how to move up silently, cross a crest on their bellies, dig in and take up all-round defensive positions. To a man, they took it seriously, learning that loose shovels and weapons can make one helluva lot of noise in the stillness.

"You know something, sir," I said to Lieutenant Claude Nadeau, our chain-smoking I-C, "they're going to make one damned good platoon."

"I knew that, Cederberg. I knew that right from the beginning."

"I'll bet you didn't notice they're beginning to walk like infantry-men, Mister Nadeau, did you?"

Nadeau lit a cigarette. "How do infantrymen walk?" His close-cropped black moustache twitched when he exhaled.

"Well," I said, "you know how artillerymen walk. Like they take themselves seriously. Like they'd like to know who owns the place. Infantrymen," I added, watching him carefully, "swagger a bit, like they don't give a goddamn who owns the place."

Nadeau chuckled. "That so? Guess I've never noticed."

The first light showers fell in mid-month, instantly soaked up by the parched land. The new brigade concentrated in the Foligno area and the no-name battalion lost A Company for several hours while en route. Exercise Canyon came and went, the entire unit practiced assaults and night relief tactics while vehicles were lost, and platoons wandered around aimlessly until redirected by tireless junior officers and sergeants who had to be everywhere at once.

Five Div commander, Major General B.M. Hoffmeister, judged the drill a "working success" then reminded the colonel and his company commanders that we had to maintain better spacing on the attack and avoid skylining. "Spacing," he declared (according to Nadeau), "is critical, because when men bunch up, inevitably there are heavy casualties and Canada is not prepared to accept the kind of casualties inflicted on the country during World War One."

"It's known as thin on the ground," I explained to the platoon, "meaning we should stay three to four yards apart when advancing. The general also means that if we don't, we could be thick on the ground, thick with the dead and dying. OK?"

It was named the Gothic Line and stretched some 200 miles across the Italian peninsula, anchored in the west on the coastal plains south of La Spezia and in the east at Pesaro on the wind-whipped Adriatic Sea. The offensive called for the 1st Canadian Corps to assault the eastern end where the Germans had sown more than 105,000 mines, strung almost twenty miles of concertina barbed wire, sited 2,375 machine guns, 479 antitank and assault guns, miles of antitank ditches and constructed more than 3,500 shell-proof dugouts, manned by an entire army group.

During the third week of August, the men of the 1st Canadian Light AA Battalion — as one small formation in the 1st Canadian Corps — crawled and clanked in endless columns to an assembly area fifteen miles inland from Ancona. Armored vehicles travelled the 120-mile track carved out of secondary routes (because their steel tracks would destroy Italian auto highways) by night only and without lights. One thousand tanks and ten divisions backed up by 1,000 guns would be launched in what was known as the Adriatic Corridor.

The four-mile-wide front centered on Montemaggiore. And 1st Div infantry, the generals said, would force a crossing of the Metauro River, and advance ten miles to the Foglia where the 5th Armored Div would slam through the gap.

"It will be a piece of cake," said a senior officer. "We won't even use the artillery until the river crossing has been pulled off — silently and at night. You fellows in the 12th Brigade? It'll be a splendid way to break in." He laughed. "You'll just be rounding up prisoners and riding on the backs of our tanks all the way to the Lombardy plains. Then the armor will break out and we'll be in Venice in no time at all. How about that, men, winter billets in Venice!"

The moon went to bed early the night of August 25th, but the shimmering stars watched as units of the Canadian 3rd Brigade waded the shallow Metauro River and pushed through the olive groves on the northern side. Easily, with minimal enemy opposition, they occupied the first line of villages, covered by a storm of artillery fire that erupted on schedule at midnight.

Following four days of heavy fighting, the corps with the 1st Div leading had reached the Foglia, poised to break the line. Opposite them, dug in, were elements of the veteran German 76th Panzer and the doughty 1st Paratroop Division. And the 26th and 19th Panzers were moving up to bolster the enemy lines secured to 500- to 1,000-foot ridges and small peaks dominating the river flats.

Enmeshed in huge minefields and resisted by a stubborn defense, six battalions slogged their way forward despite mounting casualties that reduced 110-men companies to as few as fifty. It took both the Toronto Irish and my old outfit, the Highlanders, to elbow the Jerries off Point 120.

It was at Point 204 — a 1,300-foot height which joined up with Tomba Di Pesaro — that the 11th Brigade together with the British Columbia Dragoons Armor took on the 26th Panzer in a firefight that forced the Canadians to the limits of their endurance.

With the Perths stymied by a rain of shells and mortars that cost them fifty-two casualties in a matter of hours, the BCDs launched their own assault. Their headquarters was virtually wiped out, their colonel mortally wounded. Only eighteen Shermans remained while forty-nine men were killed and wounded before they reached the crest, supported by the infantry. And they held all night despite determined Jerry counterattacks.

The Gothic Line had been breached.

And we knew it the next day, listening breathlessly to a crackling radio exchange on the big 36 set in the platoon lead carrier.

"You'll get shit for goin' off the regiment's assigned wireless frequency," warned Sergeant Morrison.

Nobody paid any attention to this remark. It's doubtful if even he did.

"Zebra One...Zebra One" a voice crackled.

"I hear you A-Okay, Charlie Two, go ahead," replied the other.

"You sure that hole's been punched clean through?"

"That's the way we read the situation, Zebra One."

"How's it going on the right?"

"First Div's gone in and, with point 253 in our hands, it'll be a pleasure trip."

"But we got to have Point 204, Mount Peloso."

"Yes, well, the PLDGs and the Lord Strathcona Horse did that yesterday."

"Casualties...?"

"Say again, please..."

"Were there casualties?"

"The Dragoon Guards had over a hundred, I'm sorry to report — thirty-five fatal — and the Straths lost thirty."

"Goddamnit!" exploded the first voice.

"Agreed, Zebra One. But the enemy has disengaged. We think they've had enough."

"Well, that's good news. Now we take the ball and run with it."

"Drive carefully if you want to see Venice, Zebra One."

"To hell with Venice, I want Vienna! Roger, out."

"Better get back on our frequency, heh?" said Morrison, hoarsely.

Signaller Bert Cuthbert expertly moved the tuner until he was sure he was on. "That's it," he announced, popping up in the carrier, "I had it marked with ink. OK?"

"Christ!" sighed Norm Hall, "sometimes I thought those guys

were talking about a football game. Like you punched the hole, an' we'll take the ball."

"Who do you think they were?" persisted Norm.

"Probably generals," offered Crawford.

"Probably."

"An' saying it right on the radio — what if the Jerries were listenin'?" asked Crawford, shrilly.

"What's the difference?" responded Albert. "We know what we gotta do and the Jerries know what they gotta do. It's no secret there's a war on. It's the timing that's critical."

"Where'd you catch onto that little trick…listenin' in?" asked Morrison.

"In the Liri," replied Albert. "Only, because of all those big friggin' mountains and rock, we could only get bits of info, just enough to make us more curious."

That evening, we took down our divisional patches and scraped Canadian Corps insignia off the sides of all vehicles. "Nobody, but nobody," said Nadeau, "is to speak to any civilians because our English will give us away and the Fascists still have informers on our side of the lines."

Sergeant Graham demurred when he was told to remove his DCM ribbon. "That's a personal award," he argued.

Colonel Dick didn't agree. The ribbon was tucked carefully inside Graham's small pack.

The 98/109 "no-name" outfit moved up, assembling south of Montecchio. The muted thump-thump of shellfire from the fighting front reminding them that, ready or not, their time was coming. And it had a quieting effect.

I finished a letter home and one to Francine.

"Letter writin' isn't easy," said Kerr. "Sometimes I got to start 'em two and three times before I get the hang of it."

"Agreed."

"And the people at home write funny ones."

"Yeah," interjected Crawford. "My old lady is always reminding me to wear my friggin' rubbers. And she's never even seen an army-issue rubber… What kinda letters do you write, Sarg?"

"Let me see," I replied. "To my mother and father, I tell 'em I'm fine, the weather's fine, we're out on rest and not to worry about me."

"An' your girlfriend?"

"I tell her to keep her legs together until I get back."

"Jeez," Crawford wheezed, "I wouldn't write that in my letter."

Corporal Howie MacLeod winced visibly when, like prolonged rolling thunder, the harsh sound of artillery fire echoed in the warm late-evening air.

"How're the new guys gonna take it?" Kerr whispered.

"You noticed MacLeod, too?" I half asked.

He nodded.

I lowered my voice. "You can't tell by looking at them. It's uncanny. One guy you think is a shit-hot soldier, he just can't tolerate it. But most can, somehow. If you're asking me about the platoon, hell, they'll do fine." I glanced around at fifty men and boys, from the prairies, the valleys, the cities, some cleaning weapons, others packing gear or topping up vehicles, smoking, just sitting, dozing.

I felt good. "They'll do just great. And they know it in their own way."

Tomba di Pesaro, the walls of the casas a flat white in the cloudy weather, sat on a spur, running easterly toward the Adriatic a few miles to our right. We moved tentatively along the dirt track, the ex-ack-ack gunners staring curiously at the evidence of the bitter infantry fighting — a shattered motorcycle, a knocked out jeep, helmets, Jerry weapons.

I halted in the lead carrier.

"What the hell are ya stopping for?" shouted Morrison from three vehicles back. "We're supposed to push right in and back up A Company!"

Holding up my hand, I searched the spread of the valley carefully with my eyes. "OK...OK, Scotty, but something out there stinks."

Morrison was 175 pounds of nervous energy. He sprinted up beside me. "Whatta you see?"

"Nothing."

"Well, fuck it, let's move. Orders are to get to Point 250." He jabbed a thick finger at the "X" circled by a chinagraph pencil on his sit-rep map. "An' that's where we're going!"

I looked behind at Albert. He shrugged. I tapped my driver, Crawford, on the shoulder. "You heard him, let's move it."

Point 250 was a saddle of ground 250 meters above sea level, supporting typical solid stone farm buildings which dotted most of rural Italy — sturdy, tiled and flanked by two straw husk stacks and a cesspool. We laagered the carriers behind the south-facing long wall and posted lookouts on the north face.

Albert and I walked the track, noting a second rutted road crossed it just to the west of the main casa. Four platoon had already caught and killed a dozen chickens. Kerr was squatting in front of a growing pile of plucked birds, working swiftly with the Halls. Chicken feathers rode the gentle breeze.

"Better start diggin' in!" I yelled.

Albert shuffled over to his carrier, pulled out his spade and began shovelling dirt in every direction.

"What're you worried about?" croaked Morrison. "We ain't seen hide nor hair of any Jerries."

"Yep, that's right. But we're straddling a defined point on our maps an' the Jerries probably have the same friggin' maps. Worse than that, we have two dirt tracks crossing right over there." I nodded in their direction.

Albert and I dug while Kerr and the Halls plucked and Johnny Belanger built a fire under a can of well water. It was warm work. I stripped to the waist, noting that Greenwood was digging, too.

Everybody looked up as what was obviously an enemy shell swooshed overhead, exploding with a sharp carrump! about 100 yards to our rear. "Shit," shrilled Crawford, "they couldn't hit a barn door with a shovel full-a coal."

The pot of water was beginning to simmer. Frank Hall coolly dropped in half a dozen legs and wings. He sniffed at the fumes. "That's going to taste just fine," he announced.

A second shell exploded about fifty to sixty yards ahead of us and off to the left.

My slit trench was down about two or three feet. "Go, buddy, go!" I panted in Albert's direction. "Those bastards are ranging." I cursed and yelled: "Goddamn you guys, start digging!" I stood up and moved several feet from the trench, waving the shovel. Then the stonk came in, hissing menacingly like a dozen ruptures in a steam line.

I wheeled for my slit trench, but three soldiers had already landed into it in what made me think was a ridiculous dead heat. Throwing away the shovel and taking a flying header, I slid under the nearest Bren carrier. The ground heaved as the 88s exploded one behind the other in sheets of pale yellow flame, spraying the platoon area with shards of white-hot metal.

Then silence. I lifted my head. Water was spurting out of the chicken stew can where shrapnel had punctured it. A small cloud of chicken feathers hung in the air where Kerr and the Hall brothers had been. Sheepishly, three members of the no-name unit crawled out of my slit trench. Helmeted heads poked up from behind vehicles, folds in the ground and out of the husk stacks.

"Anyone hurt?" I called, dreading a reply.

Outside of the can and some holes where the steel slivers had penetrated two of the carriers' armor plate, the platoon escaped without a scratch. "Sorry about that," muttered Belanger, standing upright in my trench. "I guess I didn't think — just ducked."

"Forget it, but the next time when I say 'dig' I expect you to dig. OK?"

Belanger dusted off his trousers and went for his shovel. Seconds later, the platoon was all wordlessly digging, except for Al Hall. "What'd they do that for, Sarg?" he asked, curiously, no trace of fear in his sharp voice.

"Just to let us know they're around and ready to fight," I replied.

"Probably just unloading their ammo because they're retreating and they don't want us to have it," he said, ambling indifferently over to his brother. He sat down. "You can make it big enough for both of us, if you like."

Norm Hall grunted and licked some perspiration off his upper lip. "You're crazy," he said, bending to his work.

On September 3rd, we received orders to cross the Conca River, a mere trickle of water moving slowly down the center of its broad, heavily pebbled bed, encased in steep banks.

"TAC says the leading rifle companies are already over that road across the river and beyond the next ridge. So we just catch up," reported Morrison.

The road, two lanes wide, ran parallel to the Conca, in front of a thick stand of trees, then easterly to a blown bridge over a wide creek that emptied into the river.

"We blow that bridge with a bomb?" asked Moose.

"Nope. More like the German sappers did it as they backed up," Albert replied.

A squadron of 8th New Brunswick Hussars' Sherman tanks clanked into position on our left.

Sergeant Morrison joined Albert, Eddie and I. "Tommy Graham got it last night with A Company. The sergeant from the Rileys — who took on the RSM — remember?" His ringing voice was tempered by remote sorrow. "He lives one long, long day at Dieppe. And mebbe a few hours more in Italy. Kinda makes you wonder what was the point of surviving the first time, heh?"

We were twenty yards from the riverbank when the German Tiger tank, squealing and roaring, surged out of the stand of trees, its 88 belching fire. The lead Sherman was hit before it could return a shot, the others swivelled quickly on their steel tracks and found cover behind squat farm buildings before returning the fire with their stubby-barrelled 75s.

The Tiger slewed left and clanked ponderously along the roadway, its 88 swung forty-five degrees and pumping armor-piercing and high-explosive shells as it moved. The vehicle commander was half out of the hatch, directing fire.

"Christ! It's like watching a movie!" breathed Albert, hoarsely.

Flame spewed from its long barrel. The Shermans had recovered from their surprise and slammed shot after shot at the slow-moving Panzerwagon that outweighed and outgunned them. Twice the Sherman gunners registered hits, but the Tiger, engine screaming, rumbled on.

"That sonuvabitch is gonna get away!" yelled Morrison.

A corner of one casa protecting a Sherman was blown away. Smoke erupted.

"He gonna shoot at us?" asked Crawford, shrilly, suddenly realizing we were in plain sight of the tank gunner and commander.

"Would an elephant kill a fly when he's fighting lions?" someone yelled.

At the last moment, just when it appeared inevitable the enemy tank would run right out onto the blown bridge and plunge through the shattered decking, the commander realized he couldn't make it. Slowly, belching shells, the Tiger backed up. Gears clashed. The engine revved higher, a last shot was fired and the tank veered to its left and, sticking its lightly armored rear high in the air, began snorting and chewing its way off the road down the dirt track detour across the creek.

It was the moment the Sherman gunners had been waiting for. In rapid succession, three shells ripped into the Tiger. It coughed like a stricken rhino, and smoke and flame wreathed the turret, followed by a series of muffled explosions.

The Shermans poured a withering barrage of shells into the stand of trees.

"What for?" squealed Moose. "They think there's more of 'em in there? Shit, I thought the infantry companies had already cleared the next ridge."

"That's what TAC said. Hell I was talkin' to the looie an' he said we were supposed to get our asses up and support B Company because it'd lost a couple of platoons," Morrison blurted.

"Lost a couple of platoons?"

"Well, mebbe misplaced 'em is a better word. Anyway, they lost contact."

But Moose wasn't placated. "Well, if all we had to do was mosey up and help B Company, whereinhell did that big bugger of a tank come from?"

Greenwood interrupted. "Easy, Moose," he soothed. "You heard the sergeant. We lost contact with a couple of platoons. Well, Germans lose contact with their units, too. That big bugger, you called a Tiger, he might have lost touch…didn't know his infantry had dropped back."

A swirling eddy of black smoke rose from the burning Tiger. Two NBH Shermans chugged slowly through the shallow Conca, halting after snorting up the far bank. We watched while two crewmen scrambled out of their turrets and cautiously approached the smoldering Jerry tank.

Four platoon carriers splashed through the shallow riverbed, pulling in behind the panting Shermans.

"Any survivors?" yelled Morrison.

"The Jerry tank commander," one crewman yelled. "But I hope he dies. He cooked up one of our crews!"

I looked back across the river. The burning Sherman seemed to glow in the sunlight.

CHAPTER ELEVEN

THE Coriano ridge bulged out of the rolling land like an elongated groundhog, dominating the vineyards and bristling with the guns of the 29th Panzers. It took the Toronto Irish, CBH, Perths and the N.B. Hussars, plus the New Westminsters and Straths, several Desert Air Force strikes and accurate shooting by the Canadian arty for almost thirty-two hours before the dogged defenders were pushed back and over the Marano River on September 14th.

Bulldozers dug mass graves for the enemy dead who littered the savaged ground while scores of Canadian dead were carefully recorded, wrapped in army-issue blankets and trussed up with assault cable for burial.

At the same time, the men of the 1st Div — the West Novies, the Royal 22nd, the 48th Highlanders, the Seaforths, the Carleton and Yorks, the Hasties, the RCRs — had crossed the Marano and stormed up against San Fortunato. The rolling, flat earth was devoid of cover and men and machines were blown to pieces locked in a death struggle against strengthened German artillery units and "old enemies" — the paratroopers and Panzer Grenadiers.

And Canadian artillery lit up the boiling nighttime battlefields with searchlights when the moon hid its face.

By the 23rd of September, the corps had marched against the cream of the German 10th Army for four weeks. But the price had been high: 3,896 officers and men had been hit (of which 76 were ours), 1,016 fatally. An additional 1,005 had been evacuated because of sickness.

The 89/109 no-name unit, rumored to become the Lanark and Renfrew Scottish, got a new C.O., acting Lieutenant-Colonel Buck Buchanan while Colonel Dick went to Div HQ as senior staffer of the Ops group.

Our platoon crossed the Uso River just north of San Vito in a drizzle. We did it without antitank support because the rapidly rising

157

waters had washed out the only culvert-style bridge. Finally, one antitank gun was manhandled across, then, after the engineers had strung together a Bailey bridge, the tanks made it.

Despite two company attacks, thickened by our section's automatic weapon fire, menacing German Tigers and heavy machine-gun fire stopped us cold.

The armor pulled back and laagered behind our forward positions and our section joined them as night, thick with clouds but without rain, closed in. Crawford backed our carrier into a haystack while the other three snuggled against a friendly casa wall.

Jerry shelling was sporadic, mortar fire almost nonexistent. We dug in. A reinforcement spaded out a shallow slit trench a few feet away from the stack, then climbed in after wrapping himself in his blanket.

I walked over. "That's not deep enough, kid," I allowed.

He grinned. "I know my way around, I'm from the 48th Highlanders," he answered, briskly.

"What's your name?"

"French."

"Well, French," I said, grabbing a fistful of his blanket and literally unravelling him, "dig your fuckin' trench deeper. OK?"

"Ah, shee-it!" he groaned, "you ex-artillery guys don't know from nothin'."

"That may be, but *dig*."

"What was that all about?" Kerr asked.

"Nothing."

An 88 roared in and exploded, throwing up great clumps of dirt.

"If that's all the Jerries do tonight, I'll sleep just fine," commented Albert after the explosion died away.

Two 88 airbursts, timed to explode before they hit the ground, tore the darkness apart, angrily spewing sheets of flame and shrapnel. Then one of the tanks, its hatch open, erupted in a sheet of flame, followed by a series of explosions as its ammo went up. The glare from the burning Sherman lit up the vineyards.

"Jeezus!" breathed Albert, "that'll do it!"

"Do what?" asked Crawford.

"Now that the Jerries have hit one tank, they'll know for friggin' certain there are more of 'em here! Even if they don't, they'll shell the shit out of us!"

Half a dozen pale faces were turned toward the fiery torch that had been a Canadian tank, their skin dirty yellow. The tankers, who had been outside their vehicle, smoking around a brew of tea, had scattered, throwing themselves flat into the muck.

I looked up into the sky, sensing the horror of the inevitable barrage. "Dig! Everybody dig like you've never dug before!" I shouted.

Two minutes later, we cowered in half-finished slits, rolling mud-balls with feverish fingers and cursing while exploding 88s marched back and forth, crisscrossing the vines in crazy tic-tac-toe patterns.

In between stonks, we dug. Albert and I shared a double. Solid-steel armor-piercing shells slammed into the ground and drilled their way clean through the walls of the stone casa for what seemed like hours. I tried to burrow into the dirt. "Christ!" I mumbled, "there's no escape!"

I rolled over on my back. "I've had it," I groaned.

"Yeah?" Albert hissed, "but what're you gonna do about it?"

"Lemme think," I panted, digging deep inside of me for my sense of humor which seemed to have deserted me. "I got it! I'll stick my leg out an' get a piece of shrapnel. Just enough to get me out of here as wounded."

"Y're nuts. But suppose you do, then when you pull it back in, all you've got left is a bloody stump!"

We both laughed, nervously.

A series of exploding 88s staggered across the farmhouse yard, the last one showering us with dirt. We both grunted, punched by the concussion. It was followed by a blessed silence that lasted several minutes. We climbed out cautiously. I shouted for Kerr. "Over here, Fred!" he answered, rising from his slit, stained with mud.

The stricken Sherman was only glowing now.

"You check out your section an' I'll do likewise. OK?"

Not one of our men had even a bruise from flying debris. But their pride had been wounded. "My God!" breathed Norm Hall, "wasn't that something!" He adjusted his steel helmet, bellowing for his older brother.

"I'm right behind you, little brother," he said, tilting his soft forage cap back on his head. "Don't worry about me...my time's not going to come in this damned war."

Norm scowled. "Yeah, well dear brother," he rasped sarcastically, "you don't know that. And I think the sergeant should make you wear a damned steel hat!"

Al Hall had a steel helmet. But he had never worn it, complaining it was uncomfortable. It was a standing joke in the entire section that if he did, it would be time for everybody to go home because the war was no longer tolerable.

"Nope, sorry, Norman, but I can't do that," I said.

Walking around the corner of the casa, we peered into a shell hole, the biggest we'd ever seen in the lines. I bent over and touched the dirt. It was still warm.

"That must've been that big explosion that jolted the area halfway through the stonk," said Albert. "Looks like they're using mediums ..."

"No way," said Kerr. "I know my artillery. And gunners aren't gonna throw that big a shell into the line positions because the beaten zone is too large — it could land among their own men." He paused. "But just mebbe, if they got an angle and they're desperate ..."

I looked at Albert. "Let's dig a new slit, right in the middle of this crater and, on the basis that lightning doesn't hit twice and you can't drop two shells into the same hole, it should be the safest one in Italy."

Albert shook his head.

"Why not?"

"Because I don't like it," he said slowly, "an' don't ask me why."

Another barrage of 88s, this time mixed with Moaning Minnies that sobbed hysterically as they arched through the cloudy night, drove us back into our trenches.

"Lord Almighty, I'm never gonna get used to those fuckin' Moanin' Minnies!" sobbed Albert as the thin-shelled, electrically fired clusters of 60-pound mortars howled and danced through the lines. "Every goddamned one sounds like it's gonna land right in my hip pocket!"

I went on clenching and unclenching my sweaty hands, gritting my teeth in time with the explosions and hanging onto the damp earth.

Shells were still raining on us, intermittently, when I fell asleep. I had no idea of time, despite the fact I had a wristwatch, because the irregular yet sustained thump-thump-crash of enemy high explosives seemed to make it immaterial.

Oddly enough, when I awoke in warm sunlight, I felt refreshed. Maybe relieved was a better word. I pounded the sleeping Albert awake, loped from trench to trench rousing the others. "Wakey! Wakey! Rise and shine! It's daylight in the swamps! Palms of your feet on the dirt!" I shouted, oddly exhilarated.

The hulk of the Sherman was charred.

Kerr and Albert began a fire and we brewed tea. Two loaves of bread were lifted out of the battery box, two messtins filled with canned Armour packed-in-Chicago-Illinois bacon. Some of the boys began shaving.

"Get that new kid up," I yelled at Norm Hall, motioning toward the shallow trench near the haystack, so shallow I could see folds in his blanket above the line of the ground.

"Hey, kid, get up, it's chow time!" scolded Norm. The blanket remained motionless. He bent over the trench, poked at the still form under it. Exasperated, he lifted the lower end of the blanket, grabbed one foot and yanked. The leg came away in his hand and he nearly went over backwards.

"My God, Sarg, come here! The poor bugger's cut in two!" He flung the cold, hairy leg back on the blanket. "Ughhhh!" He wiped his hands on his trousers.

Private French, the ex-48er who knew everything there was to know about the front lines, had been sliced bloodily in half by an armor-piercing shell that had gone through his shallow trench.

"If he'd-a dug the thing a foot deeper," sighed Kerr, "it would've missed him. Poor, sad bastard!"

It clouded over and the rain began, drenching us. It followed us back into a rest area and was still falling when we bathed in the Marecchia River. Lieutenant Nadeau got his third pip to become Captain, and Lieutenant R.T. Ambrose joined us as platoon I-C. And seventy-one reinforcements arrived to replace the latest unit casualties.

We had just settled in when Sergeant Morrison came galloping into our bivouac. "Hey! Cederberg...Kerr — your carriers are all topped up ain't they?"

We nodded.

"OK, well, we're going right back in."

"I thought we were gonna have some kinda holiday," whined Crawford.

"Is Jerry on the move? At the Fiumicino? Like comin' at us?" someone yelled.

"Nah. Nothin' like that. Seems like the Toronto Irish gotta be relieved. They lost a friggin' company — 'A' someone said — after they crossed the river without any support and ran into some Jerries and tanks. By the time help got up, they only found ten bodies. The rest had been taken prisoner. So, the whole regiment's comin' out, an' we're taking their place in the line along with the Highlanders and Perths. OK? Now let's get a move on, heh?"

By noon, the platoon was in a large two-storey casa, about 100 to 150 yards short of the Fiumicino.

"Some people think this is the Rubicon River," allowed Kerr. "You know, the river Caesar crossed with his legions when he marched on Rome and seized power."

Greenwood nodded. "He's quite correct," he said amiably. No one ever demurred when Alex Greenwood said a statement was true.

A partially paved road split the sunken fields between us and the river, glittering behind a row of poplars. It led eastward to San Mauro, a town the like of which we'd never before seen in all of rural Eyetieland. The neat houses had blue, pale yellow, red, even green-colored roofs. And directly across from us, more than halfway to the river, was what appeared to be a deserted casa, bigger than we'd ever seen before.

Because we had acquired two Vickers .303 medium machine guns, our first telephone call informed us we'd be required to carry out harassing shoots when necessary, using the new long-range ammo. Obediently, we sited them in two vee-shaped pits west of our casa and on our side of the road. In between them and our building, I ordered two large, deep slit trenches.

"Whatta we gotta do this for?" complained Belanger.

I straightened up. "Because," I explained, "if we're ever caught between the pits and the casa by a stonk, we'll have somewhere to go. *Capeesh?*"

"I understand," he said, "but it doesn't make sense."

It was cloudy with little showers late in the afternoon and night, right in the middle of stand-to, the shelling began — Moaning Minnies, mortars and the hated 88s.

"I heard," said Kerr as we flattened behind the casa's thick stone wall, "that our generals were thinkin' about launching another offensive. Well, somebody must've told the fuckin' Germans 'cause they sure are touchy."

Dawn brought peace and quiet. And more showers. At night, the shelling resumed. Two days later, TAC ordered a shoot so we zeroed in on the reference points provided and the two guns began to thump-thump-thump. Kerr and Albert triggered the slow-shooting guns while the Halls and Elmer Verch and Belanger fed the belts through. I directed fire, calling out the taps.

Three mortars soared through the sky and exploded among the British forward troops on our left. TAC had ordered 2,000 rounds, so that's what they got, before we quit.

Each nightfall brought down sporadic, sometimes intense, shellings which raked the platoon area. In between times, we maintained standing patrols and sent contact parties out to check with our Brit friends on the left and C Company on the right.

"The Brits are a strange bunch," reported Kerr, returning from patrol, "they're in a graveyard..."

"You won't always get the best site selection," I interrupted, sarcastically.

Kerr ignored me. "They've hauled the bodies out of a crypt, piled 'em up, and turned it into a cozy little platoon headquarters. Better'n that, some of 'em are even sleepin' in the caskets, enjoying what they called plush livin'."

"With the bodies still in 'em?" asked Crawford, shakily.

"Nah. God, y're a dummy. The bodies are still in the inner wooden boxes, piled outside."

"I don't care. I could never even lie down in a casket, let alone sleep in one."

During mid-afternoon of the fourth day, we often heard sometimes shrill, sometimes quavering cries drifting on the breeze across the soggy furrows, obviously coming from the large casa between us and the river.

"Girls!" breathed Belanger. "Or mebbe women!"

"Nope. Cows," said Crawford.

"Horses," stated Kerr flatly.

"Yeah," agreed Al Hall, "but I think I also heard a cow, or perhaps a steer, bawling."

"I thought I heard horses late yesterday," said Norm Hall.

"How'd you know they were horses?" asked Crawford.

"Don't be so damn ridiculous."

"They coulda been cows," insisted Crawford.

"There's a difference. And if you never heard 'em, then you wouldn't know," replied Norm, evenly.

The sun came out briefly later, outlining distant rain clouds sharply.

"Sarg," said Norm, "me'n Al would like to go out and put those animals out of their misery. You got any reasons why we shouldn't?"

I did, but couldn't use them. "No," I said, slowly, "but MacNeil and I will go with you. OK? Eddie'll be in charge."

We moved cautiously and bent double, each man independently and one at a time, across the sunken road until we closed with the casa barn, then made a dash for it. Inside, three of the most magnificent black horses I had ever seen were lying on the concrete floor. Two of them tried frantically to get up, winnowing and neighing. Black blood clogged the ragged shrapnel wounds in their flanks and backs.

"My God!" breathed Norm.

What looked like a cow to me stood in a corner, its large brown eyes fixed on us.

Single shots in the forehead put the horses out of their misery.

I gulped. "Now, let's get outta here before the Jerries hear that and we wind up in a firefight we can't win."

"Nope. Not yet," said Al. He ran a hand over the cow. "This is good beef, 'bout two years old. We should haul it back with us." He twirled a length of stout rope he had lifted out of a bin. "Take just a couple of minutes an' Norm an' I'll have him quartered for easy carryin'."

I looked at Albert. His expression was noncommittal.

"OK, if you can do it as quick as you claim," I said.

That two-year-old was killed, bled, skinned, butchered and quartered while I watched uneasily. Each of us shouldered a quarter as we worked our way back to our lines in a spread-out diamond formation. We had less than thirty yards to go when my inner alarm system clanged noisily.

Shifting the meat, I yelled: "Let's move it!" and we broke into a jolting, ragged run, arriving through the rear doors as the first of a short stonk of mortars exploded in the field behind us.

"Goddamn! That was great! An' good timing!" exulted Kerr.

"Good timing, nothing," panted Albert, "Cederberg heard that German gunner holler 'Fire!'"

That night, while shells and mortars forced our standing patrols out of their slit trenches, Howie MacLeod came apart, mentally, and we had to ship him out. I had never seen that happen before. And it frightened and puzzled and saddened me.

The next afternoon, the sun again broke through the leaden sky and Kerr and Albert and I decided to go to San Mauro, using the deep ditch on our side of the road for cover. It was more curiosity than a desire to loot although its modern appearance through our glasses hinted there might be some special pickings.

San Mauro hadn't been fought over. That much was obvious because the sleek, well-cared-for homes weren't shattered, the neat small lawns weren't chewed up by mortar explosions.

"Looks like the Jerries pulled out before our guys got here," noted Kerr.

But the pickings were almost zero. Most of the airy, bright-colored rooms were empty. Even the mirrors had disappeared. And while there were sheets and blankets on the comfortable beds, the closets were empty except for odd shirts and ties and simple dresses. We rapped on the stuccoed walls just in case some valuables had been cached away. Nothing.

"Funny," said Albert, "an' from the looks of things, the people who lived in these houses must've had lots of cash."

We approached a pink-colored house larger than those we had searched while working our way across the town. Kerr wrinkled his long nose. "You smell something?" he asked, glancing around.

"Yep," I replied, "and it's rank. I'll go inside, and you guys head round to the back and see if you can find what's causing it."

I poked the front double-doors open with the barrel of my Tommy gun and stepped into a spacious center hall. There were a couple of broken chairs in the large room off to the left and the floor and heavy table were littered with broken glasses and bottles. Signs of a big party, I thought. Upstairs, the bedrooms were a wreck, sheets and coverlets and pillows scattered in all directions. I was trying to flush the handle on the toilet (because I hadn't seen one in an Eyetie house before) when I heard Kerr's shout: "Fred! Fred! Out here...in the garage! Jesus Christ!"

It was a four double-door garage with a paved drive. As I trotted toward it, the foul odor of death grew stronger. Kerr and Albert were standing outside.

Kerr waved his Tommy gun. "They're in there — all of 'em and dead as hell," he said, pure horror in his voice.

"Who's in there? Some Jerries?"

Kerr shook his head, slowly. "Women...girls...my Gawd, Fred, it's awful, just awful."

I stepped halfway into the garage and there, lying on their backs, almost nude, their legs apart, nine young Italian girls lay side by side as if asleep. But the pasty color of their bare breasts and faces and the cloying stench of death said they weren't. And the clouds of flies that swarmed around their partially covered swollen bellies and between their thighs confirmed it. I fought a powerful urge to vomit as I hastily backed out.

"My Godalmighty! Who could've done a thing like that?" croaked Kerr, tears in his eyes.

I shook my head, numbly, but I was thinking "Germans." (Only years later, I found out they had been brutalized by Fascist youth following a wild orgy during the thirty hours between the Germans' departure and the Allies' arrival.)

Albert lit a cigarette and sat down on the pavement. "They've all been shot...right up between the legs," he said softly. "The men who did that should be hung like dogs...by their balls."

"Now what do we do?" asked Kerr. "We just can't leave 'em here — like that!"

And all we had wanted to do was liberate any goodies if they were to be had. "There are a lot of sheets, upstairs. I saw 'em. We'll get 'em and cover 'em up," I said, finally.

"That all?" mumbled Kerr.

"Jesus, Eddie, what else can we do? We can't be around here when it's dark, burying them while the Jerries bang away at us with 88s and mortars. No. We'll cover 'em, get outta here an' report what we found to TAC, and then it'll be their problem."

I didn't wait for their replies, but jogged across the parking area and into the house, upstairs, and began gathering white sheets.

"Now for the worst part," said Albert when I handed he and Kerr several, "we got to go back inside that stinking garage."

Taking huge lungfulls of tainted outside air, we needed several quick-in, quick-out trips before all the dead *senoritas* were draped under white linen covers. Then we closed the door. "Just in case some starving dog — or something — gets in there," allowed Kerr.

The careful walk through the ditch back to the platoon casa was in complete silence. And the Jerries didn't fire a single shot.

Captain Nadeau, back at TAC, didn't want to believe our story at first. And he couldn't believe that the Panzer grenadiers who were opposite us could possibly be guilty of such an atrocity. "They're soldiers, Cederberg, good ones. Not animals. However, we'll report it to brigade."

During the unusually quiet night, just two hours before dawn, an enemy patrol slipped into C Company's lines and surprised 15 platoon, getting away with eight prisoners.

"Somebody goofed," Albert said. "If the outside slits had been manned, they'd never been surprised."

Belanger, who didn't like the overnight two-hour shifts in the trenches outside our casa, sighed. "I guess them outside slits are what the doctor ordered, but I still don't like 'em. Even when the sergeants bring out a mug of coffee laced with rum. It's too damned spooky."

The New Zealanders relieved us late on the afternoon of the 10th of October and, the next day, Colonel Buchanan sent a runner for me. He pointed to two officers with spotlessly trim uniforms. "They're from Allied Military Government — AMGOT legal people, Sergeant Cederberg. Take 'em up to where you found those women and give 'em any details you might have." He then said, softly to me, "By the way, when you were doing that...ah... reconnaissance in San Mauro, did you happen to see any working pianos? We're having a mess do shortly, and a piano would come in handy." He spread his hands, flexing his long fingers as though playing an invisible piano.

"I'll get a 30 cwt to follow us. And, sir, consider it done."

The two faceless AMGOT officers made notes while Kerr and Albert and I related what we had found. And because the Kiwis had crossed the river when the Germans pulled back, we drove easily to the big house with the four double-door garage where the nine young women laid beneath their impromptu shrouds. The stench was even worse because a full sun was out and heat had built up inside the building.

They went inside. Thirty seconds later, their mouths and noses engulfed in khaki handkerchiefs, they burst through the door, slamming it behind them. "Holy Mary Mother of God!" the youngest wheezed, "this one tops them all!"

There's a practicing Roman Catholic I thought, watching as both men fought the urge to upchuck. "Germans?" I asked.

The RC officer wiped his eyes with his handkerchief. "Germans what?" he coughed.

"Did the Germans do" — I nodded toward the garage — "that."

"I couldn't say." He looked over his shoulder at the closed door. "But we'll sure as hell find out," he grated, grimly.

They went inside the house, coming out a few minutes later, still making notes.

"Looks like there was a big party in there," I said.

They were as talkative as a pair of priests who had taken a vow of silence. "Thanks men, thanks for your help," the RC said. "You want a ride back?"

"No sir," replied Kerr, "we're waiting for a 30 cwt."

It took the three transport men and driver and the three of us to manhandle the piano into the truck.

"What stinks around here?" panted the driver. "Smells like there's somethin' awful dead."

"There is, fellow, there is," answered Kerr, soberly.

And we buried our dead, twenty-two men-boys who would never again feel a warm sun on their backs or taste wet rain in their faces. And while the Pipe Major from the Seaforth Highlanders played "Flowers of the Forest," and an honor guard paced rhythmically and deliberately up before a symbolic grave, the men of the 89/109 watched curiously under a bright but cool sun.

It was odd, I thought later, but no one mentioned names. Perhaps it was the music supplied by the corps band, or the plaintive wail of the bugler who wrenched the "Last Post" out of his shining brass instrument, but everyone was silent after parade was dismissed.

That evening, there was a boisterous party under the large marquee signed "Officers' Mess". And Lieutenant Ambrose asked us to supply a pair of barkeepers — "men who won't get likkered up or make asses of themselves."

I took Norm Hall with me and, after the celebration was cooking on all eight cylinders, visiting nurses and their officer satellites in full orbit, we began requisitioning the pungent army-issue rum for our platoon's use. Nine empty vino bottles were topped up and carefully stashed outside the tent for delivery to Albert and Kerr. By the time Norm and I had departed the scene for our lines via motorcycle (supplied by a compassionate Ambrose) the men's party around a gas-fueled fire was in full swing.

Greenwood, sitting in the darkness, tilted his mug filled with rum to his mouth and drank in great gulps. He didn't even bother to wipe his lips, just sat and stared up at the waning half moon. "I'm drunk," he slurred, "drunker than an Irishman at a wake." He grinned, his small eyes glistening.

Crawford reeled by, a mongrel he had befriended at his heels. "Hi, old-timer!" he laughed shrilly.

"I like your dog, Master Crawford," Alex belched.

"He's a good dog."

"We're all dogs, after a fashion, my friend," replied Greenwood, smiling crookedly.

"Aw come on, Alex," soothed Kerr, "we're not, really."

"Then we're fools. That's it, fools." Greenwood let his back sag against a carrier shrouded in the gloom. "Churchill didn't say 'Give us the tools and we'll finish the job!' " The words slurred out of his thin lips. "He said, 'Give us the fools and we'll finish the job!' " He smacked his hand on the ground. "And here we are — the fools."

"You're drunk, old-timer," said Crawford, gathering up the dog.

Greenwood was slack-jawed. "What do you call him, Master Crawford?"

"Stupid."

Alex peered at us. "There, gentlemen, further proof. If it's needed."

And from the mortar platoon lines, beyond a row of leafless trees, drifted snatches of a dozen voices singing in ragged unison:

> *When this fuckin' war is over*
> *O, how happy I will be!*
> *When I get my civvie clothes on*
> *No more soldierin' for me!*
> *No more church parades on Sunday*
> *No more askin' for a pass!*
> *We will tell the sergeant-major*
> *To shove his passes up his ass!*

"Do you know that tune?" Greenwood asked no one in particular. "That's a hymn tune. I sang those same notes in church a long, long time ago." He began to cry.

Albert and Kerr stood up, looking down at the veteran from the Loyal Eddies who had marched so far for so many months.

"Leave him be," I said, "he's got a crying jag. And you got to let those things burn out."

The platoon finished off the nine bottles of rum before the dawn streaked the skyline. And we drank water all afternoon after the noonday sun woke us up.

A week later, balmorals were issued to all ranks who didn't already own them. And the paymaster hustled Victory Loan bonds.

"You know," commented Crawford after buying $200 worth, "I got a letter from my girl the other day..."

"Whoee! Crawford's got a girl!" squealed Belanger, "I don't believe it."

"Yeah, well, there's this girl who lives on our street in Saskatoon. And she writes to me. So, she's my girl friend. Anyway, she said she had bought one of these things, said it was her contribution to Canada's war effort. Hell, I buy 'em too…and get shot at…and do the fighting!"

As October lengthened, so did the rain and cloud, turning streams into swollen rivers, washing out bridges, even the signallers' telephone lines.

CHAPTER TWELVE

TRUCKS loaded with seven-day-leave parties rolled toward Rome and Florence under bright, early November skies, while the one-time artillery 89/109 ack-ack no-name unit officially became the Lanark and Renfrew Scottish Regiment of Canada, confirming the issue of balmorals, sometimes referred to as cowflaps. Especially when Al Hall wore one. It literally folded itself around his narrow head.

I opted for Rome.

Rome was the Eternal City, the Open City the Germans chose not to defend, the city of broad avenues, narrow streets and shops half-filled with shoddy goods. And it was a city peopled with mostly shabbily dressed men and women, bare-legged urchins, black marketeers, AMGOT personnel, black- and brown-robed clergy and whores (proving all the ruins weren't carved out of marble or stone). It was Rome with an autumn nip in the air and venereal disease rife in unlicensed cathouses; where hawkers peddled dirty pictures and blessed rosaries outside the massive ruins of the Colosseum; and the jagged remains of long-ago temples where old crones and cats lay down to sleep even on chilly nights.

During those nights, red-capped British and white-helmeted American military police patrolled the dark streets, checking for deserters, muggers and soldiers improperly dressed or drunk. And airborne troops and infantrymen fought over young prostitutes, crooked crap games or real or imagined insults.

Staff at the Canada Club, which occupied the impressive Italian National Art Gallery on the Via Nationale, recommended a pensione. It was full, so I located a smaller one down the narrow, cobbled roadway. The concierge was a stooped but cheerful little man whose English was better than my Italian. Idly, as he passed me an ancient key after insisting on six nights' rent in advance, I wondered if he was also fluent in German.

"On the third floor," he said, expansively, "the bathroom is at the end of the hall. Don't forget to turn the light off after you use eet."

I was stiff and tired after the jolting ride from Tavoleto where the unit was on rest.

"You would like a girl, perhaps?" he asked, his dark eyes bland.

I clumped up the two flights, carrying my big pack without answering. Following a trip to the bathroom (where I turned off the single-bulb light) I stripped and climbed into bed without even having a cigarette. I rose at noon the next day, refreshed in body, but for reasons I couldn't come to grips with, low in spirits.

That afternoon I headed for the Colosseum where I got a whiff of the kind of power the Romans must have generated eighteen centuries earlier. And in my mood, I was in no condition to argue with a self-appointed tourist guide, a skinny Italian so emaciated his shirt and sweater couldn't disguise the fact his chest had caved in at some point in time.

"My name ees Guiseppe," he intoned, "but you should calla me Joe because that's what the Yankees all-a call me. And, please, thatsa 300 lira. OK?" He extended his thin hand.

"How do I know you won't take my money and run? Hell, how do I know y're even a guide or know anything about Rome, let alone the Colosseum?"

His eyebrows sagged in anguish. "Joe ees a 'onest man. You ask-a anybody..." His hand remained extended.

I sighed. "OK, Joe, you're an honest man. Here's the lira. Now tell me about this heap of stones."

It was begun by Vespasian and finished by his son, Titus, he told me. And sixty thousand people could be seated to watch games that included gladiators in combat, Christians thrown to the lions or even an elephant hunt.

"Sixty thousand?" I asked.

"Well, mebbe only forty thousand."

In one single set of games, he continued, five thousand pairs of armed men had fought to the death. In another, eleven thousand beasts, all from north Africa, and brought in at great expense by the patrons, tore each other to shreds before the sated, bloody survivors were despatched by merciful attendants.

I could almost hear the Roman masses cheering and a shiver rippled down my back as I thought of the waste.

Joe took me to what he swore was the original site of the Forum.

"It was on thees very spot that Rome, itself, was founded, almost eight hundred years before the birth of Christ," he rattled on, blessing himself almost absently.

"Here, too, was the Golden Milestone on which all the distances to the faraway cities in the empire were inscribed, and there was the senate and temple of Vesta in which lived the six Vestal virgins." He swung his arms in a wide arc.

All I could see was a bare spread of land that looked like it had been clawed from the covering earth.

My eyes followed a trim Italian girl, hips swinging gently, on the arm of an elderly gentleman with a Tyrolean-style hat pulled low, almost to his thick grey moustache. The faint traces of the words U.S. Army ran crosswise down one side of her cloth coat.

"Now," intoned Joe, "do you steel theenk I am-a not truly a guide?"

"You're truly a guide, Joe," I replied.

He beamed. "Now, I show you the baths. They are *magnifico, Sergente!*"

The remains of those built by Caracalla must have originally covered a huge city block. "Two thousand Romans could bathe here at once," Joe exclaimed. "And another three thousand in the baths of the Emperor Diocletian. They were known as Thermae and, all told, there were eleven of them, fed by the eleven mighty aqueducts carrying water from the mountains to Roma!"

I had a mental vision of thousands of Romans, fat, thin, muscular, bald headed, ugly, handsome, bathing, shaving, splashing, swapping rumors and inside stories in what must have been canyons of stone and mortar and marble. Christ, I thought, the whole damned brigade could've held shower parade in either of them.

"And they had hot water," finished Joe, emphatically. "Next, we shall go to the Pantheon, built I am sure by Hadrian."

"If you say 'you're sure,' then mebbe you're not," I suggested.

"I am only a guide. Not what you call a heestorian. *Si?*" Then he went on. "Eet was built of brick by Hadrian. And eet ees the oldest, standing roofed temple in the world. The interior ees a perfect circle with an open eye in the dome which allows the sunlight to enter. And because the sun rides through the heavens, eet allows the light to ride slowly around the inner walls. Clever, no?"

Sensing my lack of visible enthusiasm, he shrugged. "Well, even the popes who destroyed most of the ancient city for reasons I do not understand, even they didn't pull down the Pantheon. So, it must be special."

We stood in front of what looked like a stumpy turret on the banks of the Tiber.

"That," said Joe, "was originally Hadrian's tomb. Then eet was crowned with marble statues and trees, growing right out of the earth on the roof. Later, eet became a papal dungeon, known as the Castel Sant'Angelo. And from eets parapets, the great Italian silversmith, Cellini himself, fought a French army besieging Rome over four hundred years ago!"

I could sense that Joe was getting patriotic and, perhaps, expecting a fat tip. All I could picture were the dungeons crowded with miserable humanity and jailers whose only claim to their humanity was the fact they could go home each night.

Finally, he walked me to the arch of Titus and I gazed indifferently at the legions of Caesar carved in cold relief and loaded down with the spoils of war.

"They are carrying in triumph the honors of a war against the Jews," said Joe, "after the emperor's great cohorts had sacked Jerusalem." He searched my face. "You weesh to see more?"

I shook my head. "Not today, Joe." I gave him an extra 200 lira and a pack of Export cigarettes.

"You are a good *sergente*," he said, gratefully. "Not like the others. They drink too much, fight, and always look for women. Why are you not an officer?"

I chuckled for the first time since leaving Tavoleto.

That evening, I had dinner at the Canada Club, then found a *trattoria* about two blocks away, bounced down the half flight of steps and ordered some *vino bianco*. Two drinks later, I let myself out through the crude bathroom when a fight between a Canadian gunner and a British paratrooper turned into a mass brawl.

The concierge greeted me hopefully. "You would like a girl tonight, maybe?"

I hesitated.

"She's only seventeen...maybe twenty...with big..." He cupped his hands in front of his chest. I shook my head. "No? Then I have something veree special. But she is expensive. Very much lira."

"What makes her special, old man?"

He rolled his eyes and dropped his thin voice to a whisper. "She is Engleesh, *Sergente*. Real *Englessi*..."

"English?" I echoed.

"*Si*. On my sister's grave, I swear it. But she is expensive — some say 2,000 lira."

"Send her up. And if I don't like, I'll send her away. OK?"

"That is impossible. You must go to her." He reached under the counter and produced a piece of paper. "Here is her address."

I read it. "Where is it?"

"Out the door, two blocks to the left and half a block to the right. The number is 137, apartment 44. You are interested?" When I didn't answer, he said, "I shall telephone her; it is by appointment, only, *signori*." He disappeared into the little office.

Fuck me, I thought, now I'm a *signori!* And right in the middle of a friggin' war, in the middle of Rome, there's an English whore who works by appointment only.

He was grinning when he emerged. "*Signori*, the lady can see you in an hour. Isn't that good?"

He was so goddamned happy, I figured she must kick back twenty-five percent of her fee to him. "I may be back in a while," I said, indifferently. "May I have my key?"

I was halfway through the door out onto the street when the concierge called to me. "*Signori!*"

I turned.

"You should bring something to drink, *si?* I have some fine spumante, from before the war. Or just after it started. Only 300 lira." He hitched his shoulders high.

"What's the English lady's name?" I asked as I paid for the sweetish bubbly wine and tucked it under my arm.

"Ah, the lady will introduce herself. I don't like names. They only cause trouble, you understand?"

I didn't, but that was OK.

Apartment 44 was on the fifth floor of a narrow building which had seen better days but wasn't run down enough to be classified as a dump. The hall rugs were worn, probably because ten thousand customers have used them, I thought inanely.

Her blond hair outlined a sharply angled face and wide-spaced blue eyes. Her skin went with the color of her hair, pale and clear. Her teeth were small and very white in thin lips when she smiled. "Good evening, I'm Gail Rigby. Do come in."

She took my glengarry and looked at my shoulder flashes. "Hmmm," she said, pleasantly, "Canadian."

I handed her the wine.

"Isn't that sweet of you," she said, "or should I say wasn't it sweet of Signor Topazzinni?"

The room was divided by a curtain strung from a rod, a coffee table on our side. The rug reminded me of one I had seen at my grandmother's — Persian by pattern, worn by age. Lacy doilies were in place on the arms of the furniture and what looked like a fern sprouted from a brass pot. A kitchen alcove led off one corner.

I began to unbutton my battle-dress jacket.

Gail's pale eyebrows went up. "Wouldn't you like a glass of spumante first? After all, you paid for it." Her small laugh was genuine.

I raised my eyebrows in return. "Why not?"

Gail Rigby even had ice.

After one bottle of spumante and almost two hours of very small talk that left me with the feeling she was buying and I was selling, I found out what was on the other side of the curtain: a large bed with clean white sheets. And for the first time in over a year, I shared sheets with a woman I actually enjoyed.

We lay together in the gloom. I lit two cigarettes and placed one between her lips. She snuggled against me. "Thanks love," she murmured. "Aren't you going to ask me what is a twenty-one-year-old English girl doing in Rome...whoring?"

"Nope. I don't care."

"Ah, love."

We stubbed our cigarettes. She sat up and for the first time I noted how her large firm breasts seemed even larger because of her slender body.

She giggled. "I wondered when you'd pay special attention to my titties. They're my crown jewels. And look between my legs. I'm really a blond." She took my hand. "Come love, let's have a shower. I always shower after I make love."

"Are you gently telling me to get lost?"

Her smile was quick. "I'm not telling you anything of the kind, Freddie, I'm asking you to have a shower with me!"

The shower was smaller than a telephone booth and the water was only a trickle. But after a little coaching, the washing and love-making was sensational. And I didn't tell her how much I disliked being called "Freddie."

Hard early morning sunlight was poking through the window when I awoke. Gail was already dressed.

"Where are you going?" I asked drowsily.

"To work. I do have a job, you know. I'm an interpreter with the

AMGOT people. There's a pot of tea on the table for you. Don't waste it, got it in the black market, real English tea."

"I...er...well...what about...?"

"Leave the twenty-five-hundred lira on the table, love. Just be sure you lock up when you leave." She opened the door.

"Will I see you tonight? I asked.

"If you wish."

"What time?"

"Well, I'm off at five, so I'll be back about five-thirty or so. If you're sure, I'll see you then."

"I'm sure."

I walked for hours, revisited the site of the ruins of the Forum below the Palatine Hill and it looked different than it had the previous day. I could almost hear Cicero, Scipio Africanus, Augustus Caesar, the only names that came to mind from my lessons. Then I scrounged a bottle of Johnny Walker's Black Label from the mess sergeant at Canada House, following an hour's wheedling.

"Boy, she must be some friggin' special for you to ante up this kind of money for a jug of Scotch," he leered, sarcastically, passing it to me wrapped in thin wartime paper.

"I'm a solitary drinker," I returned.

Gail and I had dinner in a restaurant she knew, pasta laced with Canadian or British ration bully beef and sitting atop tasty filet mignons originally destined for an American Army officer's club. And two glasses of chianti,

Gail Rigby had been orphaned when she was nine, she told me, and brought up by Aunt Agatha Hockley, her mother's maiden sister. And she and Aunt Agatha had been on holiday in the Italian Appennines when Mussolini decided to jump into World War II via hapless France's unprotected back. By the time Aunt Agatha had taken the events seriously, they drove to Rome. But it was too late for any escape to her beloved England. It was all too much for dear old Aunt Agatha. Upset, outraged and befuddled, she succumbed to a stroke, leaving her seventeen-year-old niece on her own.

"They didn't intern you?" I asked, astonished.

"They were going to," she said, sweetly, "but a little favor here, another one there — and I got the proper papers. But I had no visible means of support. Isn't that the expression?

"Anyway, considering how I had managed to get the papers, I

decided I did have a visible means of support — all I had to do was
use it, ah, judiciously, until better times."

"So, you took to the streets."

"Don't be crude, lover, I am not a streetwalker. I prefer to think of
myself as a courtesan."

"What in hell's the difference?"

"You don't know what a courtesan is — or was? Well, surely
you've heard of Madame du Barry?" she asked. I nodded. She went
on: "She used her body to become a French king's mistress. And
while she didn't accept a flat fee for each trip to the royal bed, she did
welcome trinkets such as estates, villas, diamonds — you know,
things any girl of any age would appreciate."

I vaguely recalled the lady du Barry in a movie I'd seen once, but
Hollywood sure as hell hadn't even hinted she had been putting out
for gifts.

Gail wiggled her nose. "It took a little time, but I acquired a
suitable clientele." She smiled ruefully. "After a few errors…"

"Errors?"

"I wasn't selective enough. So I learned to restrict my gentlemen
friends."

"Italians and Germans," I interrupted.

She frowned. "Yes. Italians and Germans. After all, they are men,
too."

"Enemy men…"

"We didn't fight in bed, love."

Touché, I thought, then added with a touch of what I felt passed
for irony: "Generals only?"

"Majors and up."

I grunted. "How'd I get on the list?"

She batted her long lashes quickly and grinned with an I'll-never-
tell expression on her face, then added: "Let's say I was in an
adventurous frame of mind the other night."

I ordered two more glasses of chianti.

"Well," I said after lighting her cigarette, "you've obviously done
well. You're probably one of the best dressed women in all of
Eyetieland…courtesy, no doubt, of the black market you seem to
know so well. And your friendly clientele."

"I've also got quite a bit of money put aside safely."

"Yeah, but this Eyetie money's not worth a dime outside of this
country."

"If it was in Allied script or lira, you'd be absolutely correct," she laughed, easily. "But it's in good English quid and American dollars — courtesy, as you said, of the black market. All you have to do is know the people who really know."

I shook my head. "OK, so you're one smart lady. But the war's over for Italy. Why don't you go home to England?"

She sighed. "To answer your question, love, my home was with Aunt Agatha, in a London suburb, Cheam. And, it isn't mine any more. It went to some church society. And, secondly, I need another two thousand quid or six hundred U.S. dollars. Then I shall return to England — go north to Yorkshire or wherever — and select a country gentleman. He'll never know how I came into my money, but I'll be a suitable catch."

"Just like that," I said

"Just like that."

I blinked and finished my glass of wine, feeling as though I was a mere spectator in a drama I couldn't understand.

"Why are you telling me all this?" I asked, finally.

She took my hand in hers. Her eyes had an almost wistful sheen. "I don't know, Freddie, I really don't know."

Back in apartment 44, I poured three fingers of the Scotch, took off my battle-dress jacket and boots and settled deep in the easy chair. Gail kicked off her shoes and, moving around the room, removed the teapot, cups and saucers, emptied ashtrays, carefully arranged the doilies. She looked very little without her high heels.

I had often watched my mother doing things like that — tidying up, she called it. Christ, I thought, but my mother isn't a whore. She is a lady. A mother. With children. I closed my eyes. I could hear Gail working in the tiny kitchen, the tap running. Then she began to hum something I didn't recognize.

I tried to imagine the north country English gentleman she intended to catch, but outside of a vague figure in baggy plus fours, nothing came into focus. Only one thing was certain: He'd be married and fathering kids and their mother (his beloved wife) would be an ex-whore. The whole idea struck me as utterly ridiculous and I couldn't stifle the series of chuckles that brought me abruptly back to the room.

Gail was standing in front of me. "A penny for your thoughts?"

I was going to blurt "Do they cost me money, too?" but I didn't. Instead I shook my head. "Not worth a farthing, milady," I replied. I got up. "I'm going to shower."

Propped up on one elbow, I idly placed my hand on her belly.

"Are you married, love?" she asked with a suddenness that caught me by surprise.

"Nope."

I drew slow lazy circles around her navel.

"I shouldn't have asked that."

"Why not?" I widened the circles.

Brushing my roving hand away gently, she took my face in her hands and lined it up with hers so our mouths were almost touching. "Because I'm only playing a game," she murmured, "that has no ending." We kissed softly. I slid lower as she continued to hold my face, running my lips over her breasts. "If you feel that way," she crooned, "kiss my tummy. Ah, that's it. Slowly, lover, and we'll play another game with a real ending."

It may have been another game to her, but it was brand new to me.

Each morning I left 2,500 lira on the table after I had two cups of tea. I never saw her pick the money up, but it was never there when we arrived in the evening. On the fourth, she stood in the doorway. "Shall I see you tonight, Freddie?"

"Hell, Gail, you even look great when you're dressed," I countered, knowing what I was going to have to confess.

"Thank you, but you didn't answer my question."

I glanced at my battle-dress trousers draped over the square-backed chair. I knew the pockets were low on lira. "I'm afraid I can't afford…"

She smiled. "I've been wondering when you'd have to say that, Freddie. Actually, I expected it yesterday. Why don't we discuss it tonight. Shall we leave it like that? Yes, let's do — that's if you decide to call around."

I nodded. And she was gone, closing the door softly behind her. I lay there, gazing at the ceiling. Now what the hell do I do? I wondered. And what in hell is one of Mr. and Mrs. Cederberg's sons doing, lying here in a whore's Roman bedroom anyway? And almost broke. The only answer I could come up with was that the room was a long, long way from Maughan Crescent, so I took refuge in sleep. When I woke up, I blanked my mind (it kind of ached, anyway), showered, dressed slowly and, ignoring the tea and biscuits, let myself out. Funny, I thought as I stepped into the narrow street, she never did offer me my own key.

I walked and walked and walked while my mind played leapfrog with the conscience I had been born with. She's a whore, offering me a handout, a small voice I didn't recognize said, until I decided one had nothing to do with the other.

You're getting in over your head, you'll be beholden, the voice persisted. I sighed, oblivious to the hint of history in the tiny *piazze* I plodded through, the sounds of the living city. Idly, I thought of my brother, Reg, and wondered if he had ever managed to get overseas. Poor bastard, I reflected morosely, he couldn't get over and I...?

Responding to sudden hunger pangs, I gulped down noodles and black-market Spam in a smoky *ristorante* where too many Allied soldiers drank too much vino and talked too loudly.

"Hey, Sergeant, you lose y'r best friend?" a half-cut British corporal asked me, reeling unsteadily up to my table.

I stared at him.

"Cat got y'r tongue, too?" he continued, cheerily.

"None of your fuckin' business!" I said, icily.

"Friendly bugger," he lisped, wobbling over to a bench circled by drinking Tommies.

I paid my bill, walked up the stone steps and into the street. It was raining lightly, spitting on the cobblestones. I turned up my jacket collar and headed for Canada House. Once, I was certain I could see Gail walking in the throng moving ahead of me. I quickened my pace, closing in on a woman walking alone, her blond hair bouncing lightly on her shoulders. I enjoyed an expectant high feeling of elation as I caught up, but it desolved into genuine disappointment when she looked at me indifferently, a complete stranger. I hurried on, driven by I knew not what, but my mind was made up: A handout or no, a whore or no, I was going to be at apartment 44 at five-thirty.

I knocked once, twice, before the door opened.

"Well, my wandering sergeant is back!" she laughed, swinging it wide. "Do come in."

Clumsily, I took a long step inside the room, engulfed her with my arms and hugged her. As we came together, I kissed her in a faint cloud of her fragrance, my *vino*-laden breath, even the scented soap she had used that morning in the shower.

"Easy, Freddie," she gasped, pushing against my chest with her small hands, "you're going to crush me to death with all this affection."

She had it all figured out. "First, you go and see Signori Toppazzini and get a refund on your room. That should free up your cash.

And you'll stay here, with me, as a house guest. We'll call it my contribution to the Allied war effort."

I tried to say "I'll pay you" but she shushed me quiet. "Not to mind. Remember, there's a war on, and everyone must do one's bit."

We made love with a slow-building passion I had never experienced before. Later, while Gail Rigby slept, I left her bed, got the Scotch and a glass and, listening to her regular breathing, stretched myself almost horizontally in the lone easy chair.

Pleasantly tired, sipping the silky whiskey, I closed my eyes, luxuriating in a feeling of well-being, like a fighter who has gone the distance and won. Growing up isn't easy, I thought, recalling that my old father had once written to me, pointing out that it involved knowing the difference between being loved or mothered or laid. I had been slightly shocked when I had read his words, scrawled in an architect's straight line across the page, remembering, too, he had never once offered me advice at all when I was a teenager.

I poured another drink. I still might not understand the strict lines between my father's three categories, I acknowledged, chuckling to myself, but I'm learning, pops. Opening my eyes, I gazed in the gloom at Gail's gently rounded form under the sheet and blanket. She was on her side, as if in stride, a slender, pale arm folded under her pillow, her fine blond hair half over her face.

What the hell, I said almost aloud, she's wonderful to look at. And she's wonderful to be with. Who cares whether she's a whore or not? Certainly, the north country squire who will father her children won't give a goddamn so why should I? "Fuck 'em all, fuck 'em all, the long an' the short an' the tall!" I hummed quietly.

I fell asleep with shapeless dreams of England, home, school and sunlit rivers I couldn't place chasing each other through my head.

I woke up alone under a blanket, drier than a Death Valley water hole. I drank most of the trickle of water from the shower head and washed with what was left.

We said goodbye on the sidewalk at the foot of the broad steps leading up to Canada House. In the lowering darkness, beside a convoy of idling Canadian Army leave trucks, I kissed her lightly.

"Will I see you again?" I asked, realizing I was playing the game she had referred to a million years of nights earlier.

"We'll see, love," she whispered, but her eyes said no.

"I'd like to — besides I owe you about ten thousand lira if you include the dinners." I was trying to be sauve and, I sensed, flunking terribly.

"You didn't have to say that."

I mumbled something unintelligible.

She put her arms around me. "Love, you've been fun...very much fun..." and kissed me so warmly I was startled. Before I could react, she pulled free and walked quickly down the Via Nationale without looking back, her high heels clicking rhythmically on the pavement.

The transport officer yelled: "OK! Let's move 'em!"

I climbed over the tailgate and finding room on the wooden bench-styled seat along one side, sat down.

"That was a right good-lookin' dame," a faceless Perth Regiment sergeant next to me said cheerfully. "She wasn't Eyetie, was she?"

"Nope. English."

"With an entertainment troupe?"

"Something like that."

"Lucky you. Say, you gotta cigarette? I'm fresh out."

I handed him one side of my pack. "Here —"

"Thanks, buddy, thanks a lot."

I knew what had happened to his cigarettes. He had sold them for a small fortune when his cash gave out. And I wondered why I hadn't thought of doing that when I was going broke. But then, he didn't have a Gail Rigby, lady whore.

The return trip to Tavoleto was long and tiring. And by the time I had checked into the regimental orderly room, I was no longer sure of her apartment number.

CHAPTER THIRTEEN

THE rains came in December, warm at first, then chilled. And in between the damp clouds and wet ground, rumors blew hot and cold.

"The whole corps will be pulled back and shipped to northwest Europe to be united with the second corps to create the first ever all-Canadian army in action," stated Greenwood, enunciating his words precisely.

Everyone clapped and cheered.

"Where'd you get that?" asked Kerr.

Alex's pale eyes widened. "Shall I say at a certain…ah, let's call it an emporium of fine wines and excellent food."

"You mean a vino dive?"

"Shee-it!" exploded Morrison, "I heard las' night we're going to Burma on account of we're specialists. We can climb mountains, cross rivers. Hell, we can do anything!"

"Me?" parried Kerr, "I don't know, except that we're definitely being pulled out."

Colonel Buchanan settled it. "We're going to cross another river, a couple of canals, and capture the village of Godo for starters — just to straighten out the corps line, then we'll head for winter quarters."

Only Al Hall demurred. "We were told by the generals we were going to spend the winter in Venice. Or was it Vienna? Anyway," he grinned whimsically, tugging at his lopsided balmoral, "I've already made my plans. And they include Venice. So, that's where we're going."

It sounded reassuring.

Training absorbed most of our daylight hours, but at night we sold blankets for vino, gave most of our chocolate rations to black-eyed *bambini*. Or offered families a dozen cans of bully beef in exchange for a hot, home-cooked meal of what we called spaghetti, but the natives referred to as noodles. Our summer issue had given way to battle-dress serge, swathed sometimes in denims or coveralls or sleeveless leather jerkins which deflected the brisk mountain-born winds gusting through our lines.

Buchanan, who ruled with a firm but tolerant large hand, put it all in perspective: "Between the tough training in weapons, traffic control, battle drill and the endless business deals with the locals, this regiment is ready for whatever the Germans can throw at them."

Sergeant Morrison's square hands rested on his hips. His helmet clung to the back of his head and there were mud stains on his clean-shaven, pink jaw. He looked at his wristwatch. Then again. "Almost 1600," he said, "an' no sign of Kerr." He squinted at me. "You tell him to be here for 'O' group at 1600?"

"I told him."

It began to rain. Scotty stared up at the low grey clouds, so low they gave the impression they wanted to lie down on the flat earth. He scowled.

"No good looking for blue skies, Scotty, they been that dirty grey color for 'bout two weeks now," Albert said, shifting his feet in the mucky, alluvial loam. He deftly toed a clot of mud at the once-white long wall of a casa our carrier was parked against.

I studied the casa. Only the long wall remained. The splintered ends of the heavy beams which had once supported the red-tiled roof protruded beyond the line of the wall like jagged stumps. Crawford's steel-helmeted head was barely visible above the armor plate of the carrier — Betsy III. Betsy III had three shiny and small oblong scars on the commander's side where an exploding 88 had flung shrapnel through the armor plate.

I shivered in the damp, late-afternoon chill. It seemed to amuse Scotty. "Need a hot water bottle, sonny?" he asked with mock solicitude.

"Screw you, Scotty." I thumped my feet on the ground and slapped my arms.

Hooking my thumb under my Tommy-gun sling, I snapped it against my chest and returned to studying the blasted farmhouse. Spotting a sliver of broken mirror, I absently picked it up. Staring into it, all I could see was the soft stubble of a faint, reddish-blond beard, and bleary, tired eyes. I flung the reflection into the rubble littering the ground.

"Can't stand yourself?" cackled Scotty.

"I'm no Miss America, if that's what you mean. But you have to concede I'm not getting the proper diet or my beauty rest."

"Ahhh," consoled Scotty, "it's the war, heh."

"Where we going this time, Scotty?" Albert asked.

"The Senio River."

"Where's that? Near Venice?"

Scotty laughed loudly. "Hell, no. Just a few miles north o' here. But there's a few rivers an' canals, even a couple of big run-off ditches — the Eyeties call 'em *fossi* — before we get there."

"Another Lamone?"

"Nah. First we gotta cross the Naviglio Canal." He paused, then added, "I hear the First Div took a kickin' at the Lamone."

"That so..." Albert said, cupping his hands and lighting a cigarette.

"Couple of old buddies — First Div arty — visited the other day. Said the RCRs an' Hastie Ps got over them big dykes, but everything got snafued and they had to back up. The Hasties did it without permission, so the RCRs had to back up, too. Also said some senior officers got booted out."

"It can happen," I said, "but maybe now they won't be giving us the razz about the 11th Brigade in the Arielli."

"You mean when you guys promised the moon and Pescara and delivered nothin'?"

I had forgotten Scotty was ex-First Div. "Yeah," I said. But I hadn't forgotten the approaches to the Lamone, splashing in its rush to the Adriatic between thirty-foot high grassy flood-control banks. We had jumped the Montone River with the Plugs, been held up by severe mortaring and machine-gun fire at the Via Cupa canal, outflanked Godo and cut the road to Ravenna. The pressure had forced the Germans to retire to the Naviglio and allowed the Princess Louise Platoon Guards to capture Ravenna, the one-time seat of the imperial court of The Western Holy Roman Empire.

It began to rain harder. Scotty looked up into the boiling clouds, the raindrops splattering off his cheeks. "Ah, hell, let's get into my jeep and wait until that dumb bastard, Kerr, gets here."

Albert and I pushed into the back seat, Scotty got behind the wheel and the three of us watched while Crawford yanked an edge of the carrier tarpaulin over his head.

"Whatta you think of our new looie, Mr. Lafferty?" Scotty asked.

"He's a boy," replied Albert, wheezing and coughing. "Friggin' cigarettes. I'm going to quit one day!"

"He'll do," I offered.

"Got the smarts even if he's a kid," said Scotty.

I pictured his lean boyish face. They're all beginning to look like kids, I thought — except Ambrose. He had a face that insisted he had been born old. But most had one thing in common: They were willing, sometimes to the point of being foolhardy. And death or promotion came quickly. A wound had been Mr. Ambrose's ticket out.

One in particular, stuck in my mind's eye. Sallow-complexioned, he had come up with the reinforcements two days before we were relieved at the Fuimicino. He had had no pips on and carried a rifle. I thought he was a private.

"Hey, kiddoh," I had yelled at him the next morning, noting he was unshaven, "get out your issue razor and do a job on your kisser."

"Why, Sarg?" he had asked, wide-eyed.

"One, because it's good for your morale. Washing and shaving makes you feel better every morning, if you have time. And, two, sonny, because I told you to. OK?"

He shaved. And he struck me, at the time, as a cut above the average newcomer. He was curious. Always asking questions, why this? why that? followed by OK, Sarg, whatever you say. I gave him shit for the condition of his rifle, pointing out it had to work every time or he'd be just another statistic.

Oddly, he had disappeared after we had been relieved by the New Zealanders and reached our rest area. The next morning, I had checked out all weapons, ordered vehicle maintenance and reported to platoon headquarters when Scotty introduced me to him. He was the newest of our rookie looies.

"Why didn't you tell me you were our officer up in the lines?" I asked.

"Well," he allowed, smiling lazily, "when I came up to TAC, I asked Sergeant Morrison what I could expect in a forward position. And who was running the show. His advice was to keep an eye on you and Sergeant Kerr, that both of you knew what you were doing. So, being green, I found a rifle, left my pips and revolver in the platoon carrier, and did what I was told. I learned a lot."

"Scotty," I said as the rain battered the jeep's canvas top, "what was the name of that little, white-faced looie who came to us at the Fiumicino? The one who got it next time we were in when he stood up to direct fire?"

Morrison frowned. Ah, Mr., ah...I don't remember."

Neither did I. But I had liked him in the short time he had been around.

The growling noise of an armored carrier moving through the slop, its tracks and bogeys squealing, the steel links spanking its underskirt, broke the silky silence of the falling rain. We watched Kerr's stubby vehicle nose around the wall of the casa, Moose behind the wheel. Kerr stood in the commander's spot, his back to the slanting rain. Belanger crouched next to the roaring motor in the observer's long seat.

Moose rocked the carrier to a halt beside Betsy III and Kerr leaped out and scrambled into the jeep's front seat beside Scotty.

"Sorry 'bout being late," he said, rapidly, "but we threw a track and had to repair it." He rolled his eyes and shuddered violently. "God! but I'm cold. Couldn't we have done this at TAC?"

Scotty shook his head. "We'd never get in. There's more brass in there than you'll find on poolroom spittoons." He produced a heavy talc-faced map case from beneath his seat. "This one," he said, soberly, "is going to be a big one, heh."

Rapidly, he sketchily outlined the plans of the corps' attack, then reduced it to the regiment's role within the 12th Brigade's axis of advance.

"You know we're kinda thin on the ground, heh? Well, to beef up the assault, your sections — now a machine-gun group — will be goin' in as X-ray four, with the assault companies. We cross the start line at 2115. Every man."

Scotty coughed. Then he said almost apologetically, "I won't be going up, ah, tonight. I've been ordered to stick around TAC just in case...ah, you know...just in case."

"Will Mr. Lafferty be leading?" asked Kerr.

"Hold your questions till I'm finished, OK?" He righted the map case against the wheel. "Now, you birds, look here, heh."

He squared the one-inch-to-the-mile map, jamming a forefinger against it. "Ah, shee-it, Mr. Lafferty should be doin' this!" he snorted.

Moving his finger around, he halted when he located what he wanted. "This here," he intoned, "is where the platoon is now." A small, imperfect chinagraph circle marked the reference points. "And here," he shifted his finger, "is the Vecchio where you kick off at 2300. It's nothin' but a low-banked little ol' canal." The finger slid across the talc. "An' here's the Naviglio. Now that's a big bugger, with twenty-five-foot dykes on either side. There may or may not be any Jerries defendin' the dykes. Recce patrols say they ain't, but you know by now that info could be dead wrong, heh."

Scotty sighed. A drop of rain fell off his helmet and flattened on the talc. Impatiently, he wiped it away.

"Anyway, the Naviglio ain't gonna be your big problem." His forefinger jumped inside an oblong, red chinagraph circle, slightly open at one end. "This here is an *osteria*, a row of inns — high, solid stone casas. An' if they're manned by Jerries who don't intend to leave, then you got a problem. Heh?"

"How come?" asked Albert, slyly.

"Because it controls the approaches to the canal. An' you'll never get across with them there!" Scotty gushed.

"Ah, Scotty, don't take it so fuckin' serious, we know that."

Scotty's return grin was strained. He continued. "You'll go in alongside Able Company. Charley'll be on your right. Baker an' Dog'll be in reserve. An' this is important. You guys gotta take every weapon you got. An' that means packin' the Vickers!"

Kerr groaned.

"Yeah, I know, the barrel weighs in at about forty pounds an' the tripod goes at fifty. So, you split 'em up. One piece per man an' everyone else carries ammo. An' when I say every man goes, I mean carrier drivers, too. Except the kid with the looie's vehicle at TAC. He'll be with Mr. Lafferty." He snorted. "Now you know where he'll be."

"How about Simpson?" I asked.

"Simpson?"

"The new kid. He was pretty jittery at the Lamone. I had to send him out. He was bawlin'...."

"Where's he now?"

"Working for the support company cooks."

"Leave him there, then." Scotty's eyes shifted from face to face. "Any more questions?"

"Yeah," Kerr said, "we're all under strength."

"Replacements will be up at 1900. They were having their dental and medical checks at LOB this afternoon."

Kerr snickered. "Can't send 'em up to be shot at unless they're healthy."

"How about support — like arty and tanks?" I asked.

Scotty grunted. "You got div and corps artillery. And the heavy mortars, the 4.2s. And the armor will be up soon's the Vecchio and Naviglio can be bridged by the engineers. Shouldn't take long an' they'll be right with you."

"When does the barrage go in?" I persisted.

"Not till you need it."

I sat back. "If the armor has to wait for bridges, so will the antitank guns."

"When you figure a way how to get 'em over water hazards without bridges, you can take 'em with you," squeaked Scotty. "Until then, you'll have to rely on your PIATs."

"I'd sooner have some Jerry bazookas," said Kerr.

Scotty ignored him. "Keep y'r heads up an' y'r tails down an' good luck."

By chow time, the rain had ceased. And the meal was hot — beef, potatoes, carrots, thick slices of bread and messtins of heavily sugared coffee. Dessert was rice. In the raw chill, it was satisfying.

"No raisins in the rice," observed Albert, "the cooks are makin' their own booze again."

It was the only complaint.

Lieutenant Lafferty brought three reinforcements with him when he came to see us. I got one, Kerr and Albert the others.

"What's your name, buddy?" I asked.

"Boutlier." He had a somber face, pale and black-eyed.

He didn't look more than eighteen. And he gave the appearance of someone who had been fitted for a battle dress too large for his thin but long frame. Too thin, I thought, to carry half a Vickers.

"There's a Bren in the number two carrier," I said, "it's yours. So, go get it and leave your rifle there. And fill your ammo pouches with mags. Your water bottle full? You got your chocolate and beef?"

"Yes, Sergeant."

"And there's a spare shovel in beside the Bren. Make damn sure you take it, too. One of the guys'll show you how to hook it to your web gear. When you're set, go get yourself something to eat before it's all gone."

Boutlier half turned to go, then stopped. "What's it like, Sergeant?"

"What's what like?"

"Up there."

I shrugged. "Don't worry about it, kiddoh. You just stick with the section. Do what everybody else does. And then all you'll have to do is get used to the noise."

"The noise?"

"Yep. The noise. That's what it's all about; they just try to blow you away with lots of friggin' noise."

The looie passed out mail. "Anyone who wants to fire off a personal letter has exactly forty minutes. It'll be going back with the platoon carrier then."

We scattered in the darkness, each to his own vehicle, each to read and think, even briefly, about a distant home or woman or family. Mine was from Francine. The almost illegible address was a dead giveaway. I turned it over in the light of the gas-burning fire. It's odd, I thought, it's her scrawled handwriting I remember about her most. Opening it, I smoothed out the single blue page and read words I could make out to her sign-off "All my love, darling." It startled me. She had never before been anything but casual, closing with "as ever."

Gently disturbed (by what? I wondered) I slowly read the text again, but it was her usual letter about the weather, tennis, volunteer work (aboard a garbage truck of all things!), her son, Hunstanton, the shops. And "All my love, darling." It triggered a warmness for her I hadn't felt in months. I shall write her, now, and sign off the same way, I thought, then see what develops.

I was rooting in Betsy III for my gas-proof pouch containing writing paper when I heard Lafferty's high-pitched shout. "Sergeant Cederberg! Sergeant Cederberg!"

"Sir!" I yelled back, automatically.

"Over here!"

I fought back an urge to yell "But I got a friggin' letter to write first!" and went over to him, picking my way carefully through the puddles.

Lafferty sat on a box of belted Vickers ammo. "Check out the men, eh, right now."

"They know what's expected of them. They aren't first-timers, they've been there before, sir," I began, my words faintly tinged with sarcasm.

He nodded wearily. "I know, Sergeant, but check 'em anyway. This is going to be a long, long night."

Slowly, I opened the tab top of my ammo pouch and jammed Francine's letter inside, trying to ignore a tenuous tugging deep inside me that had reminded me without warning there were still strings tying me to other places and other times.

By the time I had returned to our area, I was beginning to get worked up. I yelled at Kerr and Albert. "Check those buggers out an' make sure they're all carrying the maximum," I shouted.

Of the eleven in my section and nine in Kerr's, only two were what we called "cheaters." The others grumbled while we stood over them until we were satisfied every pouch and pack was loaded to capacity. And they cursed silently when we made them produce their emergency chocolate and tins of bully beef.

"Now the water bottles!" I snapped, angry more with Lafferty than the men.

Each uncorked the stoppers and tipped a few drops on the ground. "Wait a minute, MacIntosh," I said to a beefy, moustachioed dispatch rider, conscripted for the night. "Give it to me."

He unbuckled it from his web belt, passing it over tentatively, his eyes shining in the gloom.

I sniffed at the neck. "Vino?"

He shook his head. "Eyetie brandy, like wartime stuff."

I poured it on the ground. His bland expression, barely masking a sad grin, didn't change. I gave it back. He knew and I knew he had more of the stuff squirreled away; that as soon as my back was turned, he'd fill up again.

"Why do you drink that rotgut?" I asked him.

William MacIntosh shrugged. "Let's say, it helps ease the pain when everything's going wrong," he said.

Kerr was watching me under his blond brows. "What's the matter with you tonight?" he asked, mildly.

I shouted at Crawford, his dog motionless at his feet. "Get rid of that goddamned pooch!"

"I ain't takin' him up with me, if that's what you mean, Sarg," he replied steadily.

"You're fuckin' right you're not. Tie him up to the carrier. And make damned sure it can't get loose. You can get him back when we come out."

Crawford bent over and almost lovingly gathered the scrawny mongrel in his arms. "C'mon, Stupid ol' buddy, you're gonna have to be alone for a while," he crooned. Lowering it gently into the Bren gunner's side of the carrier, he sat it on a stack of blankets then arranged the tarp so it covered most of the dog's scraggly body.

"I said 'tie him up to the carrier,' not inside it!" I barked.

Crawford faced me slowly. "Sarg, he ain't hurtin' anybody in here. An' when we get back, if he's messed it up, I'll clean up, so good you'll be able to eat off the armor. OK Sarg?"

I shivered. I was abruptly cold and tired and sorry. "OK, Crawford, just be sure he's tied up with enough rope so he can get out and crap or lift a leg when he has to."

Crawford beamed. "Thank's Sarg. I'll do just that, an' I'll carry some extra grenades."

Ah, hell, I thought. I reached out and loosened Kerr's shoulder straps and looked at Belanger and Greenwood. "You all got extra grenades?"

They nodded.

"Where the hell are we going? All the way to Berlin?" Albert asked.

"Yep. And walking."

Alex Greenwood was philosophical. "Ah, I said to myself when I transferred to the armored division, my walking days are over. I shall ride into war, saving my strength for the battles ahead."

"Now you know different," interrupted Albert. "Hell, we aren't even infantry, we're pack mules. We carry medium and light machine guns, grenades, ammo, rations, shovels and the generals' best wishes — then we fight."

In the chill of night, the muddy ground was thickening. And cold air rushed out of the high passes in the Etruscan mountains, touching us with its icy breath. Without direction, we shuffled into a circle around the now-flaming fire and the unseen smoke began to blacken our faces.

"We move off at 2125," I said after looking at my wristwatch. "Anybody got any letters to go?"

Someone said, "Belanger took 'em over to platoon headquarters a couple of minutes ago."

The men's shadows reeled grotesquely on the sides of the laagered carriers. Lafferty was still seated cross-legged on the crate of belted Vickers ammo, staring blankly into the flames leaping and hissing out of the sawed-in-half biscuit tin clogged with gas and muck when I reported the section guns had been checked out.

I could hear the platoon carrier grunting through the darkness, heading for TAC. Perversely, I was relieved and angry, but I didn't try to sort it out as I returned through the darkness to our section lines. Albert was dozing, flat on his back in the gunner's compartment of his carrier, his wide mouth open. I halted beside him and he opened one eye then the other.

"If it rains hard, you'll drown," I said.

He snorted and closed his eyes. "When did you say we move out?"

"About two hours."

"Then go away. I need my sleep. I've just passed my thirty-first birthday. And when you get that old, you need more rest."

"Happy birthday."

Walking around Albert's vehicle, I crossed over to Betsy III, patting Stupid before selecting a handful of Tommy-gun mags. I stuffed them into my pouches, crushing Francine's letter. And I wondered if Albert was still writing the letters he didn't mail before every assault. I was trying to guess who would post them if anything happened to him when I realized I couldn't picture him getting killed. Climbing into the carrier, I snoozed fitfully until we loaded up and trudged into the night.

CHAPTER FOURTEEN

WE reached the ten-foot first bank of the Fosso Vecchio without a shot being fired. And not a single mortar exploded as, shoulders hunched, the section plodded forward. No one spoke. The silence was broken only by the occasional hushed oath, the clang of a shovel striking a weapon, the rasping breath of a man straining under the weight of a Vickers barrel or tripod or case of belted ammo.

We moved with a gentle hiss, heavy boots lifted up and lowered almost rhythmically in and out of the gumbo muck. It was a gentle sound, a repetitious sound, like the endless sigh of calm waves lapping against the sandy shore in some secluded cove.

All of us sensed what was going through the mind of reinforcement Henri Boutlier, moving up in his first attack. To him, the clink-clank of gear sounded enormous, as though some madman in a church tower was driving the bells one against the other.

I could hear Albert swearing with each step. The forward pair of thick iron legs of the Vickers tripod was biting into his shoulders. Boutlier slogged alongside him. And we could actually smell the new man's fear and it bothered us because it heightened ours. And to a man we were repelled by it because it could infect us, strip us of our self-imposed discipline, leaving only panic.

It began to drizzle and a mist crept between the men of the Lanark and Renfrew, almost isolating four- and five-man clusters.

The solid wall of the nearest embankment channelling the *fosso* was a brown gash before us. Then it was real, a rising mound of dirt with tufts of grass clinging to its smooth lines. Without hesitation, we staggered up the steep slope, doggedly pulling ourselves to the crest.

"See anything?" panted Kerr, staring into the rain and gloom.

"Nothing. But the Naviglio is supposed to be just another six or seven hundred yards ahead," I hissed. "Let's go."

We waded through the cold, calf-deep water, clambered up the far embankment, slithered down its side and resumed our plodding advance.

"Recce says there's nobody holdin' the canal," wheezed Kerr.

"Screw recce," I snorted, hefting the Vickers barrel to another spot on my shoulder. "The Jerries probably let 'em in and out so's they'd go back with the wrong info. We do it, so why wouldn't they? Ah, my God, my back aches."

A flare burst high in the night sky, reflecting off the covering layer of clouds. Its bright, fierce glare made every furrow seem like a ridge, every half-flattened blade of grass stand out like a British Columbia fir.

We froze. "Ours?" someone whispered.

"Theirs, I think," Kerr shushed.

Drifting lazily below its tiny parachute, the burning magnesium chased the darkness away, fizzled and went out. The black of night clutched us again as we began moving forward once more.

It was cold. But not a man shivered. Each sweated profusely. To our left, I could hear the rifle companies surging across the flat, treeless approaches to the canal. It sounded as though someone were dragging a gigantic tarpaulin across the ground.

Nerves tightened. We planted our heels firmly in the soil to steady our balance. Left-right, left-right, one laborious step at a time, fighting to suck the damp air into aching lungs, we lurched forward. A large, long casa loomed up on our left, pale and ghostly in the mist.

"Not far to go now," grunted Kerr. "I saw that on Scotty's map."

No one answered. And as silently as it had appeared, it disappeared while we pushed relentlessly on.

In the gloom and mist and rain, the first dyke containing the canal looked like a mountain — grass-covered and almost perpendicular.

"Holy Christ!" rasped Albert, hoarsely, "we'll never get up that friggin' wall of dirt!"

I held my free arm up. We halted. Albert and the two men loaded down with the Vickers sank gratefully to the wet ground; the others stood, shoulders heaving, staring up into the forbidding shadowy line of the embankment.

"Wait here," I hissed at the machine-gunners and lowered the Vickers barrel. "C'mon, Moose, we'll take a look-see from the top."

Wide-legged, clutching at heavier clumps of dying grass, we made it, gasping, to the dyke's broad, flat crown. Thankfully, we lay there, then bellied to the side of the canal. I peered into the black almost-dry channel. "My fuckin' nerves!" I hissed, "Germans!"

Moose reacted first, snapping off quick shots from his rifle as two Jerries, apparently spotting us at the same time, lifted their Schmeissers in surprise. First one then the other, arms flailing, went over backward.

At the same time, heavy gunfire shattered the night to our left. Long strings of tracers slit the darkness, followed by a series of detonating Jerry potato-masher grenades, the eye-blinking pin-points of flame scarring the ground mists. Hoarse, maddened shouts were flung at the forbidding sky. The slow, rhythmic thump-thump-thump of a Dren gun, spouting incendiaries, sprayed the faint outline of the dyke, followed by the intermittent harsh crack of our own 36 grenades.

Kerr and Greenwood scrambled up beside us. "That's tore it!" wheezed Kerr. "Where in hell are they?"

We flattened against the damp grass as Jerry gunners burped strings of bullets, whining madly along the length of the dyke. Others, from another Spandau to the right, thumped into the embankment. We slithered backward until — except for our heads — we had the protection of the dyke's upward slope.

"We netted into A Company?" I snapped.

Kerr nodded. "Well, have Cuthbert tell 'em there's Germans all over the goddamned dyke — even on our side. Quick!"

Kerr slid down the soggy embankment on his rump, I could hear him yelling at the signaller. Then he was back. "Done," he said. "Now, what's the lay of the land an' what're we going to do next — keepin' in mind, we're supposed to get across this Godforsaken canal."

"Yah, Sarg, an' how come there's no water in that fuckin' canal?" gasped Moose.

"Mr. Lafferty said the Jerries have dammed it up south of here 'cause that's where they're expecting the main assault."

We pushed ourselves higher between bursts of enemy fire, until we could see about twenty to twenty-five yards in both directions, along the dyke's crown. "I'd reckon it goes straight away toward the rifle companies, over that way," said Kerr, pointing to his left, "but it's gotta sonuvabitch of a bend the other way, slanting almost to that casa — at least I think it's a casa — to the right."

"Aren't the Plugs on our right?" I asked.

"Yep. But just where on our right, I dunno. Things get off line in the friggin' dark."

The firing on our right picked up in tempo. But, in the darkness, we couldn't be sure who was firing and in which direction. Enemy mortars danced across the plowed fields, shredding the ground, the mist and rain, flinging the shattered earth upward in great geysers of mud.

I had to shout at Kerr and Moose. "We can't stay here! Christ! I forgot! Jerries might be tryin' to climb up the canal side of the dyke!"

Moose pulled the pins on two grenades. "Well, we're gonna find out right quick!" he shrilled, rolling them through the thin grass with enough force to send them over the lip of the dyke. Two sharp explosions followed and we flung ourselves across the ten-foot crown. Machine-gun fire chewed into the embankment.

"Where in hell's that comin' from?" I panted, sensing the hairs on the nape of my neck were trying to crawl up under my steel hat. For protection? I thought giddily.

Kerr stabbed a finger toward our right, along the bend, at the outline of a row of tall buildings.

"The goddamn *osteria*," I almost whistled.

"A what?"

"*Osteria*...an inn. It was marked on Scotty's map, remember. Shee-it, if they're manning it, we gotta lot of trouble on our hands!"

German machine-gunners were literally blowing away the mist to our right when an 88 swooshed low over our heads and careened into the fields where A Company riflemen were fighting to stay alive. It erupted like a thunderbolt.

"Christ almighty!" breathed Moose, "they got self-propelled guns somewhere. An' they're throwin' them fuckin' grass-cutters." Another pair, hooting like fast two-car expresses, roared through the rain and slammed into the long casa we had passed minutes earlier.

"We gotta get the Vickers up here. No, first let's get a couple of Brens. Hey, Boutlier! Crawford! Get up here. Bring your Brens — on the double!" Kerr yelled.

"We gonna try an' hold this dyke?" asked Moose, his little bullet eyes glittering in his angular, large face.

"We do," I said, tersely, "then we got to find out if any of our fellas are over...or get over ourselves."

We dug like demented gravediggers into our side of the hard-packed crown. It was tiring. And despite the raging firefights on our left, and so far to our right that the sound was muffled, we spaded crude pits for both the Vickers and Brens. Albert and Moose made five trips to the foot of the dyke to manhandle the Vickers and ammo into position.

Artillery from both sides hammered away at each other until we were certain the 25-pounder shells and 88s had to meet halfway, head-on in the inky arch of the night.

We waited, crouched and sweating despite the cold, staring across the canal at the far bank until our eyes ached. Mortars, laced with the whistling 88s, crashed into the fields behind us.

"You know," Greenwood said softly, "I don't believe our enemy knows we are even here, and when one considers the magnitude of the fighting all around us, it certainly gives one reason to be thankful." Then he winced, screwing his eyes hard shut and gasping as a cluster of shells exploded against the stone casa in the bend in the canal dyke, proving he wasn't as calm as he pretended.

"I couldn't have said it better," grated Albert, in the following silence, "but I'd be a helluva lot more thankful if I knew where our goddamn tanks are."

"They'll get here," Kerr pacified, "when the engineers can get bridges across that Vecchio. But it isn't gonna be easy, not with all those Jerry 88s lashing the crossings."

Kerr saw them first, a herky-jerky, ragged line of Germans, arms waving, machine-pistols spouting fire, potato mashers inside belts, on the crown of the far dyke. Sprinting, they crossed it, and, digging their heels in, charged down the canal side and splashed through the puddled canal bed.

"Fire!" Kerr screamed at the top of his lungs.

Crawford opened up. The Vickers, with the Halls behind one, began to chatter, almost in cadence, drowning out the Bren.

At less than thirty feet, I aimed straight at the belt buckle of the leading Jerry, his face straining beneath a coal-scuttle helmet. I ripped off two, quick single shots. The expression on his face didn't change when he went down sideways.

Mortars and 88s screeched and exploded in the darkness behind us.

"They're comin' up the fuckin' slope!" squealed Moose. "Get them Vickers trained on 'em."

"I can't get the goddamned thing depressed enough!" yelled Albert, glancing wildly about him. "Boutlier! Boutlier! Gimme that friggin' Bren!"

Boutlier lay face down beside the light machine gun.

Pushing him roughly to one side, Albert grabbed the Bren, rushed bent double across the crown, pointed it straight into the line of crawling, scrambling Jerries and blew all twenty-eight rounds of steel-nosed .303s literally into their faces.

I was vividly aware of the storm raging around me. I had the feeling Boutlier was dead. I watched Albert, hunched over, firing from the hip. I heard Kerr sing out warnings. I fired carefully without feeling. Out of the corner of one eye, I watched a potato masher go over our heads and explode at the foot of the dyke. Something glanced off my helmet. A German crawled laboriously out of his side of the dark Naviglio and began pulling himself up the face of the dyke. I put a short burst into his back and he shuddered and twitched before sliding down the slope until his legs jammed against another body.

As abruptly as it had begun, it ended. Someone grunted. Only it sounded more like a long, sad sigh. The misty rain, shattered by the violence, thickened, swirling among the enemy sprawled like dirty heaps of clothing on the inside faces of the dykes. Two were face down, arms spread as if in exultation.

A feeling of euphoria left me light-headed. Slowly, mechanically, I removed the empty Tommy-gun mag and replaced it with one filled with the stubby 45s. Ramming it home seemed to snap me out of my daze.

"Kerr? Albert? Greenwood? Crawford? Moose? You OK?" I hissed.

All were panting. "So much for nobody knows we're here," wheezed Kerr.

Albert bent over Boutlier, gently rolled him on his back. There was a small, darkish hole dead center in his forehead. It was almost bloodless. "He didn't know what the hell hit 'im..." he said to no one in particular.

Poor little bastard, I thought, another one who didn't have time to get used to the damned noise.

"Better get him out of here, Moose. Give him a hand, eh Crawford? Take him over to the long house." I pointed toward the bend in the dyke. "Able Company ought to be there. Or the Princess Louises." I stared after them as they carried him, Moose at his shoulders, Crawford clinging to his feet, while they worked their way down the side of the embankment.

I took a huge gulp of the misty air. It tasted of cordite. And gunpowder. "I guess, after that, we gotta keep a man on the forward side of the crest," I said softly. "So, who's it going to be?"

A gaggle of our shells sighed overhead, exploding like firecrackers several hundred yards behind the Jerry lines. And the sound jarred a silence soothed by the hissing rain.

"Christ, but when did it get so quiet?" asked Kerr in a startled tone.

"Who's going to take the first shift up on the lip?" I repeated.

"I'll go," said Albert. He wriggled into position, his steel helmet turning from side to side as he scanned the far wall of the dyke.

Moose's high-shouldered hulk dropped down beside Kerr and I. "It's Able — what's left of 'em — and Baker Companies in the casa," he squeaked. "An' shee-it, they got a lot of wounded." He spat. "And dead. Lost most of 'em gettin' across the flats an' when they hadda capture the friggin' house. I told the major we were on the dyke. An' you know what he wanted to know? When we were gonna get across the friggin' canal. Jeez!"

A gigantic swarm of Moaning Minnies whined and screamed over our heads and we instinctively clung to the damp ground — even though we *knew* they weren't meant for us. They exploded in livid sheets of flame two hundred yards to our left and behind us.

"Jee-sus!" grunted Kerr.

I had an almost uncontrollable desire to pee. Rolling over on my side, I fumbled with my fly buttons and let go. It was only a dribble, but the pain in my bladder disappeared. I wondered if anyone had seen me.

"I hope to God they don't think we got enough men to cross the canal," said Kerr, incredulously. "You tell him how many we are?"

Moose shook his head. "He didn't ask me."

The exploding Moaning Minnies triggered a prolonged stonk of mortar fire. Edgy machine-gunners ripped off strings of bullets. And, as if not to be ignored, German and Canadian artillery spewed shells at each other. Ribbons of white light flickered across the face of the *osteria* just before a hurricane of bullets peppered the canal dyke, driving us over the edge where we flattened in the wet grass, gasping for breath like floundering, beached fish.

"We just got to dig those gun pits deeper," I grated, " 'cause one of these times, we aren't gonna make it over the edge!"

Kerr nodded.

"I don't see any goddamned point," groaned Albert. "None of us are gonna make it anyway, not tonight. No way!" His words, faintly hysterical, startled me.

Reaching out, I shook him. "Don't be so foolish" was all I could say before the noise of exploding mortars drowned me out. I closed my fingers around the sleeve of his battle dress. He was twitching in time with the explosions. I sucked great gulps of air into my chest. I tried to focus on Albert's head, but in the darkness I couldn't make his face out.

Silence. Like a benediction.

Kerr abruptly yelled and pulled himself up, eyes bugging, staring to his right. The line of the canal had literally erupted, the bright explosions laced by tracers. "God almighty! Somebody's gettin' it but good!" he rasped. The rim of the night expanded, pushed by bright yellow tongues of exploding mortars and grenades until Able-Baker Company's low casa almost shone in stark relief.

"Baker Company wants all the Vickers fire we can provide laid on the bend in the dyke!" shrieked Cuthbert, slithering in between Kerr and I, his headset still around his head and under his helmet. Stupidly, I wondered if the cord was still plugged into his set.

Four or five mortars struck the bend, exploding in ragged unison and the shoulder of the embankment glowed yellow-white briefly. Tracers fled from the high windows in the *osteria*, then arched gracefully through the mist and gloom and rain like slender fingers probing the dyke.

"Can do," shouted Norm Hall, swinging his gun around and cocking it in one motion. Crawford followed his lead. Both guns began to chant — thump-thump-thump. They took their aim from every fourth or fifth bullet — a tracer — hosing the far dyke in the bend, then the faces of the buildings. The Jerry gunners in the *osteria* seemed to hesitate, bewildered by the sudden hail of .303s, recovered and returned fire in high-speed long bursts.

"Fuck 'em!" crowed Kerr. "They fire too fast! They'll never hit us at this range!"

The mortar stonk almost caught us sitting up, but the first two flattened in flame against the dyke ahead of us before the others came in. We scrambled behind the lip and rode it out, grunting and cursing and clenching and unclenching our aching hands.

It was 0100 hours plus brief minutes when the firefight ended.

We held our breath and listened to the rain, oblivious to the chill in the night.

"You'd think someone threw a switch, wouldn't ya," croaked Moose, rolling over on his back and gazing up into the mists.

"They must be comin' again," I panted.

Feverishly, we crawled back atop the dyke, fed fresh belts into the Vickers, inserted full mags in the Brens, slammed .303s up the spout of our rifles and .45s in our Tommy guns, and waited. Five minutes. Ten minutes. Until we were all aware of the cold seeping out of the wet embankment and into our stiffening bones.

"Possibly, gentlemen, our foe has run out of ammunition," whispered Greenwood.

Nothing.

"I'm goin' over the edge for a smoke, you comin'?" Kerr suddenly asked me.

The cigarettes tasted good. But the faint odor of gunpowder clung to the mists. Albert joined us.

"Who's got the handle up there?" I asked, nodding toward the top of the embankment.

"Don't worry," he said, lighting a cigarette off mine, "the Moose doesn't scare. An' he an Crawford are digging deeper pits."

Muffled explosions rippled through the night to the north.

I peered at Albert, then said slowly: "Old buddy, how's about you getting over to Able-Baker Company and collecting the rest of our section — Belanger, Verch, LeBlanc — 'cause if they're going to want us to really try an' cross the friggin' canal, we're goin' to need every man we can get. In fact, see if they got some extra bodies. OK?"

Albert peered at me obliquely. Circles had built up under his eyes. His face was paler than I had ever seen it, almost ashen in the gloom. He stood up slowly. "Anything you say, buddy." He sighed.

Kerr and I slumped against the embankment, listening to the faint crackle of Cuthbert's wireless set.

"Gettin' anything?" asked Kerr.

Cuthbert waggled his round head. "Sometimes. But it don't make much sense, like it's garbled. I don't think TAC knows whatinhell's goin' on. Hell, they think we're a whole friggin' company, if I read 'em right."

I was chewing gently on a chunk of bitter, issue chocolate when without warning a wave of mortars rained on Able-Baker Company's area. The three of us rolled over, cheeks pressed into the dyke.

Christ! I hope Albert wasn't caught in that, I said to myself.

The shower of mortar explosions continued, swinging behind us, lacing the Fosso Vecchio, then died out.

I fidgeted uneasily. Twice I crawled up to check on Crawford, Moose and Greenwood and the Halls. Even Al was digging. "Wouldn't mind at all if you could serve up some hot coffee or tea, Sarg," he commented grimly.

I felt like a nervous goddamned rabbit. "How're you feeling, Eddie?" I finally asked Kerr.

"Me? I'm gettin' cold. How about you? Worried about Albert?"

"Some."

"Don't. He's been around," Kerr consoled.

"Well, he's been gone near an hour, now. Mebbe he did get caught in that stonk..." I left the sentence unfinished.

Two more curtains of mortar and 88 fire came down behind us, then marched relentlessly toward the rear areas before petering out. And each time, we flattened face down against the embankment.

I stood up in the strange hush that followed the second one. My watch read 0335. "I'm going over to the rifle company," I said.

"Yeah? Well what about relieving Moose an' Crawford an' Greenwood and the Halls? They been up there a long time..." said Kerr, softly.

I had forgotten about them. "Right." I had turned to clamber up the embankment when Albert, Belanger and Verch, in front of a dozen Lanarks, bent double, loaded with ammo, burst out of the gloom. He was grinning his usual crooked grin.

"Drop the stuff here. An' get the Bren mags an' Vickers belts up on the dyke!" he rasped, hoarsely, poker-faced. I masked the elation I felt. "OK, Verch and Belanger, you haul it. Relieve Moose and his buddies."

Kerr posted the reinforcements from Baker Company along the length of the embankment.

The three of us, huddled together in the darkness, cautiously lit up, using Albert's U.K. wartime utility lighter. He blew a lungful of smoke out, watched it slowly dissipate. "Ol' buddy," he said, slowly, "it's better here than over in that Baker Company casa. It's filled with wounded, guys losing their minds, and..."

"Dead?"

"They're outside, against the rear wall." He shook his head, mournfully. "Like fuckin' cordwood, so help me Gawd." He puffed again. "I wasn't comin' back here. You knew that didn't you."

Kerr and I didn't respond.

"You don't have to say anything. But I knew, an' you knew, I was losin' my nerve." He suddenly laughed, harshly. "But not after I got in that friggin' casa. When I found out how many guys were really havin' troubles, I realized I didn't have many. You know what I mean? Christ! Fred and Eddie — have they ever taken a shit-kickin'. Hell, one guy thought he was havin' a baby."

"The casa been hit?"

"Yeah. But most of Able caught it drivin' the Jerries out of it. Baker? Out in the open, comin' up to help 'em."

"Where the hell are the tanks?" croaked Kerr.

"Comin'...comin'...that's all I heard. Soon's the engineers can get 'em across the Vecchio." He stared at us absently. "Scotty came up...had to go out, exhausted."

"They still want us to cross the canal?"

"Don't think so. According to Major — ah, Christ! I can't remember his name. Anyway, he said we were just supposed to hold, no matter what. No fallin' back."

Kerr grunted. "OK, then let's go up an' make goddamn sure every sonuvabitch is dug in and dug in deep. And got all the ammo they'll ever need."

Despite the chill, the rain, the mist, we worked with a will.

Dawn came slowly under the leaden, weeping sky. And with it a hail of machine-gun fire from the *osteria*. Moaning Minnies laced with mortars plowed the land behind us. We heard the ominous clanking of enemy armor before the first 88s hammered into the dyke, driving us deep in our trenches, rolling mud balls and grunting to conceal our terror.

A shell exploded violently outside the lip of the pit Albert and I were sharing. And the concussion took the air out of our chests. We shook our heads, rapidly, inhaling deeply.

"Christ!" groaned Albert and his words barely penetrated through the ringing noise in my head. "Now I know what it would feel like if an elephant stomped on my back!"

"You OK?" I managed to gasp.

The barrage of Jerry fire lifted and heads popped up in every slit trench.

"Here they come! Millions of 'em!" someone shouted.

They came over their dyke, bellowing and firing, in successive waves, right into our fire. And in the din, I could feel my blood pounding through my veins, my pulse racing. Seconds marked time.

There was no rain. No mist. No chill. Once, two Lanarks stood up, wide-eyed, indecision stamped in their pale faces. An invisible hand (or was it a fist?) reached out, scooped them up, then flung them to the ground, leaving them half in and half out of their rifle pit.

And then there were no more enemies. We panted in the stillness. From somewhere farther north on the dyke, a Bren gun chattered unanswered.

Slowly, warily, we checked out the two riflemen. Both were dead, their chests punctured by machine-pistol bullets.

"Anybody know 'em?" I yelled out at the Baker Company men. One shook his head. "Came up the other night. New guys," he replied.

"Get their ID discs and paybooks an' take 'em below the dyke," Kerr said.

"I knew one," a pimply-faced rifleman said. "Mugsy Carmichael, but he ain't ever tried to break for it before. Must've been tryin' to pull the other guy back down into the hole." He shrugged.

In the distance, behind the German-held dyke, we could hear the unmistakable sounds of enemy armor again.

"I don't like it," I whispered to Albert, "it can only mean those buggers are comin' again." I turned and yelled at Cuthbert. "Can you get TAC?"

"No way."

"Then get your ass over to Baker Company an' tell 'em to get through. We need artillery."

Cuthbert scuttled through the blasted furrows like a crab, pockets of swirling ground mist twisting smokily in his wake.

The first 25-pounders fell short and we watched in horror as they exploded closer and closer to the dyke.

"Jees-sus Chee-rist!" someone shrilled and we flung ourselves into our weapon pits.

In a staggered line, the exploding shells marched relentlessly up our side of the towering embankment, paused briefly while shredding the crown and canal bed, then resumed their explosive parade into the Germans' lines.

Shaken, but grinning sickly, a dozen steel-helmeted heads appeared cautiously out of the row of slit trenches and weapon pits.

"Holy Mother of God!" groaned a rifleman, "I'd hate like hell to be killed by one of our own shells." He shook himself.

"Y'hear the noise they make?" asked Crawford, breathing hard through gritted teeth and flared nostrils. "God I'm glad I'm on our side." Unaware of the chill rain, he lifted his steel hat high and shivered. "I don't think I like bein' shelled by those friggin' 25-pounders. Eeech!"

"Yeah? Well, you better let Baker Company know we been shelled by our stuff," Kerr said. He cocked his head. "I don't hear any Jerry armor any more, though."

"Hell, I don't even hear our stuff," Albert said.

Cuthbert was already chanting: "Baker One...Baker One. You gotta tell TAC we been dusted by our own artillery. Baker One...Baker One."

"All quiet on the Italian front?" asked Greenwood.

"Ah, Alex, y're far too educated for us."

We were forking cold bully beef out of tins and trying to make hardtack sandwiches when the first shell whistled low over our heads and exploded against the *osteria*. Eyes rounded and jaws went slack before Kerr croaked: "That friggin' thing was one of ours!"

"Where they firin' from?" asked Al Hall.

We peered through the gentle rain tumbling out of the grey clouds at the Fosso Vecchio behind us. Nothing. Another shell swooshed overhead, slamming into the *osteria*. Then a third. It was the signal for a barrage of 88s and mortars to churn the approaches to the Vecchio into a wall of stabbing yellow-colored explosions and great gouts of earth. Mindlessly, we went to ground.

"Shee-it!" grunted Kerr when it was over, "I was just gettin' used to the idea of those friggin' Jerry machine-gunners gettin' theirs in that damned *osteria*."

Albert and I went back down the embankment and resumed building bully beef hardtack sandwiches. "How long since we had some sleep?" Crawford asked plaintively.

Suddenly, I felt tired. "You didn't have to say that Crawford," I scolded.

"Too long," a voice remarked.

I stretched out, my back to the dyke and yawned, then closed my eyes, trying to ignore the muted sounds of gunfire both north and south of us along the Naviglio. My body was weary, but my alert system wouldn't let me really sleep. I gazed through hooded lids at the glowering sky. "Well," I said to nobody, "one thing's for certain — we aren't gonna get any air support on a day like this."

Someone was singing off-tune. "*I don't wanta walk without you...*

yas babeeee…no sireeee…la-la-la…no siree."

"That oughta scare hell out of any Jerries within listenin' distance," allowed Albert.

We dozed fitfully, but the staccato sound of enemy machine guns woke us each time. Once, I didn't know where I was, lying on my side, staring at the long, yellowish-brown sweep of the scarred dyke. "What's up?" I asked automatically.

Albert squatted over me. His mud-streaked cheeks sagged at the corners of his broad mouth. And for the first time since I had known him, I noted there were flecks of grey in his stubble. "Time to relieve Kerr, Moose, Norm Hall and the boys up top. Let 'em try and grab some shut-eye," he said.

"What time is it?" I asked absently, getting to my feet.

He grabbed my wrist. " 'Bout noon."

Eddie Kerr's eyes were like two pink stains in his dirty face. "Stay down," he warned, "there's been some snipin' comin' from around that fuckin' *osteria*." His large white teeth gleamed in his mouth when he forced a harsh laugh. "But so far, he's been a rotten shot. Just plunkin' 'em in close."

I glanced around at the men in the pits, their helmets spattered with raindrops. Al Hall's balmoral was a sodden blob of cloth on his head. "Well," I said, "it's good to see that crazy Hall still wearin' a soft hat."

Al heard me, looked up and scowled. "Screw you, Sarg," he said, and spat.

"We'll give you two hours. OK? Send Belanger and Verch, Crawford and a rifleman up, one at a time, an' your gang can rest up," I said to Kerr.

Two enemy shells, shushing like old women, sighed through the clouds above us and exploded deep behind the Fosso Vecchio.

I settled beside Crawford in the vee-shaped pit behind the Vickers. A bullet thudded wetly into the dyke crown about eight feet to our right. At first I thought it was just a stray then I remembered Kerr's warning. Idly, I searched the line of the canal, the *osteria* — ragged holes gaping where our guns had hit it earlier — but I couldn't see any wisps of smoke which could give him away. Fuck him, I thought.

The drizzling rain let up, but the clouds looked closer to the tortured fields than they had been. And the wind had risen, thinning the mists, chilling the living and the dead.

It was so quiet. Not a German, not a Canadian, could be seen. But they were there, waiting, watching, cold, physically drained yet tautly tuned mentally.

Only the sporadic shelling and mortaring in the rear areas shattered the clammy silence. I sighed, fighting my sagging eyelids to stay awake. Funny, I noted, the usual exchange of smart-ass comments between the men in the weapon pits had ceased. And most of them didn't even duck out of sight when an occasional mortar stonk plastered our side of the Naviglio. Helmets would merely bob in a kind of automatic recognition of the lethal explosions.

Crawford's stomach rumbled. To my surprise, I saw the lower edge of a shell dressing bandage running around his head beneath the rim of his helmet. "What hit you?" I asked.

"I dunno, Sarg." He lifted his steel hat off. There was a hole the size of a large walnut on the far side. "Piece of shrapnel, I think. Went in here," he stuck two fingers in the jagged opening, "ricocheted around on the inside and, far as I can tell, went out where it came in. Just creased me, almost right 'round." He grinned, his usually rosy cheeks streaked with dried mud. "So, I used my dressin' — just like I was told."

"For Chrissakes!" I mumbled. "Last night?"

"Some time this mornin'. Hell, Sarg, I didn't even know I'd been hit — 'cept for the wallop when it happened — until some blood ran down my nose." He laughed, a little too shrilly. "But I ain't goin' out, Sarg. I'm stayin' put. With you guys. Besides, with the stuff landin' behind us, I think it's safer up here."

I thought of the Bren carriers I had heard last night — evacuating the rifle companies' wounded and sick and exhausted. They had big red crosses painted vividly on their armored sides, but mortars and shells explode impersonally. Even in daylight.

"Yeah, you're probably right, Crawford," I said at last, "But change it when this shift is over, an' sprinkle in some fresh sulpha. OK?"

The staggered salvo of shells carrumphed into the *osteria*, kicking up showers of dust and stone chips with the suddenness of a summer storm, then a second and a third until the row of high casas was lost in the cloud of debris and flaming explosions.

"Jee-sus! They're ours!" rasped Albert. "Our tanks, firing from behind the friggin' Vecchio. Now the odds are beginning to even up."

Kerr and Greenwood scrambled up the embankment and slid feet first into our weapon pit as dozens of Canadian artillery shells whistled over our heads to explode behind the enemy positions. Then the Germans replied.

Caught in the middle, jammed inside our trenches, we were the unseeing (and unwilling) spectators to a forty-minute exchange of high explosives and armor-piercing shells that indiscriminately shattered guns, vehicles and men trying to get up and reinforce their beleaguered infantry. And no sooner had it died down in our sector, it erupted all along the line.

Two hours later, a troop of British Columbia Dragoon Shermans waddled across an improvised bridge over the Vecchio and reached our side of the Naviglio, their short-barrelled 75s jutting menacingly from power-operated steel-plated turrets.

Albert sighed. "Don't they look just bootiful," he drawled, "just bootiful!"

A cluster of enemy mortars dropped from the overcast sky, exploding crisply in front of the advancing BCD tanks. Commanders dropped out of sight and hatches slammed shut.

"Nice way to fight a friggin' war," noted Kerr, "just close the lid and y're safe."

"Nope," I said, "I watched one brew up after taking a direct hit. And I could hear the crew screaming, then I could smell 'em frying. Nope. I'll stay on the damned ground where there's lots of cover."

"If you know what're y'r doin'."

"Right, ol' buddy. And now we know what we're doing."

As night draped the land, the Red Cross carriers went back to work, hauling out casualties. And the rain and chill mists held everyone — the living and dead, enemy and friend — in their soggy clasp. Lieutenant Lafferty arrived with ammo and bully beef, hardtack and chocolate. In the gloom, he looked ten years older.

"Your people seem to be surviving, Sergeant," he greeted, tiredly. "How many casualties?"

"Three, not counting Crawford."

"Crawford? Isn't that him on the dyke?"

I nodded. "Just a slice off his hard head. You won't believe it Mr. Lafferty, but the fragment went through his helmet, raced around on the inside and went out the same hole, an' he just got skinned."

"I'd believe anything after last night."

"Baker got badly mauled, eh?"

"I don't have any company counts, but I heard someone at TAC say we've lost over 130 all ranks, not including the sick or...ah... exhausted."

The noise of gunfire to our south echoed through the night sky like rolling thunder. An 88 rushed overhead to explode in a sheet of flame against the Vecchio dyke. We bent our knees like punch-drunk fighters and hunched our shoulders. But not a man went to ground.

"Sorry to hear about Scotty."

Lafferty licked his lips. "Just went over the edge, for a while. He wasn't the only one." He unhooked his water bottle, "Got a sip of rum for all of you, just a sip. Keep away the chill. Even my good mother who won't allow the demon in the house would approve on a night like this."

Each gulped back a swallow, muttering, "Thanks sir."

"How long are we holding, or..."

Lafferty took a swig, stuffed the water bottle inside his dirty jacket and exhaled slowly. "We hold. An' tomorrow, providing the weather lifts, the Desert Air Force will hit the Jerries hard. An' with tanks for backup, the colonel says, late in the day the Westies will pass through the First Div bridgehead and right hook the bastards out of their positions across from us."

Suddenly, I knew the reason for the violent, explosive firefights to our south: Canadians had got over the Naviglio.

"I think, if I remember correctly, the Carleton and Yorks and Loyal Eddies secured it. Anyway, the Westies will exploit it, an' we'll jump across the Naviglio soon's we know they're breaking out, moving north toward us. OK?"

Kerr and I crawled from slit trench to slit trench. "Eat biscuits, chocolate, bully beef, whatever you got, an' conserve your water, OK?"

"I'd rather sleep, if you don't mind, Sarg," countered Crawford. "I'm so doggone tired."

"Everyone's tired, little fella," said Kerr, irritably, "but unless y'r on our side of the dyke...up here, you stay awake."

"How come I gotta eat?"

" 'Cause it's good for you, an' you can stay awake longer. OK?"

"When we moving across the canal?" hissed Al Hall.

"Early this evenin', mebbe later. It all depends on how fast the Westminsters can move along the friggin' dyke."

The runner from Baker Company gave us the word at 1930. "Go when the searchlights are turned on and the BCDs open up on the *osteria*."

The word passed.

And we waited, forgetting our fatigue, beginning to sweat despite the frost on the night air.

"You ever get used to this?" whispered Belanger.

"If you mean me, the answer is no. If you mean Al Hall, I don't think he even thinks about it one way or the other."

Belanger giggled.

The gunfire to our south was louder, even driving some of the men to ground. They'd rise, slowly, grinning sheepishly.

Waiting, I told myself, grimly, is worse than fighting. And there's only one thing worse than waiting, that's dug in too close to a nervous soldier, like Belanger. For an instant, I hated him. Where in hell was Albert? Or Kerr? Or Crawford?

"You think a couple of prayers might ease the pain?" hissed Belanger.

"Little buddy," my words were evenly spaced and brittle, "if it'll make you feel better, you can even take a shit in your steel hat." In my personal darkness, I cringed at my own callousness. Apologetically, I added: "Belanger, you do what you have to do. An' praying might help, if you can think of any."

I pulled myself out of my slit trench, patted his helmeted head and clambered up the slope of the dyke where out of the shadow of the high embankment I could make out the rest of the section manning the pits and trenches.

"Kerr?"

"Over here, with Albert and Alex."

I slid into the weapon pit on my buttocks, pulled my knees up and rested my back against the damp dirt wall.

"What's up?" asked Kerr.

"Nothing."

We sat in silence, listening to the crackle of machine-gun fire to our left. Two heavies shuddered overhead toward our rear areas.

"Some general or colonel is in for a surprise when those things land in," mused Greenwood. Thoughtlessly, we listened, waiting for the explosions sure to come. They were dull, like faraway booms.

"What's with the searchlights Lafferty was talkin' about?" asked Albert of no one in particular.

"It wasn't Lafferty, it was the Baker Company runner," I said. "Anyway, they're used to give us directions."

"Shee-it!" gritted Albert. "Who needs it? All you gotta do is head for where the firin's comin' from."

"And if there's an overcast, they can bounce the beams of light off the clouds and light the front up."

A star shell exploded in the night, and drifted, hissing and glowing toward our lines. Without the low clouds, its light was faint and fleeting. "But we got no overcast," noted Albert dryly.

"MacIntosh got it the other night," Kerr said, quietly as the darkness closed in again.

"Ah," I grunted. "Bad?"

"He was still alive when they took him out."

"Ah," I repeated. We had never been very close, but I had liked the burly west coaster. Even if he liked his vino and brandy too much. And I remembered the night Kerr and I had emptied our Tommy guns into three huge tins of *vino rossi* so their contents would spill across the muddy ground rather than wind up in any section water bottles. He had looked at me sadly, shook his head slowly and walked away in silence.

"What do you think?" Kerr persisted in talking.

"About what?"

The blond-haired son of a Saskatchewan homestead farmer nodded toward the enemy lines.

"Can't be a helluva lot more of 'em," I said, pausing to cluck my tongue against the roof of my mouth, " 'cause there must be forty or more of 'em lying on that friggin' canal bed."

"Nope," interrupted Albert, morosely, "Moose said he took a look just before last light an' they're all gone. They must've snuck out an' collected every one while we had our heads down sometime."

"And we never heard 'em?"

"Guess not."

"Christ!" I snapped, "they could've kept right on coming and overrun us."

"But they didn't, my Sergeant," droned Greenwood. "And think about it...the age of chivalry is not dead, if you'll excuse the non-intentional pun, not yet."

"Christ!"

Automatically, we checked our weapons, ammo pouches, hooked up our shovels and waited, huddled in the dank, growing gloom.

Heartbeats and seconds pounded by. I could only shake my head. I remembered the Highlanders' pipers and I couldn't rationalize why. But where, oh where, were they? Billy Gillis, Piper MacMillan, the MacLean? And I vividly remembered the sun-splashed, mortar-shredded Liri valley, the pipers, cheeks hard, sweat rolling down their faces, high-stepping across the ragged ground, each in his own cloud of the shrill, defiant notes of "Highland Laddie."

"We got no pipers," I muttered aloud.

Albert looked at me quizzically, then closed his eyes.

The searchlights' sudden dazzling light caught us by surprise. And the crash of our guns completed it. But, obediently, we rose to our soggy feet and, white-knuckled fighters clutching Brens, Tommy guns and rifles, we surged across the top of the dyke. Shovel handles hanging below small packs, water bottles gurgling on swinging hips and web gear straps biting into aching shoulders, Baker Company, reinforced by Dog and our section, plunged down its steep side on to the Naviglio's almost dry bed, then up the far embankment. And as we reached its towering crown, I flinched, half expecting a withering storm of machine-gun fire. I looked to my left at the line of Lanarks, strung out, panting, slipping and sliding as they crossed the flat ground, then in ragged confusion, plunged down the far side.

Tank shells slammed into the *osteria* on our right, driving long slivers of brilliant light through the eerie glow from the searchlights bathing the land. One building exploded in flames and burned fiercely.

At a lope, eyes darting from one shifting shadow to another, we labored forward toward a long, low shadow dominating the line where the black sky touched the rim of the earth.

One hundred yards. Two hundred yards. The black, squat shadow began to take shape. A casa.

Thirty yards to go. I swung to my right. "We're veering too far in that direction," I thought as I peered into the gap between us and Dog Company.

A single tracer exploded out of the casa and streaked between us. There was a stunning brief silence. We froze. The sound of the shot was still in our ears when half a dozen tongues of spitting flame seemed to erupt out of the casa wall.

Hoarse shouts and curses mingled with angry cries. The night air was filled with singing and hissing bullets. Men fell in mid-step, as though driven into the soggy ground by flailing fists. I dove frantically for a small fold in the ground. Aiming at the wall, I squeezed off two short bursts, rolled to my right, squeezed off several more. Goddamn Tommy gun! I thought savagely, they don't have the hitting power at this range! A string of bullets screeched over my head, and I almost burrowed into the muck and loam.

I scuttled further to my right, bullets chasing me. In a brief lull, I could make out Albert and Kerr and the Hall brothers, hugging the ground. Cautiously, slowly, I wriggled toward them.

"Holy Mother of God!" someone breathed.

I reached out. "Who's that?"

"Me. Crawford."

Two rifle company Bren gunners rose on their haunches to my left and cut loose long bursts into the casa's face. They hit the dirt face first, rolling sideways, when several quick-firing return strings of fiery tracers sliced through the night where they had been.

We lay on the ground, aware of the bullets following each other in the night, sweating, alternately panting, holding our breath and wincing.

"Well," said Kerr, stolidly, "we can't stay here, an' we can't get up. Now what?"

"Dog or Baker Company could swing 'round and hit 'em from the back side," I started, but repeated Spandau fire shut my words off. I buried my face in the dirt. Cursing, I lifted my head. "But I don't think we can wait that long."

"Like we're gonna have to turn this situation around?" hissed Kerr.

"You said it." I did a cautious pushup, peering to my left and right. "How many you think we got?"

"All of 'em," said Albert. "I think Dog Company took most of that opening fire."

"Okay," I grated. "Tell you what I think. We'll take 'em with the old game of cops and robbers."

"You mean cowboys an' Indians!" I recognized Moose's shrill, thin voice.

"Eddie, you take the Halls — no, leave Norm here. Ah, hell, take 'em both. They aren't afraid of anything when they're together, but one always worries about the other when they aren't. Take Alex, Albert, Crawford and Moose. It's just like you've practiced it, only for keeps. OK?"

Kerr nodded.

"Crawl off far's you think you got to, then go 'round to their back side. Use grenades and every automatic you got when you rush 'em. But get in as close as you can first, so you can lob the 36s inside the casa. When we hear 'em go off, we'll hit 'em from this side."

"That ain't cowboys an' Indians," squeaked Moose.

Kerr needed what seemed like years to get in position while the nervous Jerry gunners alternately fired over our heads or into the ground, chewing up our precious dirt protection. But when we heard the grenades exploding in the casa, we gathered our legs underneath our heaving bodies and literally catapulted low through the air and straight at the building.

It went off in perfect army pamphlet fashion. Only Crawford's head cut began to bleed after he bounced off the stone sill of a window, diving into the rear room and, helmetless, he stripped the scab off his forehead.

"Fuck me!" he panted, "that wasn't so tough." Reaching up with his free hand, he brushed some blood off his snub nose. "Shee-it! I'm comin' apart again."

Five Germans died in the explosions and follow-up fire, three were wounded and four survivors surrendered, still dazed by the ferocity of the short firefight.

An eerie glow from the battlefield searchlights pervaded the large, litter-strewn living room of the casa, outlining the four German prisoners, hands clasped atop their heads. I counted my slowing heartbeat. About eighty thumps a minute, I guessed, then wished Zwicker was handy to ask the POWs some questions.

Outside, the howl of Moaning Minnies and machine-gun fire was incessant.

Moose plunged into the room. "We got company comin'!" he panted.

"From which direction?" crackled Kerr.

Moose pointed through a shattered window. "That way."

We crouched low, staring through the unnatural half-gloaming, half-night and watched them closing the casa.

"There's seven, for sure!" hissed Albert.

They hesitated as if undecided, bunching up, crouching.

"Morning!" rasped Kerr, *sotto voce*, gently offering the password.

"Glory!" was the response, and you could almost feel the relief. Led by a corporal, his two hooks almost invisible under the mud staining his battle-dress jacket, they jostled into the room, stopped and gawked at the prisoners.

I didn't recognize him. "Dog Company?" I asked.

"Baker."

"Where's the rest of your platoon?"

"This is it — all that's left," he said, "me an' the six."

I was going to ask him who his sergeant had been, but the words caught in my throat. I didn't want to know. Instead, I said: "You got anybody who can speak German?"

He looked at his men. "Anyone?" They shook their heads like toy soldiers.

Kerr swung around, facing the prisoners. "Any of you guys speak English? *Versiand?*" he added in his own brund of pidgin German. For a brief few seconds, they returned his stare, impassively, ashen faced.

"Anybody?" repeated Kerr.

"A little," muttered one, "perhaps a little."

They were the survivors of a seventy-man company of the 117th Panzer Regiment which had defended the Naviglio for two days. Their orders had been to delay our attack to the last man, if necessary. Studying the German's sallow-complexioned features, I noted the lines running out from his thin nostrils to the corners of his mouth. They gave him an expression of utter resignation. And I wondered what he had looked like maybe three years earlier, marching or riding along sunlit roads, peering curiously at French or British or Russian prisoners heading toward the victorious Panzer armies' rear areas.

"We were gonna get over an' give you hand," the corporal was saying, "but we couldn't get regrouped quick enough." He grinned, exposing a gold tooth. "Anyway, you got it done. An' that's what counts, eh." He shuffled his feet. "OK, gang, we gotta get our asses up on that next canal." He prodded them toward the doorway, stopped, half turned and added: "We got a couple of Red Cross jeeps comin' up. I'll tell 'em you're here. Hey! You got any casualties? Besides them Jerries, I mean?"

"Nope," I said, "just the Jerries."

The corporal stood in the shattered doorway, his Tommy-gun butt on his shoulder, his right fist wrapped around the stubby barrel. "What a fuckin' week it's been," he said, smacking his thick lips together. "You know we're down to 'bout two companies, mebbe three. We got every guy who can breathe up front, pioneers, scouts, even spare cooks and clerks." He eyed the prisoners with smoldering contempt. "Christ! An' you guys think you got it tough! Me? I don't think I give a fuck anymore. Just do what I gotta do no matter who gets in the fuckin' way." He shouldered his way past the riflemen blocking him, walking quickly. "C'mon, gang! Like I said, let's haul our asses."

We listened to them until we couldn't pick up the sounds of their footsteps.

"So," said Greenwood, squinting at the empty doorway, "it's come to that."

Suddenly bone weary, I wasn't in the mood to listen to the educated Edmontonian's rhetoric. "Tell your men to sit down," I growled at the English-speaking Jerry, "an' smoke if they got 'em."

"I'm sorry, but we have had no cigarettes."

Albert extracted four Exports from his pack, tossing one to each. "Don't light 'em till you're sitting," he cautioned.

"What has it come to, Alex?" Crawford asked while the POWs lit up.

"He doesn't know," I grated, irritably.

Greenwood lifted his eyebrows. "Ah, but the great generals of history knew, like Napoleon who said when good soldiers get desperate, they are capable of doing anything, anything asked of them. They might die, but they must be victorious."

He rolled his pale blue eyes. "Translated into the vernacular of the Canadian infantryman, it suggests the men of the Canadian First Corps in Italy has reached the 'aw fuck it' point, meaning they can't stop. They're desperate."

"Jesus!" Moose's reedy voice, dripped with awe.

I couldn't tell if Greenwood was being glib or really knew what he was talking about, so I squatted on my hunkers and gazed moodily across the windowsill at the ribbons of shellfire and tracers sparkling in the distance. It reminded me, I thought, of the 24th of May.

We laid the German dead in a neat row under waterproof capes beside the wall they had tried to defend, then loaded the wounded and prisoners into two Red Cross jeeps and a Bren carrier and took stock.

"We hold here?" asked Albert.

"We move — up to the next friggin' *fosso* or canal, whichever comes first. Then dig in," I said, tiredly.

We had plodded two hundred yards before the night literally erupted in our faces. "Dig you bastids! Dig!" shrieked Kerr. And while Canadian heavy mortars and 25-pounders lobbed choking smoke shells across the sodden Fosso Munio, smoke that blew back into our positions, we forgot our terrible fatigue. Bent low, we dug mechanically, spading the wet earth out of the Godforsaken land, too exhausted to fling it far and wide, just shaking the sticky globs of earth off our shovels onto the ground beside the deepening pits.

Ammo parties brought up fresh mags and clips. We passed them from slit to slit, throwing empties into the darkness. I reached into my left pouch. Balled up at the bottom was the air mail from Francine. For a moment I considered smoothing it out and packing it carefully back in the pouch. Instead, I tossed it over the lip of the trench and, opening a pack of biscuits, munched slowly on a tough cracker, wishing idly that the Canadian Army bought its supply from the Yankees rather than the Brits.

"Yankee biscuits," I said to myself, "taste like arrowroot cookies, not goddamn concrete."

Twice during the next three days, weary Lanark riflemen staggered to their muddy feet and launched themselves across the thirty-foot wide Munio at the enemy-held far bank.

Both times, heavy machine-gun fire drove them back despite 4 platoon's attempts to neutralize the nests of Spandau gunners.

Finally, the Plugs made it, securing a small bridgehead about 1,000 yards farther down the waterway. It was the signal for an 11th Brigade assault by the Highlanders, the Perths and Toronto Irish — who dogtrotted through our positions shortly after 2000 hours.

"You'll be the foot-on-the-ground people," Lafferty messaged, "the firm base in case anything goes wrong."

"Good luck!" Kerr called hoarsely as they disappeared into the chill night. "And they got no artillery barrage, either," he whispered to me. "How come?"

I scratched my stained forehead. "I think I have fleas," I said, sadly.

"To hell with your fleas. How come there's no barrage?"

"Mebbe they've run out of shells..." coughed Moose.

Before I could consider those words, the distant night was streaked with flickering lines of hard light, followed by the shrill yammering of dozens of quick-firing Jerry automatic weapons.

To a man, we peered into the gloom with straining eyes, a gloom now punctured by the harsh, erratic drumming of exploding grenades.

Albert yelled first. "Christ! Here they come!"

Vickers were cocked, rounds rammed up the barrels of rifles and Brens. We hunched behind our weapons, half out of the slits. My scalp tingled under my steel helmet when I finally made out the dim forms of dozens of men lurching across the plowed ground toward us.

"Don't shoot! For Chrissakes don't shoot!" It was a despairing, high-pitched scream.

. In our instant of indecision, they tumbled among us, Irish infantrymen who had survived the scathing fire that had blown away their leading buddies. One landed feet first in my slit, almost breaking my right leg with his steel-shod issue boots. He was panting like a miler who had just finished his run, his shoulders twitching violently.

I stared into a round-eyed, dirt-smudged face. "What happened out there?" I managed, yanking my leg from under him.

He wheezed. "Hundreds of 'em! Spandaus! All over the fuckin' place! We never had a friggin' chance!" I thought he was going to cry, but he took a big breath and shook himself. His heaving chest told me he was fighting for self-control, digging deep inside himself for the reserves of nerve that had carried him through the endless days and nights since the first time he had gone into action. Slowly, like a man coming out of shock, he lifted his head.

"We should have had an artillery barrage," he said, dumbly. "We should have. Then we'd have made it." His words trailed off and I saw the three hooks on his sleeves.

In the darkness, I wanted to reach out and pat his shoulder. Instead, I stood up. "Eddie! Albert!" I hissed.

Like crabs, they scuttled across the uneven ground. "I know," Kerr whispered, "the Jerries could be comin' any minute. I've already passed the word, but how're we gonna sort out these Irish guys?" He swung both his arms in a semicircle where the panting riflemen clung to the dirt, flat out behind slabs of turned-up earth and small hummocks.

"Tell Cuthbert to contact TAC. Get the word back on what's coming down," I said.

Albert nodded and, turning, disappeared up on the low crown of the Munio dyke.

The Irish sergeant had won his personal fight. He climbed awkwardly to his feet and cocked his Tommy gun. One corner of his mouth twitched. "Can you ask 'em to contact our company? I saw our signaller go down, so we got no wireless."

"Can do," snapped Kerr, breaking for the dyke.

"In the meantime," the Irish sergeant said, "my guys will dig in." He took a large breath and blew a stream of steamy breath into the chill night and extended his hand. We shook.

Only the sounds of shovels biting into the thick soil broke the stillness while we watched and waited for the usual German counter-attack. My eyes watered and shoulder muscles cramped and the minutes dragged by. A small rivulet of sweat ran down my back and I was idly wondering how far it would go when the skyline to our left was torn apart by fiery fingers of heavy machine-gun bullets, followed by muffled explosions.

Kerr executed a perfect hook slide before collapsing into my slit trench, as two parachute flares exploded dully above us, turning night into glaring day.

"TAC says they contacted the Irish and they're calling up artillery so's they can have another go!" The words gushed out of Kerr's mouth.

"What the hell's goin' on to our left?" I asked.

"The Perths have gone in."

The flares fizzled out, hissing, while a cluster of our 25-pounders whistled over our heads, exploding in shrill cracks! three or four hundred yards ahead of us. A second then third salvo slammed into the enemy lines.

"Mebbe that's why we didn't get a counterattack," I offered.

"Yeah. Mebbe. Just the same, I'll tell that Irish sergeant what he's expected to do...where is he?"

I pointed to a hump of black shadows. "This side of that..."

We watched the Irish riflemen rise silently out of their makeshift slits, fan out to our right, then plod stoically forward until they were lost from sight. And as the violence on our left dwindled down, it erupted again directly to our front.

German and Canadian artillery were dueling in the gloom when the Irish runner came panting into our position. "We're pinned down again," he spluttered, " 'bout one hundred yards ahead of here — but diggin' in." He cocked his head, listening as shells slithered overhead. "Funny," he observed, "they never seem to collide, do they?" He shrugged, "Well, I gotta go, Sarg, see ya!"

First light followed the sleepless long night. Intermittent firefights raged all along the line before the appearance in the fast-clearing skies of the Desert Air Force. It was the strings of whistling Spitfires, their 20-millimeter cannons spewing shells into enemy positions, that put an end to them.

"MacNeil," I said, lighting my first smoke in hours, "you look like a sixty-year-old man."

He picked at dried mud on his sleeve. "I'm even older than that on the inside."

My stomach rumbled. "I could eat a horse and chase the driver for the second course," I said.

"Cuthbert says there's grub comin' up early this afternoon," said Kerr. "Anybody got an extra cigarette? I'm out."

I threw him my last pack. "Take a handful."

Kerr lit up and handed it back. "What for? They'd only bust up in my pocket." He exhaled a thick cloud of smoke. "Where in hell's the armor? First, we got no artillery, now there's a shortage of Shermans. Everybody goin' home to leave us to finish this friggin' war on our own?"

It was so quiet, we began standing up, yelling across the gaps between slit trenches to each other. "Hey, Sarg," Moose squealed, "you think the war's over?" He laughed shrilly.

"Yeah," yelled Crawford, "an' the generals are leavin' us here to find our own way out."

The troop of Lord Strathcona Shermans was almost on our positions before we were aware of them. Chugging and grunting, the twenty-eight-ton tanks played follow the leader along the narrow road flanked by leafless poplars. We waved. The first tank halted, forcing the others to pull up.

"Hey!" shouted Kerr, "where ya been? It's all over now!"

The tank commander waved back. "We're headin' for the Senio where the action is!" he replied, good-naturedly. The Shermans snorted, blowing puffs of black smoke out of their tailpipes, and moved slowly forward.

Lieutenant Lafferty arrived in a Bren carrier as the pale winter sun slid toward the horizon, followed by six of the low-slung armored vehicles and a company jeep stacked with a dixie of still-warm stew, another with tepid tea, biscuits and cigarettes.

"You ride from here," he greeted, "like you were supposed to from day one."

Messtins and enamel cups were lifted out of small packs in the carriers. Lafferty spilled what he termed a "warming dollop" of rum into each mug of tea which was thrown back in a gulp. Then we ate with relish.

Kerr wiped his mouth with the back of his right hand. "OK, Mister Lafferty, what's coming down?" he asked, quietly.

"Jerry's pulled back to the Senio. Beaten. That's what's come down." He blinked tired eyes in a tired, lined face. "The Highlanders, Perth and Irish are on the Senio. The enemy caved in after the First Div turned their right flank."

It sounded like a piece of cake, I thought morosely, the way he says it.

"Where was the artillery when this thing started?" I asked.

"Or the tanks?" chipped in Kerr.

Lafferty bit his lip. "The tanks couldn't get across the Munio below here. They needed medium artillery to clear the way. Our artillery? The 25-pounders? Well, to be honest, I don't know. But I hear rumors...rumors that we're a little short of ammo. Temporarily."

"An' what about that firefight to our left? Where the Perths went in?" asked Albert.

Lafferty shook his narrow head. "Took one helluva beating, I hear." He sighed. "We got off lucky. Just a couple in the rifle companies," he said, unconvincingly, because he was only too aware that we weren't involved in the 11th Brigade assault. We just sat, firm on the ground as the issue pamphlets would state. Digging and ducking, we called it.

"By the way," Lafferty continued, "we're going to get Wasps, flamethrowers. The fuel will be carried in special tanks mounted behind the battery boxes. The Perths have 'em and said they scared hell out of the Jerries."

We laagered through the night, moving off the next morning, the large wireless in Lafferty's set spluttering faintly. We crossed through the vineyard where the Irish had been ambushed, each man alone with his thoughts when we glanced at the bodies of those who had been cut down at the moment the advancing riflemen had come under the heavy fire.

It was the sight of more than thirty Perth infantrymen, huddled in death along the length of a stretch of roadside ditches, that froze my mind. I watched as Lafferty deliberately turned his head away, then rapped his driver's steel-helmeted head to speed up. Despite the cool wind rushing by my ears, I could hear him say: "They took a helluva beating."

One hour later we reached the Lanarks' battalion area. "We're goin' out for Christmas," Lafferty said, emerging from TAC, "Ravenna."

I looked at Albert. "What day is it?"

"I dunno. Must be near Christmas."

"It doesn't feel like it," I said. "Hell, it doesn't even look like it should be Christmas."

"What's Christmas supposed to look like, Sarg?" asked Crawford.

I looked up at the grey skies, at the yellow-brown ground, a shattered casa standing in a scarred orchard.

"I don't know any more," I said.

Neither did I know that 2,344 Canadians had been killed or wounded in fewer than twenty days of savage fighting.

CHAPTER FIFTEEN

T HE 23rd of December 1944 dawned chilly and cloudy over Ravenna, just inland from the grey and often whitecapped Adriatic. And outside of the officers and men on duty, what remained of the Lanark and Renfrew Scottish Regiment of Canada slept in, blissfully unaware that it was the eternal resting place of Dante Alighieri who had composed the immortal *Divine Comedy* sometime toward the end of the thirteenth or beginning of the fourteenth century.

The ragged, dirty odds and sods with the "Canada" patches on their shoulders were also blissfully unaware that Dante's classic was the narrative of a journey through Hell, up a mountain named Purgatory which led, eventually, to the presence of God.

I shaved the face reflected in the broken mirror, carefully scraping the suds off my lean jaw, wondering if the bloody veins in my slate-colored eyes would ever totally disappear. The mobile bath was next, turning in dirty socks, underwear and shirts for scalded, steam-cleaned issue.

"I was beginning to wonder if the only change I'd ever get would be with you or Albert," grinned Kerr.

"Yeah, well I'm going down to stores to get our beer and whiskey rations and chocolate," I said, feeling ten years younger and a century fresher than I had in three weeks. "You know what God says: 'The first man in gets full rations, the last gets what's left after the one-thousand-mile snipers at echelon have skimmed off more than their share.'"

"An' I'll see how much mail's waitin' for us," said Kerr.

It was half a bottle of gin and a quart of VO per sergeant and three bottles of beer per man, plus British milk chocolate bars for all. The mail hadn't caught up, the postal clerk, a paunchy twenty-one-year-old with rickets who shouldn't have been allowed to even enlist, told Kerr regretfully.

"Let's stash the booze an' beer for a section party later tonight," offered Albert.

Colonel Buchanan talked easily that afternoon, pointing out there was a men's club, the Maroon, five cinemas (which made Albert comment that we used to call them shows, but we've been away from home so long we didn't know any better), and an overabundance of fresh air for all ranks.

"That, men, wasn't planned, I can assure you," he said, referring to the shattered windows in our billets — a collection of community buildings, baths and schools. "But being a trifle cold is one helluva lot better than being shelled."

He also told us what we already knew: The Lanarks had suffered horrendous casualties, wounded, killed, exhausted and sick. "Consequently, we're going to have to reorganize, for the time being."

Reorganization for the time being meant the scout and antitank platoons would be converted to riflemen to beef up understrength infantry companies; that the remnants of Baker would be divided among Able, Charlie and Dog, giving the regiment three fighting companies of 110 men each.

"The machine-gun section will be used to thicken our line next time in, the other support company platoons form our reserve," he said, then paused, peering into his men's faces. "You've done every goddamned thing you've been asked to. And more. I'm proud of each and every one of you, down here in a sideshow war, tying up and whipping crack enemy units." He paused again. "And no matter what the future brings, I know you — all of you — can handle it."

He looked at his watch. "There'll be reinforcements. The general says so. And mail. And Christmas dinner. Enjoy yourselves, you've earned it."

We broke up, shuffling each toward his own billet. Curious, I reflected, times are changing. We used to cheer when the Old Man spoke, now we just listen.

Reinforcements were trucked in late that afternoon. Albert and I were ordered to parade them to an Eyetie public bathhouse, temporarily operated by the service corps. Albert recoiled like he had seen a column of ghosts when they marched up to the company office. "My God!" he coughed, "they're just a bunch of children!"

They stood in three ranks, floppy balmorals at every different angle on every different head.

"An' either the goddamned army is runnin' out of uniforms, or bodies, because not one of 'em fits inside his damned battle dress." He shook his head, sorrowfully. "OK, let's hike — by the right, quick march!"

Inside the long shower room, the recruits stripped quickly, their pale, untanned bodies almost obscene in their whiteness. Hot water pushed faint clouds of steam in all directions. Albert and I undressed. "I'm never turnin' down a shower," he said, "because you never know when you're gonna get another one."

It began as horseplay, flying soap and snapping towels.

"Wait'll we get them friggin' Germans in our sights!" shouted one scrawny nineteen-year-old with his brush-cut lathered in suds. "Hell, we'll drive 'em all the way to Berlin."

I towelled myself vigorously, thinking back to a year earlier (was it *only* one lousy year?) when we had bragged our way through the 1st Div lines, telling the men with the red patches on their shoulders how we'd show the Jerry paratroopers what real men could do.

"I'm gonna get me one for my brother!" whooped a chunky, swarthy kid with so much hair on his chest that it even sprouted on his shoulders. "I promise!"

"What for?" yelled another.

"Them bastards killed him in Sicily, that's why!"

Yeah, I thought, you'll be too damned busy ducking and digging to keep that promise.

"Hey, Corporal!" shouted a muscled youngster with a pretty-boy face, molded in perfect proportions around a mouthful of gleaming white teeth, "how many Nazis have you stuck like pigs?"

Albert, his solid body and legs still marked off in tans and whites, was bent over, drying his feet. He straightened up slowly, scowling, "What'd you say, soldier?" he asked tautly.

"How many of the friggin' Nazis you pig stick?" He repeated the words distinctly, but nervously. His white teeth disappeared behind compressed lips.

There was an odd silence, broken only by the hiss of water.

Albert began talking softly. "Nobody pig sticks anybody, sonny. They dig, run, duck, scream, roll mudballs and hope to hell they stay alive." His voice rose an octave. "An' that's what y're gonna do, if you're gonna stay alive. Whatta ya think this is? Some kind of fuckin' game? Like in Hollywood? Where guys roll around, clutching their bellies and flailin' their arms? Where everybody gets up after it's all over?" Now his voice was carrying from one end of the bathhouse to the other. "You'll just do what you gotta do, when you gotta do it. An' if someone gets killed you won't remember it. An' if you get killed, you'll never know what hit ya. You'll just be another goddamned casualty," he shouted. "You understand?" He glared at them all. "Now get dried and get your fuckin' clothes on. You gotta be checked out by the MO and dental officer. We don't want no damaged merchandise in this regiment!"

We won two of them, Tex O'Leary and Tiny McKee.

Tex stood two hands higher than a pony. "Everybody calls me Tex," he drawled, " 'cause that's where ah hail from, Texas." He beamed for the first time since he had gone to the bathhouse. "An' ah'm gonna be y'r Red Cross soldier." He lifted the armlet from his tunic pocket and held it up for us to look at.

"Good," said Kerr, "we ain't had that luxury for a while."

"What in hell would a Texan want to join the Canadian Army for?" asked Crawford, sensing the sturdy American was younger than he was.

"Ah couldn't get into the U.S. Army. They said ah was too short an' too young. Seventeen."

"You coulda lied a little."

"Ah didn't think-a that in Texas, but ah sure knew better when ah tried in Canada," he retorted. "How old're you?"

"None of y'r business," sighed Crawford. He reached down low on the rope he had in his left hand and yanked his dog roughly. "C'mon, Stupid, let's get outta here."

"Nice dawg you got, friend," responded Tex.

Tiny McKee stood over six feet in his army-issue boots and weighed in at about 175 pounds. "But I'm strong, Sarg, strong's a horse."

"Where's home?"

He grinned, amiably. "Toronto."

"Beach?"

"Parkdale."

And Howie MacLeod was back. "You look fit like a bull fiddle!" greeted Kerr. "And the medics must've thought so too."

Howie's face smiled, but his eyes had a haunted look. "I had two offers: go to a permanent work crew or back to the unit." He stared at the wall. "I'll be okay," he said softly, "don't worry about me."

Albert, Kerr, Greenwood and I sat together in the half light of the late afternoon, swigging from a bottle of VO.

"Yuh, know something?" Kerr said, "I think the colonel was counting those reinforcements when he said we'd have three companies instead of the usual four and a full support group."

"Figures," Albert said before throwing back a gulp, wiping the neck of the bottle and passing it over to Greenwood who took a long pull, sighed and smacked his lips.

"Well, they look like nothin' at all," he allowed, "but they're better than the Zombies sitting at home, refusing to go."

Albert spat. "Who needs 'em? They can sit on their tails till hell freezes over. We'll do alright. I don't want anybody with me I can't trust."

Crawford broke up our party before the VO was half finished. "The mail's in, Sarg!" he shrieked excitedly. "It's at regimental HQ. I saw the trucks an' they're loaded for bear!"

I shuffled my letters in order of their postmarks, with the oldest on top of the stack. Those from my mother and father read like each one I had received since leaving the U.K. "We all worry about you ... everyone's fine...one of the McAlister boys is reported missing in action over the North Sea. The youngest Wilson lad was killed in Holland." It's odd, I mused, I barely recall what they looked like. "Your father doesn't say much, but I know in my heart, he's thinking of you all the time," penned my mother. "Your mother is always talking about you, telling anyone who will listen what a happy little boy you were," noted my father.

"Your sister joined the Women's Air Force, did I tell you?" my mother asked. No, she hadn't. "And your brother, Reg, he's been shifted from Labrador (on guard duty) to Niagara-on-the-Lake where he's driving for the camp general, I forget his name, my son. And I pray for you, every night, every Sunday at mass. It's so quiet in the neighborhood what with all the boys away." Away. That's my mother, I thought, she simply can't say overseas.

Francine's first letter was all news, and her sign-off, I noted wryly was back to "as ever." I chuckled inwardly, as I concluded she must have been randy the night she wrote the earlier letter. Her second gave me hell in no uncertain terms for neglecting to write. I chuckled again.

Swiftly, I penned two fold-up airmails, one to Francine, pointing out there was a war on and I was involved in it. To my parents, I repeated the words I had used for months: The regiment is on rest, I'm fine and my love to all.

"There!" I said, "my duty's done."

"I should make carbon copies, enough to last till this friggin' war's over," chortled Kerr, "and make a deal with the postal clerk to send one home once a week until further orders. Except, I guess, they need 'em — whatever we say."

"Ah, the cynical sergeants," drawled Alex. "You need them, too, whether you admit it or not. They are links with the real world at home."

Silently, I confessed he was right because if he was not, then why didn't I tear them up? I glanced at Kerr's bland face. It signalled he agreed.

I had two parcels from home, one packed with canned butter (that made me drool), stuffed olives, cigarettes, candy bars, socks and a mickey of Dewar's Scotch packed inside a cake that had long since hardened. The contents of the second caught me by surprise. In it, neatly fitted together, were tin paint boxes complete with brushes, coloring books, a small box of Tinker Toys, bundles of lollipops, a wooden duck on wheels that quacked when pulled across the floor, three Raggedy Ann dolls and half a dozen red-mesh Christmas stockings. The note in my mother's neat handwriting was explicit. "These, my darling son, are for some Italian children who, if everything I read in the papers is correct, won't have much of a Christmas. Do find a family and be a Santa Claus for a few minutes."

While Kerr, Greenwood and Albert stared wordlessly at the gifts, I was so overwhelmed by my mother's loving thoughtfulness that I couldn't think of a word to say. There, I thought, a million miles away, living with her own personal terror and fears, she could still feel for people she didn't even know, wouldn't even understand. And I could see her, poking around in Simpson's or Eatons, or Woolworths, peering at the toy counters, mentally saying "That will do, nicely" as she attached each item to an imagined Italian child.

"Well, I'll be goddamned!" exploded Kerr, "who'd have ever thought of that!"

I shook my head. Only Katherine Sarah MacNeil Cederberg, I replied to myself.

Christmas Eve, the four of us prowled the windy, dark streets of downtown Ravenna until we intercepted an Eyetie woman we judged to be a mother.

"*Aspetta!*" I said in my best Italian.

She was in her early thirties, full bodied, her dark eyes took me in quickly, reflecting a mixture of uncertainty and fear. She took a half step, but Kerr blocked her off.

"*Aspetta, Signora.* And ah, *Buon Natale!*" he said, grinning.

Whatever the woman replied, we didn't understand. "*No comprendo*, lady. *No comprendo* at all," said Albert.

Greenwood was carrying the box of toys. He opened the interlocking flaps, holding it almost up against his chest. She shrank back, her mouth wide open and for a second I was convinced she was going to scream.

"Toys. See, toys, *per bambini. Su bambini per Natale.* See?" soothed Greenwood.

In the gloom, the woman lowered her face almost into the box. She looked up, bewildered, glancing from face to face.

Albert lifted out the wooden duck, set it on the pavement and walked a couple of paces, pulling it behind him. The wheeled duck obediently quacked repeatedly. "*Per su bambini* ... see, lady?"

She gasped. "*Si!*"

"*Avete bambini, signora?*" Greenwood asked.

"*Si, si. Tre.*"

"How many'd she say? Three?"

"Yep."

The woman laughed nervously. "*Buon Natale!*" she said, trying to turn away from us again.

"Jesus, *signora*, it's *Natale* ... and these goddamned toys are for your kids," said Albert, exasperation all over his homely face. "*Per su bambini!*"

"*Dove su casa, signora?*" asked Alex, politely and patiently.

Cautiously now, comprehension flooding her face, she lifted two coloring books and a Raggedy Ann doll clear of the box. "Ah, *per Natale* ... *Grazie, Canadesi signori, grazie.*" Her words tailed off. She sighed, shrugged, then spoke in rapid Italian. We shook our heads. "Ahhh," she signalled, taking Greenwood's arm, "you come with me."

Her name was Anna and she lived in a one-room ground-floor apartment with her ancient mother and three children, two girls, nine and eight, and a boy, six. Mother, shawled against the chill in the over-furnished room, watched us like a hawk through hooded eyes. Her husband, an officer, had been shipped to north Africa four years earlier and she hadn't heard a word from him, or about him, since 1942.

The children, shy in the beginning, warmed to us quickly, following the first round of lollipops and finally climbed unabashed into any available lap after the coloring books, paints and stockings had been handed out.

Albert made a quick trip to the Regimental cookhouse, scrounged half a dozen tins of bully beef and Anna cooked up noodles. It was a hot, cheery meal, broken by the kids' squeals of delight and our awkward attempts to carry on a conversation with their mother.

The quacking duck was a howling success — except for grandma who never took her suspicious little eyes off us.

Out in the street, sober, stuffed with home cooking, feeling better than we had in months, we returned to the billets, shrouded in utter darkness behind windows hung with blankets to block the chill winds. I almost stepped on a dozen snoring sleepers before I got the half bottle of VO, Kerr's issue quart and the mickey of Dewars. Fully armed for serious drinking, we located a small empty room, sat on the floor, backs to the walls, and sipped.

"So," grunted Kerr, "it's back to the Senio in three days." He wiped his mouth with the back of his hand. "I hope the hell the 11th Brigade has pushed the Jerries right off those big banks and 'cross the friggin' river."

"Betcha they haven't," rasped Albert. "They're too damned tired, just like the rest of us."

"Even our enemy may be too tired," commented Alex, "too tired to retreat any more."

"It reminds me of two punch-drunk fighters, waitin' for the final round, all beat up, but they gotta go when the bell sounds," Kerr said, sourly. He stared at Albert as he passed the quart to him. "You got nothin' to say?"

MacNeil shivered. "Somebody just walked over my grave," he said, quietly.

Alex sniffed at the air. "Only one of a Celtic origin would make such a superstitious statement."

A flicker of annoyance flitted across Albert's face. "I know what I know," he said, doggedly.

I lit a cigarette off Kerr's glowing butt, inhaled and blew a cloud of smoke toward the ceiling.

"Do you consider yourself fey?" persisted Alex.

Albert frowned. "You mean queer?"

"Certainly not. It's fey. F-e-y, and it means doomed. Do you have a sense you are doomed?" Greenwood spoke softly, like a sensitive surgeon probing for a piece of shrapnel or a bullet.

"No. But I got a feeling."

I took two swallows out of the mickey. "Oooof! That's got some barbed wire in it!" I gasped, trying to change a subject I instinctively disliked.

"Tell me about it," said Greenwood, extending his right hand for the bottle.

"All he said was somebody walked over his grave, Alex," I interrupted, testily, "an' you're trying to make a friggin' federal case out of it."

Greenwood held the mickey to his lips, staring at Albert, a small smile playing on his thin lips. "Tell me about it, Corporal MacNeil."

Albert shrugged. "I got a feeling 'cause we've been too god-damned lucky since 'way back in September. And that tells me the law of averages has gotta catch up — sometime."

"Bullshit!" The word exploded out of my mouth. "We're not lucky, we're good. An' you better believe that!"

"Amen," mumbled Kerr.

Albert was agitated. "I'll buy that, but so were a lot of other guys. And they bought it!"

I started to sing softly, "*When this fuckin' war is over...*"

Greenwood giggled, poured back a mouthful, giggled again. "You always sing that rude song when you're getting loaded, don't you."

"*Oh, how happy I will be!*"

He reached over and tapped me on the knee. "Sergeant, do you know that I am the most faithful husband in the entire Canadian Army, excluding Catholic padres, of course. I have never had intercourse with any woman since leaving my wife in '39."

I stopped singing in mid-note, "What in hell brought that on?"

"If Corporal MacNeil is correct, then we could all be doomed."

My mouth opened. I sat bolt upright, looking straight into Kerr's face. "Eddie," I said, feeling like a base runner leaning the wrong way during a pick-off, "I also got a feeling. They're both goofy."

"And if we are all doomed, I must tell you that I — on this Christmas Eve, 1944 — I not only crave feminine companionship, but I insist on one last piece."

"You want to throw a perfect record away just because a dour Canadian of Scottish descent gets down in the mouth when he's drinkin'?" I shouted.

Someone in the next room pounded on the wall and yelled: "Go to sleep, ya drunken buggers! Go to sleep!"

Eventually we did. Vague fragments of troubling dreams tumbled through my head, fragments I couldn't remember when I got to my feet, blinking, stretching my stiff arms and legs. My breath was so strong, it almost knocked Kerr down.

"Sheesh!" he moaned, "go brush y'r friggin' teeth before you kill somebody."

On the theory that drinking was too personal and serious a pastime to be enjoyed during a regimental spree, Kerr, Albert and I drank moderately Christmas Day. But we began sipping with a purpose early on Boxing Day. We paid for our purpose, waking on the 27th amid cigarette butts and empty whiskey bottles while the December sun shone feebly.

"Ah, dear God," muttered Kerr, "what would make a man do a thing like that?"

"It must've been the sleep that did it," grunted Albert, "because the last thing I remember was feelin' right good."

Bren carriers piled high with ammo, packs, rations, weapons, we clambered in to gaze numbly at the rolling, flat brownish country-side while the regiment rolled north and east along Route 16 toward the Senio River where we would relieve the Highlanders.

"You know the Jerries strafed and did a little bombing over Ravenna last night?" shouted Crawford as the cold wind whistled around my aching head.

I shook my head. "Nope."

"I didn't think so." Crawford's rosy cheeks had been nipped even rosier by the biting breeze. I could hear him laughing to himself.

The sounds of enemy vehicle motors were muffled by the twenty-five-foot high grassy flood-control dykes flanking both sides of the Senio. And from where we were holed up — in a casa some 100 to 150 yards south and east of them — the embankments looked like sheer walls even in the shadows of night.

"Trucks, I think," said Kerr, cocking his head, "but I wonder what in hell they're up to."

"Long as they aren't comin' our way, I couldn't care less," quipped Howie, tensely.

Our casa was sturdy and two-floored, set back a few yards off the Via Rossetta, a paved road running roughly parallel to the Senio River. Leafless rows of shell and mortar-shredded peach trees rose unevenly between the road and the first dyke. Sited on the regiment's extreme right — attached to Dog Company — we were fourteen men, two Vickers, an assortment of Brens, Tommy guns and rifles.

Mr. Lafferty had told us: "There's one thousand yards between you and the Plugs on your right. You'll make sure no Jerries exploit that gap, and you'll support Dog when they try to clear the embankment on our side of the river. Dog's platoon on your left is led by Mr. Bodnaruk; you've got him if you get into trouble. And there's always your 19 wireless set to TAC."

The relief had gone without incident minutes after the short winter dusk: no enemy interruption or fireworks of any kind. "He's been pretty quiet the last few days," a sad-eyed Highlander platoon looie I didn't recognize said, wearily. "Celebrating Christmas, I guess. Just like you chaps."

We laagered our three carriers behind the south wall and a husk stack before the last of the Highlanders had trooped out, foot-slogging to a pickup area.

Kerr posted lookouts in the perimeter slit trenches, while Albert, the Halls and I manhandled the Vickers and ammo to the upper storey where Moose had sledgehammered two traverse firing slits, punching them through the sturdy stone wall.

"Goddamn but it's cold," I snorted, the exertion not enough to fight the chill. "Let's have a small fire."

And while the flames chased away the wintery chill, we smoked.

I turned to Albert. "You recognize that Highlander looie?"

"Nope. An' I didn't recognize even one of the men, either. Not a single one," he said sadly. "An' think about it, I used to be a corporal in Able Company — a long, long time ago."

"An' there were only eleven of 'em."

Albert shrugged. "We're supposed to be more'n thirty, aren't we?"

Howie's face was pure grey even in the firelight.

"This better be a nice, quiet night," I said, at last.

Howie's grin wasn't reflected in his eyes. "That CBH looie said it was quiet up here."

I was thinking. Four men in the holes, one up top, that's five. We can manage three shifts. "Two on, four off," I said aloud, "everybody takes a shift. OK?"

Nobody replied. They were listening to the sounds of the enemy vehicles again.

"Eddie? You make contact with Mr. Bodnaruk's platoon?" I asked.

"McKee an' I. You gettin' forgetful? Right after I posted the sentries. They're snug like bugs."

I sighed and closed my eyes. "I'll take the next go-round, Eddie, wake me at 2100." Then I remembered Cuthbert and his wireless. He was propped up against the wall beside me. I nudged him. "You make damned sure that set of yours is working, OK?"

"Sure, Sarg, sure."

The high, pale stars and full moon gave way to dawn. We stood-to, manning the upper storey and slit trenches. And as the sun rose, Jerry snipers peppered our casa with bullets while we cautiously scanned the embankment for their positions.

"What's that fuckin' red-brick tower over there?" asked Crawford, pointing several hundred yards beyond the dykes.

"A church tower, what else? An' they're probably using it for an observation point," someone replied.

"Shee-it!" lamented Crawford, "they can see right down our throats!"

Swooshing briefly before impact, a stonk of Jerry mortars crashed down between us and Dog Company, flinging shrapnel, pebbles and dirt off our casa walls. "An' they just proved it," said Crawford, lifting his head, slowly.

I was rousing the sleeping men for stand-to when the first armor-piercing shell struck the casa's front wall, rocked the entire building, and whistled across the room, exiting through the rear-side stable. Then I heard the hollow clang! "Jesus Christ!" I thought, "that's comin' from an enemy tank or SP!"

The second round, high explosive, didn't quite make it through the AP hole, exploding in an eyeball bulging sheet of flame that bathed the room in a brilliant, brief, pure white glare. Fragments of searing shrapnel zigged and zagged off the stone walls amid the horrendous blast of noise.

Someone howled like a banshee. I twitched, face down on the dirt floor, my head ringing. Wham! Wham! Two more HE 88s flattened and exploded against the outside wall, filling the room with dust. Holy Jesus! a small clear voice inside me said, so clear it startled me, if that gunner does put one through the AP hole, he's gonna kill every mother-lovin' one of us! I was starting to raise my head when another explosion shook the casa, higher up on the wall. A shower of stone shards fell through the boiling dust and my face was buried in the floor again.

In the following silence, I heard the muted clash of gears, the grunting rumble of a powerful engine. "Christ!" I thought, "he's across the river, comin' straight at us!" Getting to my hands and knees, I noted, curiously, that the blasts had blown the fire out. "The guys outside!" I yelled.

Kerr picked his way through the dust and raced to the side door. "I'll check!"

I rose on shaky legs, glancing around the room. Cuthbert was flat on his back, eyes closed, grey faced, his arms flung outwards. "Tex!" I shouted, "Tex!" The stubby American was face down, ass high, on the floor. He looked up, fearfully. "Take a look at Cuthbert, he's been hit. Quick!".

Kerr's face appeared in the open window. "They're OK, Fred," he yelled, "just shaken. An' that tank, or whatever, is moving off. I can barely hear it now, even from out here."

"Greenwood's hit!" Al Hall called to me.

"Jee-sus, no!" was all I could say.

Alex, his shoulder blades resting on a small pack, tried to grin before his face twisted in a coughing fit. I bent over him. "Where, Alex, where?"

He licked his thin lips, stifling the cough. "In the back, I think. I'm not sure, but it hurts." He said it almost wistfully. Gently I started to roll him over on his side. "Ooooh! no, Sergeant! It hurts." He frowned and coughed, then looked up at me, trying again to grin. "I said that before, didn't I?"

"I'll go get Tex over here."

Tex was on his knees between Cuthbert's legs, slitting a field dressing open. "You're gonna be alright, buddy. Tex'll fix ya up jus' fine," he crooned.

Cuthbert's face was now a dirty, pasty grey. I'd seen that look before. On dying men. Tex lifted Cuthbert's right arm, trying to get the roll of bandage under it. The sleeve was soaked in dark red blood, welling out on the floor from his armpit, moving in tiny ripples as his sturdy heart went right on pumping.

"Forget it, Tex," I said softly, "he's had it." I put my hand on the American boy's shoulder, gently tugging him upward.

Tears were running down his cheeks. "Oh no, Sarg, that ain't so. He's gonna live and ah'll save him."

I tugged again. "C'mon, son, you gotta look after Greenwood."

Tex gasped, bawling plaintively. "No, Sarg, ah can't leave him."

I was losing patience. Yanking Tex to his feet, I glared at him. "If you know what you're doing — and you told me you did — then you know you gotta save the wounded with a chance. You don't waste time. Now, take a look at Alex, goddamnit!"

Tex looked at me like a stray dog that had just been kicked, but said nothing.

I stared around the room. "Anybody else?"

Belanger and Verch had been gouged in the legs and arms. Norm Hall was sprinkling sulfa in the ragged cuts while Al opened dressings.

And Cuthbert's life drained away.

Greenwood, Tex said, was hit in the lungs. "He's spittin' blood, Sarg, but just a little."

Tex and I carried Cuthbert into the gloomy stable while the section stood-to, nervously peering across the fields at the dyke. We laid him on the cold ground. I covered him with his anti-gas cape, spreading it gently over the stocky frame. Tex peeled it back, and peered intently into the sightless face.

Lieutenant Bodnaruk appeared out of the grey light, standing stolidly in the doorway, his face expressionless. "Any casualties, Sergeant?" he asked in a surprisingly matter-of-fact tone, his eyes sweeping the room.

"One dead, out in the stable. Our wireless man. Three wounded. Kerr's trying to contact TAC for a Red Cross carrier, sir."

"Hell of an early morning, eh."

I agreed.

"A house exploded in Charlie Company's area. Filled with Eyetie civvies. Must've been booby trapped — a lot of dead." He shrugged. "Anything you need?"

"No sir."

"Well, hang in. I got to get back to my platoon." He was gone as suddenly as he had shown up.

I crouched beside Albert in the gloom upstairs beside the right-hand Vickers, my arm resting on the gun barrel. I could hear his steady breathing while I listened for the sound of the Red Cross carrier I knew would soon be coming. I thought of Cuthbert, the taciturn son of parents I would probably never know. And Green-wood, wheezing and coughing in the darkened room below. Belanger and Verch? They needed the rest while they healed.

"You ever feel spooky, buddy?" I asked.

"Lots of times."

"No. I mean real spooky. Jittery." When he didn't respond, I went on. "I don't understand. It's funny, but when those shells were exploding, I wasn't really scared. Maybe I didn't have time. Now? Now, I'm as shaky as a goddamned hula dancer, like if I don't hold on to myself, I'm gonna fly apart."

"Shaky?"

"Uneasy."

Albert's chuckle was low. "That's fey. An' you don't believe in that."

Along the line of the dyke, dull orange-colored tracers curved through the growing dawn.

I'll feel better after I shave, I told myself. And if the sun comes out, I'll feel even better than that. To Albert I said, "Nope, I don't." I didn't want to, either.

Once during the early afternoon, more 88s ripped the ground to shreds around our casa. "They're comin' from that friggin' town with the red tower in the middle of it," noted Albert. "What's it called?"

"Fusignano, you dumb bugger," replied Al Hall, "you knew that before we came up here."

Kerr contacted TAC and our artillery pounded the town for five minutes, sending up streamers of smoke and clouds of dust. The 88 shelling stopped. Still, intermittent but accurate machine-gun fire and mortaring forced Kerr and I to pull the sentries out of the slit trenches.

"It's against the rules," I said, "but we got no choice. We're down to eleven, so we'll defend from inside the house by day an' two slits by night."

New Year's Eve afternoon, Lord Strathcona Horse Shermans rolled up a dirt road, swung along the Via Rossetta and pounded 75s into a house on our side of the river we suspected was occupied by the enemy at night. Engines grunting and tracks squealing, they lumbered back to their lines amid a storm of return mortar that drove us out of the top floor and downstairs.

Howie, caught outside in the crapper, had to take a flying header into one of the trenches. When he finally got inside, I noted he was streaked with dirt from head to foot. Even his broad forehead was stained — certain signs he had been almost frantic.

"How's she goin' buddy?" I asked, shaking dust out of my trousers. "You must've had a ringside seat for that show."

He laughed, his blue eyes feverish. "Sure did. Hell, I sure did!"

"I'd give him an A for guts," whispered Kerr, "when you think he could've gone to a work gang."

Later, TAC informed us we should begin sandbagging our casa, and to mine and booby-trap each defensive area. "Yeah," added Kerr, "an' an Able Company patrol brought back positive ID on who we're facing — the fuckin' 16th Panzer SS."

"Well," said Albert, "that explains why they're so aggressive." He grinned, "We're up against the best, eh?"

No one heard the shot that killed McKee. One minute he was kneeling behind the Vickers, working the lock to make sure the film of oil wouldn't congeal in the chilly temperatures, and the next he was bowled over sideways.

"His head kinda exploded," Crawford said, "an' there was blood all over the place. It must of gone in one ear, hit something an' come out the back of his head. Sheesh! it was sudden like."

"Fuckin' sniper," Albert growled, "from offa that dyke, somewhere."

"OK," Kerr said, "we got another rule. We have to work the locks or the damned guns won't fire on rapid till they're warm. So, from now on, haul 'em out of the fire slits by the trailing legs, an' do it behind the wall."

McKee's paybook and one dogtag went dutifully to Padre MacLean.

Firefights erupted all along the line as patrols clashed and 1944 wound down and '45 cranked up. German bazooka men lobbed bombs into the area, stinging Dog Company's strong points. Regimental three-inch mortars retaliated.

"What a lousy way to spend New Year's Eve," grumbled Kerr when I relieved him a couple of minutes before midnight, easing myself into the trench. I moved over for Crawford as Al Hall clambered out.

"Ah, you'd probably have spent the night alone anyway," Crawford said, glibly. "Instead, you got private Hall, A., of Tabor, Alberta." He watched Kerr's retreating figure disappear inside the casa. "We gonna get an extra belt of rum tonight, Sarg, just for Auld Lang Syne's sake?"

"That's not a bad idea, Happy New Year little buddy. Happy New Year."

"And the same to you, old fella."

At one minute after midnight, the Canadian Army unloaded a special stonk into the 16th SS positions.

Lieutenant Bodnaruk was one of those square-built men. They made great farmers, good miners. And steady-eddie officers. And because I didn't know him, I couldn't tell why he never smiled. Maybe he didn't see anything funny about war.

He clamped his meaty fingers around the mug of tea, rocking on his hunkers. "Now here's the picture, Cederberg. Able and Dog will attack tomorrow at 0800 and the objective is to clear at least our side of those damned dykes." He sipped then swallowed a mouthful of the hot brew. "At 0500, Able will open up with everything they have as a diversion." He grunted. "I'm not sure it'll help, but those are orders.

"You keep those two Vickers of yours humping — they'll make those bastards keep their heads down long enough for us to get across the open ground and close on the dyke. Then, switch your fire to the right, so's you don't hit my people, and pin down any Jerries who might try to interfere. It won't be as easy as it sounds, because the 16th SS is a well-rested, well-equipped outfit."

He rose to his feet, drained the mug.

"There might be other opportunities to lend a hand. Watch for them, but don't get caught off-balance because if there's a determined counterattack it'll be up to you and your men to hold 'em. We'll be too scattered and in mid-stride."

He squinted around the large room. "You've tidied up somewhat since I was here last." He stopped. "Oh, yes, we might need your Red Cross man. Just in case. Now, any questions?"

"What about support?" Kerr asked.

"We got the Straths and medium mortars and arty on call."

"Do you guys fix bayonets?" asked Tex after Bodnaruk had ghosted out of the casa toward his own position.

Nobody answered.

At first light, we pulled in the Halls and Moose, worked the

Vickers until the locks moved easily, fed the belts in and Howie and Albert sat, legs spread, behind the guns. Moose and Al Hall handled the feed while we stacked ammo cases against the back wall.

It was twenty minutes before 0800 when we opened up, the barrels, hooked to their water cans, spitting .303s in a slow rhythm. And our three Brens in the next room picked up the chant.

Five minutes after Dog Company broke from the shelter of their slits and casas, straight for the towering dyke, Canadian 25-pounders poured two salvoes of high explosives and smoke into the German lines on the far side of the river. Directing our fire from the center window, I watched Lieutenant Bodnaruk lead his riflemen, clutching and clawing at the grass, up, up, up through a shower of enemy grenades until they pulled themselves frantically onto the crown.

"Swing 'em around about fifteen degrees right!" I shouted, turning to make sure the order was executed. Albert tapped his gun right, squinting grimly down the barrel. Howie had frozen, tears cascading over his cheeks.

Jerry machine-gunners, suddenly deciding we were a big problem, aimed swarms of Spandau bullets that peppered our casa, zipping through both open windows, ricocheting off stone and plaster walls. Ducking low, I yelled again: "Howie! Swing that fuckin' gun!" I never said another word. I didn't have to. Somehow, I knew Howie wasn't going to move. Flinging myself across the floor, I grabbed him by the shoulders and pushed him violently sideways.

"I'm sorry, Sarg, oh God I'm sorry," I heard his sob, "but I just can't...I can't." He ended up in a heap, his helmeted head in his arms, shaking.

I hunched over the gun, tapped right, lifted the trips and, ignoring Moose's startled, wide-eyed look, opened up. The thump-thump-thump of the shuddering Vickers, the wisps of steam escaping from the tube joining the water can and barrel surrounded me. I was conscious of Moose's great hands almost lovingly urging the belts into the ammo slot, the stream of empty casings spewing out on the floor, a sliver of the stone windowsill that caromed off my steel helmet. A wooden hydro pole in my vision took hits and, soundlessly, folded into two halves. I watched our bullets kicking up dirt as they pounded into the embankment.

We stopped to change belts. A Dog Company rifleman, sweating and dishevelled, burst into the room. "Mr. Bodnaruk's been hit, bad. An' so's one of our stretcher bearers! You got help?"

Steel-shod boots rang on the stone stairs. Kerr clomped in.

"Eddie! Take Tex an' Verch."

"Verch's out. Remember? I'll grab Norm and a couple of stretchers."

Layers of thin, blue-grey smoke drifted between the road and embankment. Lanarks, bobbing and weaving, fanned out along the grassy crown.

"Christ! Look at that!" shrilled Moose, "some of 'em are usin' ladders to get up that friggin' dyke!"

Kerr, Tex and Norm covered ten yards when they flung themselves into the dirt. "Sniper fire!" yelled Kerr, waving his right arm in the general direction of two tall poplars standing behind the German side of the river.

Albert and I poured two belts of ammunition into the trees. Kerr started to rise. Down he went. "You hit?" Moose screamed. Kerr shook his head.

Artillery shells whistled through the skies and mortars climbed higher and higher then fell sharply into the ground on both sides of the Senio. In the explosions, scuttling like crabs, Kerr and Norm got back to the casa. Tex lay still, his Red Cross armband red-and-white in the sunlight.

"Fuck me, that s.o.b., whoever he is, can shoot," Kerr gasped. "He got the kid right through the chest, and him only a stretcher-bearer."

"Two can play that game," I snarled grimly. I dug another armband out of a small pack and snapped it on, picked up a Bren, checked the mag, hefted it, and said: "Cover me."

Carefully inching sideways, exposing my banded arm toward the enemy lines, the Bren held straight up, hidden by my body, I reached the fallen Tex. I looked down at him, then at the trees. In one quick motion I straightened up, pointed the Bren at the nearest poplar and opened fire. The German sniper seemed to leap in the air, hung motionless for a split second, then plummeted straight down, disappeared behind the dyke.

Tex was dead. He had been hit twice in the chest, frontally, and through the back.

"Must've caught the first one before he went down, then got another," said Kerr, softly. "Poor, sad little bugger. He shouldn't have even been up here."

"That friggin' sniper paid for it. Right good," I said, panting after lugging the young Texan back to the casa on my shoulder. "He came right out from behind the bole of the tree and watched me, the sonuvabitch, his rifle at his side, pointin' down. He was an easy target."

Kerr and the Halls, moving in stops and starts, carried three stretchers up to Dog Company. "Bodnaruk's had it," Kerr reported on their return, "never really made it to the dyke. Shrapnel." He took a big breath. "An' they want more fire on the right, an' they've called for the Straths," he exhaled.

We sprayed the dyke with thousands of rounds of steel-nosed .303s until the upstairs floor was ankle deep in brass casings. And the stretcher bearers, ignoring sporadic mortars exploding in the fields, carried out twenty riflemen for transfer to the casualty clearing stations behind TAC.

With nightfall came another of those eerie silences which seemed to follow firefights. And Howie MacLeod sat, huddled in a corner, blurred tear stains on his cheeks. He was rocking gently back and forth, his arms hugging his knees.

Kerr said: "He'll have to go out, with Tex. OK?"

"I been thinking," I said after a long pause. "An' we're not sending him to the medics."

"Then where?"

"To help the cooks at left-out-of-battle — LOB."

"Can you?"

"I talked to TAC a few minutes ago. And told 'em he's tired, just plain run down, and that he should go to LOB. Jesus Christ, Eddie, he's a good soldier. An' just because he can't take it up here doesn't mean the medics should hang some kind of battle fatigue label on him."

Kerr looked at me obliquely. "I'm not disagreein' ol' buddy."

I explained it all to Howie in the gloom beside the idling Red Cross carrier after Moose and I lashed Tex's mortal remains to a stretcher. Howie looked at me dully. "Thanks, Fred," was all he said. "I'll work it out." He extended his hand. I shook my head. "I don't shake hands with guys I'm gonna see in a few days." I tapped the armored vehicle driver on his steel hat. "Let 'er go." He turned the carrier in its own length and, tracks squealing, the squat rear end disappeared into the night.

I checked the slit trenches. Moose grinned. "Seein' as how you're up an' about, Sarg, how's about some tea. Or coffee. Whatever's on the boil?"

Both Halls were exchanging words from their front-side pits, so I didn't bother them.

I counted the "bodies" in the one-time living room by the light of the low, rippling flames in the fireplace and shivered in the cold draft blowing through the hole made by the AP shell: three. Listening to Crawford pacing, restlessly, upstairs, I added them up. Now we were seven. Where there should be thirty-two.

Ah, fuck! I thought morbidly. The 19 set cackled. I bent over and snapped it off. "Won't have any battery left if we don't," I muttered, more to myself.

Kerr handed me a mug of coffee and I noticed how big-boned his wrist was before I remembered the Halls and Moose out in the slits. "Gimme two more, will you Eddie?" He filled them from the can of simmering coffee. I crossed the yard, almost stepped into the cesspool, lifted the issue rum jug from Betsy III's spare battery box, laced all three mugs with the strong-smelling liquid and delivered them as promised.

Glancing at my wristwatch, I said: "Stand-to will be over by the time you finish y'r coffee. Then hike inside. OK?"

It was so quiet outside, Albert broke the silence. "You think the friggin' Jerries have gone home?"

"They're probably too busy countin' their dead to fight. Just like us," I replied, glumly.

Kerr picked up a handful of peach tree twigs and placed them one at a time on the fire. It flickered, then flared, the thin smoke disappearing up the flue.

"We ought to start riggin' some booby traps 'round the casa," he said.

I nodded. "An' we got some German Teller mines stacked behind the building. We can use 'em, too, but not tonight. I'm so goddamn tired that by morning I wouldn't remember where we set 'em."

Albert opened a cold tin of M and V, and began chewing on the fat-streaked chunks.

I closed my eyes. And dozed. And dreamed I was clinging to the top of a long, long chute. A slide. I could sense my fingers going numb, that it was only a matter of time before I lost my grip. Panic-stricken, I could only stare down the glistening chute into nothingness. God, I thought, helplessly, I'm going to fall. And I knew I would have to open my eyes, just as I did when I was a little boy, dreaming scary dreams. I could hear my mother ...if you don't, you will die. Yes, that's it. Open my eyes. Suddenly, my frantic fingers slipped. I was going to plunge down the chute. I cried out and forced my eyes wide open.

Albert was bent over me, shaking my shoulders roughly. "Wake up, Fred, wake up! You're twitchin' and groanin' like a whore in a fit!"

I sat up, fists kneading my eyes until the room came into focus, Albert, Kerr, the firelight. Aloud I said: "I need a mug of coffee and a slug of rum." To myself I said, "You an' your damn fey business, you got me all screwed up."

"You got the malaria again?" Kerr asked, solicitously.

"Nope. I'm just tired."

"An' your eyeballs are back halfway into y'r head," said Albert, handing me the coffee. "I'll go get the rum." He peered at me curiously, crossed the floor and went outside.

I'm spooked, I concluded inanely, sipping the sweet-smelling cup of sugared coffee and rum. It warmed me as it went down. I felt like a guy who has heard one shoe drop and waits for the second.

The shell came in silently, scattering red clay tiles as it plunged through the roof, splintering the upper-storey floorboards before landing with a heart-stopping clang on the stone floor. It skidded across the room, struck the stone wall, bounced high and came to rest in the middle of our room.

I knew it was too late, but I dived for the corner, automatically closing my eyes tight, waiting for the inevitable explosion, the last terrible sound I would ever hear. Nothing. I turned my head. There it was, silvery, gleaming in the firelight.

"A dud!" wheezed Albert.

"Or armor piercing," gasped Kerr, rolling over on his side.

Moose clumped downstairs. "What the fuck was that?" he shrilled. He saw the shell. "Mother of God!"

A fine shower of plaster seeped out of the ceiling.

The Hall brothers and Crawford almost ran over each other coming through the door. They stood there, slack jawed, barely breathing.

The seven of us stared at the shell. "We gonna evacuate?" Crawford whispered.

"Where've we got to go?" asked Kerr.

"It's a big bugger, probably a medium, 15 centimeter, I think," Norm Hall said softly.

I had the distinct feeling it was glowing.

Al Hall walked closer, bent over it. His tam-o'-shanter flopped into his eyes. Coolly, he brushed it back until it rested on the back of his head. "It's HE and it's a dud," he said, matter-of-factly.

"Mebbe it's got a time fuse, to go off in a few minutes." Crawford's words trailed off.

I stood up. For the first time in hours, I felt strangely good. "We'll rope the damned thing carefully. Everybody'll get outside the heavy stone wall, give it a yank an' see what happens. OK?"

We did just that. Nothing. So, it was towed across the floor and, finally, rolled across the yard and into the cesspool. It went to the bottom, leaving a widening ring of ripples on the turgid surface.

"That would've made one helluva souvenir," commented Al, dryly, climbing the stairs to take the first shift behind the Vickers. "Only my parents are pacifists, I think."

Kerr lit a cigarette. "You know," he said, smoke streaming from his mouth and nostrils, "it's been some kind of friggin' day. An' I can just see it in the local Canadian papers: Canadian Army Headquarters announced that units of the 12th Infantry Brigade carried out mop-up and patrol activities along the Senio River line in Italy yesterday."

I didn't give a damn. I had heard the other shoe drop.

The next day, we set booby traps wired to 36 grenades in the ditches along the Via Rossetta and the dirt track leading to the Senio; we planted German-made Teller mines at strategic locations in the fields adjacent to our casa. And we stacked biscuit tins and gas cans in the rear stable area so even an invading cat would send them clanging down if it tried to slink inside.

For two days and nights, as the weather turned cold, spontaneous patrol fights erupted along the dyke, Lanark riflemen and SS Jerries lobbing grenades into each other's positions. On call, we rattled streams of Vickers fire across their front, chewing up the embankment cover in the gaps between our forward positions.

Three times our casa shuddered under the impact of screaming 88s, driving us downstairs into the *bono refugio* we had spaded out of the hard-packed earth. And each time the stonk ended, we would charge back up to the top floor to man the guns, staring tensely into the night, holding our steaming breath, waiting…waiting…waiting until blessed daylight.

On the sixth night of the new year, Jerry lobbed heavy incendiary shells into the Lanark lines. One erupted in glowing fingers of phosphorescent flame beside our straw stack, torching it. While Crawford and I scrambled across the yard to move the carrier parked beside it, another crashed into the roof of a Dog Company strongpoint on our left, scattering the tiles and starting a high, fierce fire that lit up the entire area.

Neither of us had time to flatten. We just froze, crouched over.

Two more thumped into the ground farther left. Something's up, I thought. Moving swiftly now, I vaulted up on the carrier's armored facing and dropped into the driver's seat, turning the key as I did. I could feel the heat from the blazing stack. Crawford stood directly in front, signalling frantically with his hands to steer left.

The carrier motor coughed. Coughed again, then rumbled into life. I slammed it into third and, gunning the engine, let the clutch out. It stalled. I restarted, revved her until she whined, let the clutch out then again and felt her lurch forward, almost ignoring Crawford's signals. At the last second, I slewed the wheel, felt the left track partially lock and headed straight for the casa where I parked, cut the motor and leaped out, ducking into the house.

"Shee-it, Sarg," panted Crawford, "ya almost put her straight into the friggin' cesspool."

I didn't have time to reply. From upstairs, I could hear the Vickers open up and I sprinted up the steps. Albert and Al were behind the guns, Moose and Norm feeding, Kerr directing fire from halfway out the large window.

From over his left shoulder I could see the Jerries streaming across the dyke in the gap between Dog Company's Bren pits, like a horde of ants, moving erratically in the light of the fires their artillery had ignited.

Dog Company Bren gunners and riflemen began firing, our Vickers chattered incessantly. And the enemy infantry, floundering in the storm of bullets, scattered before retreating slowly, the survivors trying to haul their wounded with them as the flames from the burning house died to fluttering slivers.

The hood of night gradually tightened its black hold on the tortured land. The seven of us stood-to until dawn brought with it light snowflakes that dusted the dead and dying or sizzled amid the ashes of the charred Dog Company casa.

Kerr netted the 19 set in on TAC, listening to the terse exchanges between Dog Company, HQ and TAC.

"We got some men buried under the rubble of our forward platoon position," the voice intoned, unemotionally, "an' we'd like some men — reinforcements — to help us dig 'em out."

"Any other casualties?"

"No. No. Couple wounded. One, Rankin, but he won't have to be evacuated."

The platoon commander's voice wavered, his words unintelligible.

"What did you say?"

"I say again, we got some dead Jerries lying in front of our casa. What'll we do about 'em?"

"Leave 'em there until night."

"One of 'em appears to be only wounded."

"That's different; see if you can haul him in. He might have some information we can use."

"Don't forget the men."

"Gotcha!"

"Roger."

The wounded German, shot through the shoulder, was happy to be taken prisoner. But outside of the fact his company had lost sixteen men during the past several days, he could only say it was led by two officers and equipped with six Spandaus.

Crawford and Moose and Norm, using shovels and homemade Eyetie brooms, cleaned up, brushing and spading powdered plaster, thousands of ammo casings, stone chards and ashes out the door.

Leaning on his shovel, Norm looked at the pile of ashes that had been the straw husk stack. "They burn all the way to ground, don't they, Moose."

Moose wrinkled his large, sharp nose. "Don't make no difference to me," he said. "It's the goddamn house cleanin' I don't like. It's a woman's job where I come from!" He spat.

Scattered snow flurries lashed the gaunt peach trees, dykes and shattered casas on January 7th. And rumors that we were going to be relieved livened up the usually monotonous exchange of reports on what Kerr had dubbed the "prairie farmers' party line" wireless.

"I'm so friggin' tired," moaned Albert after washing his face in his helmet, "that even if they're true, I'm gonna have to be carried out."

Crawford was curled up under two blankets, snoring.

Even the Halls were silent. Odd, I mused, they can be out on their backs, out on their feet, complaining like chronic misfits. But explode one mortar. Fire one weapon. Shout one warning. And they're instantly alert. Ready to drink, fight, hold the light. Or carry out the dead.

Rumors became facts early the next morning while our artillery and mortars pounded the German positions: The Loyal Eddies and Seaforths would take our places along the Senio.

By 1700 hours, our carriers were packed — except for the Vickers, their barrels pointed through the transverse slits at the SS positions on the dyke to our right. The Brens, full mags in place, were stacked against walls. "They gotta stay," I said to Moose, "just in case, till the last minute."

In the darkness, the Seaforth looie, clean-shaven and sporting the beginnings of a pencil-thin moustache, looked like he had just stepped out of an Army Service Corps shower.

I heard Moose giggle. "He ain't gonna look so spiffy after he's been up here for a few days!"

"How many of you, Sergeant?" he asked, politely.

"Seven: two sergeants, a corporal and four men."

"That's all?"

"We started out with fourteen. And it hasn't been a picnic, sir."

He coughed, looked over his shoulder at his men, standing against the outside wall.

"Sergeant Kerr'll post 'em for you if that's OK," I offered.

He nodded, calling: "Sergeant Parker...go with Sergeant Kerr and familiarize yourself with the perimeter slit trenches, will you?" Turning back to me, he asked: "How'd you defend with seven? I've got twenty-two."

I laughed, more harshly than I intended. "Don't go out in the fields, we planted Tellers. Don't walk in the ditches, we set up booby traps. And for Chrissakes don't go into the stable or a thousand precariously stacked cans will fall all over you."

The looie's moustache jumped. "I'll be goddamned...the Lanyard and Slaughterhouse Regiment knows how to improvise!"

"Lanyard an' what?"

"And Slaughterhouse. That's a kind of affectionate nickname you guys have earned, ever since the Naviglio." Removing his helmet, he ran his fingers through his brown hair. "Your, ah, minefield, was it effective?"

I chuckled. "Well, we got one dog and a cow; no, two dogs, a civilian and knocked out one of our own Shermans, temporarily, when it blew a track."

The looie, grinning wryly, went upstairs, Al Hall and I on his heels. "Good fields of fire," he observed. "Okay, Sergeant, I think I know all I've got to know. You want to remove your Vickers and Brens an' we'll put ours in place?"

Crawford lugged the Brens out to the carriers. The Halls, Moose and I bent over the Vickers. One, aimed to cover the far right, had a part belt of ammo in it.

"Better get it out, Al," I said.

He looked at me, grinning. "There's only a touch left."

"So?"

Al sat behind the machine gun, lifted the trips and thumbed the triggers. The barrel spouted fire. Thump! thump! thump! until the tail of the belt wiggled, signalling the ammo was gone.

"What the hell's goin' on up there!" someone screamed from the ground floor, followed by the clatter of army boots on the stone stairs. It was the looie, glaring angrily. "Goddamnit, Sergeant!" he exploded. "What're you people trying to do? Stir up the whole front in the middle of a relief?"

I deliberately shrugged. "It was a runaway burst, sir. Frank was trying to move the gun and Moose was tryin' to extricate the friggin' part belt when it just sort of took off," I replied, as helplessly as I could.

The looie swore under his breath. "Damned half-trained troops," he muttered. "Okay, okay, let's get your equipment out of here, before you kill someone."

Al didn't know it at the time, but we had fired our last shots in the Italian campaign.

POSTSCRIPT

In all, 92,757 Canadians served in the Italian theater and 26,254 were killed or wounded, figures that speak for themselves as to the ferocity of the struggle.

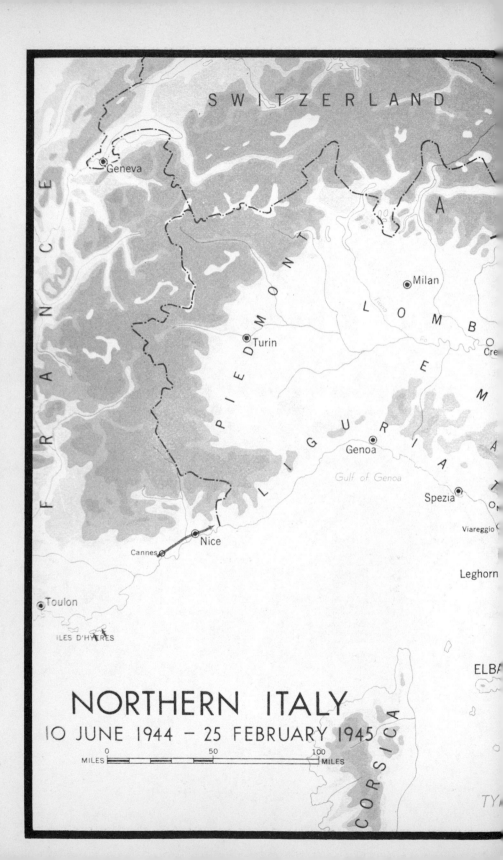

NORTHERN ITALY
10 JUNE 1944 – 25 FEBRUARY 1945

SWITZERLAND

FRANCE

Geneva

Milan

PIEDMONT

Turin

LOMBARDO

Cre

LIGURIA

Genoa

Gulf of Genoa

Spezia

Viareggio

Nice

Cannes

Leghorn

Toulon

ILES D'HYÈRES

ELBA

CORSICA

TY

MILES 0   50   100 MILES